GLORYLAND

Christian Suburbia,
Christian Nation

H. B. CAVALCANTI

PRAEGER

Westport, Connecticut
London

Library of Congress Cataloging-in-Publication Data

Cavalcanti, H. B., 1956–
  Gloryland : Christian suburbia, Christian nation / H.B. Cavalcanti.
    p. cm.
  Includes bibliographical references (p.) and index.
  ISBN 978–0–313–34812–9 (alk. paper)
  1. Conservatism—Religious aspects—Christianity.   2. Religion and politics—United States.   3. United States—Church history.   I. Title
BR115.C66C38   2007
261.7—dc22   2007027852

British Library Cataloguing in Publication Data is available.

Copyright © 2007 by H. B. Cavalcanti

All rights reserved. No portion of this book may be reproduced, by any process or technique, without the express written consent of the publisher.

Library of Congress Catalog Card Number: 2007027852
ISBN: 978–0–313–34812–9

First published in 2007

Praeger Publishers, 88 Post Road West, Westport, CT 06881
An imprint of Greenwood Publishing Group, Inc.
www.praeger.com

Printed in the United States of America

∞™

The paper used in this book complies with the Permanent Paper Standard issued by the National Information Standards Organization (Z39.48–1984).

10 9 8 7 6 5 4 3 2 1

To the *Gnostic Sisters*,
for their living *κοινονία*

CONTENTS

Preface	ix
1. Onward Christian Soldiers: The New Christian Conservatism	1
2. Will the Circle Be Unbroken? Co-opting Modernity	19
3. God Shed His Grace on Thee: Colonizing the Public Square	45
4. Blest Be the Tie that Binds: Defending Religious Liberty	71
5. His Truth Is Marching On: Public Morals and Public Faith	97
6. Shall We Gather at the River? Religious Zeal and American Pluralism	117
Notes	133
References	159
Index	175

PREFACE

This book represents a personal effort to understand an important and recent development in American Christianity. Christian conservatism, the subject of its analysis, has existed for most of this country's history, but is now in a process of reinventing itself. In its original mode, the faith was mostly practiced at the margins of the American religious scene, outside the larger sanctuaries of colonial churches, or the 1950s' growing suburban congregations of middle-class Christianity. Surprisingly, by the end of the twentieth century, what was once marginal has grown in size and importance to become one of the dominant forces in American religion. For those of us who study religion, the repercussions of the change have yet to be fully understood. How did it take place? How is it transforming the faith? How has it changed its relationship with the larger society?

Many might claim that in this book I paint conservative Christianity with too broad a stroke, and that my analysis combines traits of many groups and denominations, without the clinical sociological precision of more rigorous, empirical tests. Since this is not a study of a particular group (evangelicals for instance) or denomination (Assemblies of God, say), my approach cannot rely as readily on demographic data or survey results that may chart the changes I describe. By necessity, what is described in the following pages is an *ideal type*, the *geist* of a faith, something broader than all denominations, congregations, and religious groups that it encompasses.

This is not a book about the details of all the groups that fall within the abstract category I call *conservative Christianity*. Rather, the work examines how a large segment of the American faithful are being Christians today. It describes a certain way of looking at the world, of reacting to it, and finding a sense of calling and belonging. One thing is certain—these folks are clearly very serious about their religious calling and about bringing their faith to bear upon America's public square. Something is energizing this generation of conservative believers and that deserves our attention. Understanding their motivation, the means by which they are transforming their faith, is important.

Max Weber's *ideal type* is a useful methodological tool for the task at hand. It offers a strategy to avoid "the individualizing and particularizing approach of German Geisteswissenschaft and historicism" (Coser 1977: 223). Convinced that human reality in its empirical state was far more varied, fluid, and complex than any social science model could ever capture with scientific precision, Weber thought the *ideal type* would provide a handy analytical construct that isolated certain critical traits of a given phenomenon and then measured them against the concrete case at hand. An *ideal type* describes the broader characteristics of a phenomenon and its consequences for life in society. In *The Protestant Ethic and the Spirit of Capitalism*, Weber offers shows how sociological analysis can benefit from the use of *ideal types*. The work examines in detail the Protestant worldview found in Pietism and Calvinism, not only through its structural aspects or doctrinal disputations, but also in its *geist*. Then it connects that worldview to the economic sphere.

Weber's book models how a worldview can be captured through an ideal type, allowing the investigator to understand why people participate in society in rather unique ways, with a distinct set of values and beliefs that also affects the roles they play within their groups and the larger community. It is no wonder that Weber's use of *verstehen* is an integral part of that process. One needs to understand the religious world from the point of view of those who are living it. Following the Weberian example, this book is not an exhaustive description of the empirical phenomenon it examines, but rather an idealized viewpoint of conservative Christianity. Hopefully it synthesizes the faith's unique aspects in a clear-sighted manner. Unlike any possible statistical model, this analysis does not seek to represent the *average* form of Christian conservatism, but rather its spirit—the vision and practices that move the followers of this dynamic form of religion.

Current conservative Christians are seeking new ways to increase their presence in America's public arena. They are doing so to challenge what they perceive to be the threatening forces of secular modernity. In the process they are reinventing their faith. For the past twenty-five years conservative Christians have played an important role in America's public arena; and their reading of American reality has reoriented public debate in significant ways. But it has also affected the faith's cosmology and relationship to the larger society.

One would hope that this analysis would meet the methodological standards set by Weber, but it is extremely difficult to replicate the old master's genius. The more modest goal here is to employ his methodological construct to shed light on a recent religious development. Professor Lewis Coser suggests that "ideal types enable one to construct hypotheses linking them with the conditions that brought the phenomenon or event into prominence, or with consequences that follow from its emergence" (1977: 224). In that spirit, this book tries to do a little bit of both. It reviews the conditions that brought conservative Christianity into prominence in the late twentieth century, and examines some of the consequences of its newly gained strength.

The centrality of the conservative Church in the American religious scene is both recent and unexpected. Most sociological literature from the 1960s till the early 1980s expected secularization to continue to push religion into the private sphere of American life. There was also a clear expectation that religion would continue to lose its hold in the American imagination. What happened, in many ways, was exactly the opposite.

Since all research has an element of biography, this work too revisits parts of my personal journey. From my conservative Christian childhood, to the theological and legal training of my young adulthood, to my sociology graduate days in mid-life, I have followed the development of this new form of conservative faith with great interest. First, as someone personally affected by its developing trends—watching how its changes affected people who had invested a lifetime in the faith. Later, as a student of religion, my concern translated into a more sociological quest. The social sciences offered me a broader window with which to analyze conservative Christianity. They also added depth perception to my analysis (hopefully, taming some personal biases along the way). My concern gradually moved from the personal level to becoming an academic enterprise, dealing with a research problem.

There is, of course, a debt of gratitude to those who aided me in this journey. First, to those who interested me in the study of American Christianity: my Southern Baptist Theological Seminary professors—Larry McSwain and Paul Simmons, and my mentors in the Graduate Department of Religion at Vanderbilt University—Howard Harrod, Eugene TeSelle, and Peter Paris. My gratitude is also extended to the Vanderbilt Sociology faculty, who helped me better understand grassroots organizing and social movements (religious or secular). So, my thanks to Larry Diamond, George Becker, Dan Cornfield, and Karen Campbell.

To their names I add the names of colleagues who helped me cultivate the craft of research at the University of Richmond: Ted Lewellen and Ray Wingrove in Sociology, Del McWhorter in Philosophy, Scott Johnson in Rhetoric and Communications, and Terryl Givens and Lewis Schwartz in English.

At an experiential level, I'm grateful too to friends who have dedicated a lifetime of service to the broader Church. They inspire and challenge my understanding of American Christianity. So my heartfelt thanks to Don Steele (Pastor, Westminster Presbyterian Church in Gallup, NM), John Mack and Barbara Gerlach (Pastors, First Congregational United Church of Christ, Washington, DC), Bob Butziger (Chair, Western Region, American Counseling Association), Harmon Wray (Director, Program in Faith and Criminal Justice, Vanderbilt Divinity School), and Daniel Bagby (Theodore F. Adams Professor of Pastoral Care, Baptist Theological Seminary in Richmond, VA).

The insights and encouragement from other sociologists of religion made this book a better product. So, my thanks to Darren Sherkat (Professor of Sociology, Southern Illinois University), Rhys Williams (Professor of Sociology, University of Cincinnati), and Otto Maduro (Professor of World Christianity and Latin American Christianity, Drew University), for their timely suggestions. Thanks also to the anonymous readers whose rigorous comments added more rigor to my analysis.

Finally, a special thanks to my partner, Marie Rietmann, whose encouragement, steady support, and careful editing were invaluable in the slow and tedious process of assembling the manuscript. She, more than anyone else, lived with the preparation of this research project, its implementation, and its eventual results. Her presence and patience made the journey richer.

Writing this book was a rewarding experience. It allowed me to revisit many themes of my early journey. It's not often that one finds the opportunity to review a familiar phenomenon, this time with the insights from a variety of disciplines. Of all my research, this was perhaps the most satisfying. To the extent that I succeed, I'm grateful for the wisdom and care of my many mentors and fellow travelers. Where I fail, there is a reminder of how much remains to be learned in the journey.

1

ONWARD CHRISTIAN SOLDIERS: THE NEW CHRISTIAN CONSERVATISM

"I have been made to feel by the liberal people that my faith makes me weird."
—Midwestern voter

There is an old battle cry echoing across America, now sounded by a new group of dedicated reformers. The country is in spiritual danger; it is facing a spiritual siege. Unmoored from Christian roots, our nation risks losing its privileged status in God's eyes. This time, modernity is to blame for our condition. The secular, pluralistic nature of our society is undermining America's spiritual health. Modernity creates a spiritual vacuum that is quickly filled by "man-made faiths" or apostasy. In these dangerous times, the reformers' sense of urgency is quite understandable. Their calling is the most important a religious people could have—to "restore" the nation, to *Christianize* it. The task ahead does not frighten them. In fact, the restoration movement brims with enthusiasm, driven by its holy sense of purpose. And unlike previous generations of religious conservatives, this group has the talents, resources, educational credentials, and gumption to see the race to the end.

This book examines their story, a story of religious transformation. Once peripheral in the American religious scene, conservative Christianity is now engaged in a large-scale transformation of our social order; a change in mission that took place over the last twenty-five years. The book tries to put the change in perspective, as it explores the evolution of this new Christian conservatism. The questions are many. Who are these new Christian "soldiers?" Why is America's "restoration" so important *now*? Why is it so central to this generation of religious conservatives? What drives their disciplined and concerted effort? How is it transforming their faith? How does it change the way they relate to the modern world? Moreover, as conservative Christianity changes, how does it reshape our national arena?

The book attempts to profile the religious movement, to understand what unites these culture warriors in such gargantuan task, and to describe its current transformation. This is not the first generation of conservative believers to tackle modernity. The modern world has challenged all branches of American Christianity. In time, different segments of the Church[1] responded differently to the rationalization and secularization of American life. The most liberal denominations (churches founded in the colonial days) realigned their theology and practice to fit the modern world. Moderate churches (mostly those created in the frontier days) compromised with modernity whenever possible. Prior conservative groups retreated into a premodern faith, rejecting modernity altogether.[2] In fact, *Fundamentalism*, represented the conservative Church's theological retrenchment against the modern world.

Back in the early days of the twentieth century religious conservatives longed for the certainties of the premodern era. In fact, they did so for most of the century. But since the 1980s, the conservative community has been changing its approach. Emboldened by a rise in numbers and resources, Christian conservatives are now assuming a more direct, confrontational posture toward modernity. This book argues that conservative Christianity has developed in the last twenty-five years a two-pronged response to the modern world. These days conservative believers and their institutions are both co-opting slices of modern life and seeking to revert the impact of modernity in America's public square. The end result is a drive to *tame* the modern world, and bring it under a sectarian Christian influence. The goal is America's full-scale conversion.

Once the conservative faith was comprised of a small set of fringe religious groups. Now it boasts the largest religious network in America. At a time when mainline denominations waned, conservative groups recolonized American suburbia through a decentralized array of gathering places. By one estimate, twenty-five years ago, there were fewer than fifty churches in our nation that brought in more than 2,000 people to worship every week. Today, there are more than 1,200.[3] Numerically, Christian conservatives are the biggest winners in America's religious economy. They now represent the largest segment of American Christians, with congregations that register the highest rates of growth, literature that dots the shelves of secular stores, media outreach that equals secular channels in broadcasting power, and lobbying that keeps Washington under pressure to implement the conservative agenda.

This change is part of a larger realignment in American Christianity.[4] During the second half of the twentieth century the nation's religious fault lines shifted from the peaceful denominational coexistence of the 1950s (arranged along a mainline-periphery spectrum, with liberal churches holding the center), to the clear-cut, liberal-conservative ideological divide of the 1990s.[5] The divide has splintered American Christianity into internal warring fashions to a degree that conservative Episcopalians nowadays have more in common with their likeminded brethren in other Protestant traditions than with their own fellow faith members.

This book focuses on the changes in the conservative agenda, on the restoration drive that is re-creating America's conservative Church. Its ideological divide has realigned the larger Church, and fueled the broader culture wars in our nation. At a time of deep-seated political divisions, rampant ideological discourse, and threatened religious freedom, the new conservative agenda pitches American Christianity's dominant religious group against the secular forces that have sustained our country's pluralistic ethos.

In modern, postindustrial nations, relations between Church and State are defined by many factors. Among them the nation's *polity* (ranging from democratic to authoritarian), its *political ideology* (ranging from liberal to conservative), the strength of its *civil society* (the density of voluntary associations that mediate between citizen and nation), the degree of *religious freedom*, and the *nature* of its dominant religious groups (liberal vs. orthodox). Sooner or later, all dominant religious groups have to come to terms with the cultural context in which they operate. This Christian form of religious conservatism is no exception. As it becomes a force to contend in America's public square, members of the faith are redefining their relationship to the larger culture.

The difference is that while previous dominant groups accommodated the demands of the larger culture, this group is seeking to transform it, to bring it under its sacred canopy. This process of co-optation has lasted for twenty-five years. During this time, Christian conservatives have held steadfastly to their sectarian, unchanging Christian principles; while adapting to the country's changing temporal demands. It is a balance that challenges and complicates the faith's ongoing evolution.

RELIGIOUS PLURALISM IN A MODERN NATION

Church and State relations in the United States have historically been shaped by two distinct processes. *Symbolically*, America co-opted broad themes from mainline Protestantism, once its prevalent faith tradition, as part of its civil religion discourse.[6] *Structurally*, the country organized its religious arena as an open religious market, where multiple faith traditions competed for converts and cultural influence.[7] The mainline Protestant faith provided the nation with important patriotic imagery used to build our national identity, from the founding days through the deep divisions of our Civil War and the industrial revolution, to the hopes of the Civil Rights movement. The open religious market allowed faiths to flourish on their own. All in all, the balance between a *generic civil religion* and the *open religious market* offered the perfect formula for developing a thoroughly modern religious landscape.

Religious freedom gave American denominations room to grow on a voluntary, competitive basis, while our civil religion provided the nation with its overall ethos.[8] As the market expanded during the first two centuries, to the colonial churches were added frontier churches, and eventually immigrant churches. By the 1950s the nation's open religious market had grown to allow the coexistence of Christian and non-Christian faiths, with each tradition finding its appropriate way to promote a unifying American identity. In fact, a midcentury study of American religion indicated that being religious in the United States did not detract from being American and vice versa. In fact, the identities were quite complementary.[9] The Church and State balance seemed so stable then that sociologists described the country as a denominational society.[10] America's ability to foster peaceful religious coexistence within a single political canopy was hailed as an example to the world.

That balance was also critical to the country's modernization. The development of a multicultural, secular State, especially after World War II, demanded a cohesive set of moral guidelines, which were provided by our civil religion, along with the protection of religious freedom afforded within its borders. The formula worked so well that by mid-century the United States had elected its first Catholic president. President Kennedy ran for office on the promise that his faith would not interfere with the duties of the presidency.[11] By century's end, however, another President won his bid to the White House by flaunting his faith as a sign of fitness for office. In less than forty years, the country moved from faith being a political liability to it being a political asset. When the right religion becomes a prerequisite for leading the Free World, one knows that the balance between Church and State in America has tilted.

And the new Christian conservatism had an important role to play in that shift. Throughout our nation's history, there have always been segments of American Christianity who were tempted to push for Christian hegemony, for an American theocracy. The struggle began with our founding generation, as Federalists pushed for the establishment of Christianity, while Jeffersonians supported a strictly secular state. Every generation since has given the country a fair share of advocates for a Christian America. At our nation's birth those who sought to build a Christian America hailed from Congregational and Episcopal quarters. These days they are represented by conservative Christian communities. What those groups have always failed to understand is the crucial role that a secular public square plays in the maintenance of a pluralist society ("E Pluribus Unum"). A secular order allows different faiths to flourish, while checking the desire of some to remake America after their own image.

More importantly, they fail to learn from U.S. history. Efforts to *Christianize* the nation have always been rebuffed, at every instance, since our founding days.[12] So, the current conservative drive to "restore" America is not without precedent. What is different is that the rise of the conservative Church at the end of the twentieth century has empowered Christian conservatives to challenge the previous balance between civil religion and a competitive religious market. In the past, that balance kept Christian hegemonic tendencies in check. But the conservative movement is now powerful enough, and has enough political allies, that it can keep on pressing beyond the usual checks and balances. Furthermore, the drive to restore America these days is taking place in at least two different ways: conservative Christians are reproducing modernity *within* their Christian canopy, while seeking to colonize the nation's public square.

So, America's religious plurality is being challenged by the creation of a parallel Christian version of modernity, with exclusive conservative clubs, professional associations, broadcasting, dating services, music, and so on; and by the imposition of conservative Christian values upon secular institutions, be they public schools, clinics, the courts, the media, or the government. How is the conservative Church able to drive such large-scale enterprise? The answer is simple: As Christian conservatism grew in numbers and resources, it developed a more combative stance toward the modern world, instilling in its members a deep sense of marginality, and a bifurcated view of society ("us vs. them"). As a result, when religious conservatism rose, so did social polarization in the United States. In fact, the 2004 presidential election illustrates these two important trends rather nicely. Given their numbers, conservative Christians enjoyed an unprecedented level of political influence in that election. But those "values voters" also displayed a heightened sense of cultural estrangement.

TAKING BACK AMERICA

Who could have imagined (two thousand years into Christian history) that a presidential election in the most powerful Christian nation in the world would be marked by a strand of combative Christian conservatism *and* strong feelings of religious marginality? Nevertheless, that is exactly what happened. Conservative Christians comprised a solid voting block—at least one-third of the American electorate—and they did vote on their feelings of alienation. Though representing the fastest growing segment of American Christianity, and despite the pervasiveness of their views in our society, conservative believers felt culturally alienated, and threatened as a religious "minority."

An Ohio voter, a mother in a pro-Bush family, put it best in her post-election interview. She thought Americans saw her family as "religious kooks." Happy with Bush's victory, she was still not sure that her joy or views were shared by the rest of the American population. In their mid-twenties, she and her husband oppose abortion, favor a constitutional amendment supporting heterosexual marriage, and want more Supreme Court justices like Scalia and Thomas. They homeschool their children, and are part of a nondenominational megachurch that helps "families hold down the family fort in the twenty-first century."[13] So, their joy in victory was still mixed with a sense of alienation. Another Midwestern voter felt that liberal folks thought him weird for his faith.[14]

Ironically, it was this sense of cultural exclusion that drove Christian voters to piece together a political coalition that dwarfed all other electoral networks in the country. Their size and discipline surprised even the savviest political commentators. Their resources, organization, and steadfast commitment reflected both numerical strength *and* cultural dislocation. Moreover, post-election interviews confirmed their sense of threat: Washington politicians did not represent their interests; other Americans did not understand their urgency. Judging by their comments, the country was in danger of turning into a den of iniquity, a godless society devoid of all moral restraint. Never mind that the Catholic John Kerry was a man of deep religious conviction; or that his running mate grew up as a Southern Baptist in North Carolina. Conservative believers rallied behind George Bush as if he was the only thing keeping America from turning its back on God.

Richard Land, president of the *Ethics and Religious Liberty Commission* of the *Southern Baptist Convention*, calculated that conservative Christians made up from 30 to 40 percent of the electorate.[15] Even a more conservative estimate[16] would still represent a sizable swath of Americans voters. Embattled religious conservatives, who for most of the twentieth century had been completely absent from the political process, worked with undying zeal to pull off amazing results:

> Evangelical Christian groups were often more aggressive and sometimes better organized on the ground *than* the Bush campaign. The White House struggled to stay abreast of the Christian right and consulted with the movement's leaders in weekly conference calls. But in many respects, Christian activists led the charge that GOP operatives followed and capitalized upon.... In battlegrounds such as Ohio, scores of clergy members attended legal sessions explaining how they could talk about the election from the pulpit. Hundreds of churches launched registration drives, thousands of churchgoers registered to vote, and millions of voter guides were distributed by Christian and antiabortion groups.[17]

The hard work paid off. Bush won with 79 percent of the 26.5 million evangelical votes, the Republican Party increased its hold on both chambers of Congress, thirteen states approved amendments preserving heterosexual marriage,[18] and "Moral values" topped the list of reasons for voting in exit polls.[19] The largest segment of American Christianity gave President Bush enough support to beat Senator Kerry in almost *every religious category*. For instance, some 61 percent of weekly churchgoers voted for Bush; among those never attending church the numbers reversed in Kerry's favor.[20]

To an international observer, the most puzzling question of the election must have been: why were so many religious conservatives feeling so alienated in their own country, *even* after a majority of fellow Americans voted their way? Why were they feeling marginalized in the nation with the highest rates of church attendance,[21] whose money and pledge of allegiance honor the Almighty, and whose presidents are sworn upon a Bible? All recent American Presidents were practicing Christians. By a recent count, 491 out of 535 members of Congress consider themselves Christians. Moreover, the country boasts the largest grid of Christian churches (at least 330,000 by one estimate) and parachurch organizations in the world, in greater geographic density than anywhere else. Its network of Christian schools, from kindergarten to graduate programs, is the largest on earth!

And yet, their feelings of marginality deepened precisely as conservative Christians reached new heights in numbers and resources. It is hard to see the reasons for alienation. But religious alienation has been a hallmark of the conservative faith, no matter the historical circumstances. Christian marginality could be found in the working fields of colonial America. It fueled two Great Awakenings. It energized nineteenth-century camp meetings and the revivals of the American frontier. It launched the conservative missionary work of the late 1800s, and sustained an otherworldly religious worldview during the Great Depression.[22] Long before our recent culture wars, or the Republican takeover of American politics, religious conservatives have felt culturally marginal.

THE POWER OF RELIGIOUS MARGINALITY

Marginality is a powerful religious drive. It leads the faithful to great sacrifices. The more they feel shut out from the mainstream, the greater their zeal to overcome the challenge. The conservative Christians who helped elect George Bush exemplify that pattern. Unlike their Roman counterparts of olden days, they were never at any risk of real persecution. None faced jail, torture, exile, or death on account of faith. Their churches did not face popular opposition. Nevertheless, their sense of urgency implied a palpable threat. To them, the dangers raised by the election were not imaginary. The threat was real. Why would they feel so threatened in a tolerant nation? After all, freedom of worship is a pillar of the American compact. Luke's Beatitudes offers a good starting point in our investigation. The text presents some of the seeds of early Christian marginality. Here Jesus instructs followers that being threatened, ridiculed, and hated are preconditions for divine approval:

> Blessed are you poor, for yours is the kingdom of God.
> Blessed are you that hunger now, for you shall be satisfied.
> Blessed are you that weep now, for you shall laugh.
> Blessed are you when men hate you, and when they revile you,
>   and cast out your name as evil, on account of the Son of man!
> Rejoice in that day, and leap for joy, for behold, your reward is great in heaven;
>   for so their fathers did to the prophets.[23]

A simplistic reading of Luke might lead to the conclusion that persecution is indeed the lot of the true Christian, *the path to inherit the kingdom*. Getting along with one's neighbors, accepting one's culture, or enjoying a certain degree of social prestige are not the best way to find God's favor; "fitting in" is not the prescribed role for the truly dedicated. In other words, "real" Christianity must always be in tension with the *World*.[24] That, of course, goes against the most commonsensical norms of social interaction. In real life, the poor are not the most respected; being hungry, distressed, or reviled is a not desirable social station; and no one in their right mind would aspire to constant persecution, no matter how righteous the cause. Constant suffering, for the sake of divine approval, is a tall order. But a literal reading of Luke paints this stark picture: Those not willing to give up earthly rewards aren't fit for heaven.

To be sure, Christianity does not hold a monopoly on marginality. The sense of cultural exclusion is a common religious *compensator*[25] in other monotheistic faiths. Spiritual rewards equally compensate for life's tribulations for Christians, Jews, or Muslims. The Torah and the Koran offer similar texts, with a similar implied sense of persecution (which might explain why Fundamentalism is common to the three faiths).[26] All three monotheistic traditions promise the Almighty's blessings upon those who suffer for his sake. But the similarities simply indicate how potent marginality is as a religious drive (particularly in monotheism). In Christianity's case marginality becomes an aberration, given the Christian hold on the Western world.

Were we to contextualize Luke's narrative, it would become clear that the Beatitudes represent the yearning of a downtrodden community.[27] Early followers of the Messiah had every reason to feel marginal at the time the Gospels were written. Socially shunned, politically persecuted, they relied solely upon their faith community for survival. The text simply expresses the longing of a small band of powerless converts, suffering in an occupied and obscure Roman province. It honors their perception that God chooses the meek and lowly to work his will upon the world. But Christian marginality was real for only a relatively short period of time. By the fourth century of the Common Era, Constantine was already leading the Church into becoming the official faith of the West.

Once fully ensconced in Rome's highest circles, Christianity conquered the upper echelons of other European societies. Eventually, its wholesale adoption by the most powerful empire on earth allowed the faith to reshape all of Europe's religious practices, legal traditions, and cultural mores. So it was a powerful continent-wide religious enterprise, not a small band of powerless converts, that laid the foundations of modern Europe.[28] For more than sixteen centuries the temporal power of the Church guaranteed its ultimate reach and influence throughout the known world. Christian canon law provided the legal basis for the constitutional framework of modern European states. Organized in hierarchical layers, nationalized within European kingdoms, Christianity reached into every corner of the European continent down to county/parish level, with a power beyond compare in relation to Judaism or Islam. Backed up by worldwide trade, its missions launched an era of discovery of new lands.

Though Church leaders retained marginality as a religious compensator and the means to control their base or recruit more followers, they certainly no longer depended upon the hereafter for their rewards—there were plenty of material resources in Christendom's earthly domains. So many, in fact, that material overreach was partly to blame for the Protestant Reformation. Even prior to Luther's movement, the Church already struggled with its temporal power. Pope Leo IX's reform reflected how intertwined the Church's material and spiritual interests had become only a thousand years into Christian history. He forbade the buying and selling of ecclesiastical offices and laity interference in Church affairs.

A contemporary of the Pope, Humber, the monk, defined Christianity's power in stark theological terms: Christ established the Church as a hierarchy, with St. Peter's successor at its top; since the Church cared for the spiritual welfare of humankind, it should rightfully be placed above all secular powers, which were simply charged with the material well-being of their immediate subjects.[29] In time, the Church grew so powerful as to co-opt *entire* cultures. When the Bishop Augustine of Canterbury consulted the Papacy about the pagan customs of his English flock, his Holiness' reply showed how far Christianity had come from being the faith of the downcast:

> I have decided after long deliberation about the English people, namely that the idol temples of that race should by no means be destroyed, but only the idols in them.... For if the shrines are well built, it is essential that they should be changed from the worship of the devils to the service of the true God. When this people see that their shrines are not destroyed they will be able to banish error from their hearts and be more ready to come to the places they are familiar with, but now recognizing and worshipping the true God. And because they are in the habit of slaughtering much cattle as sacrifices to devils, some solemnity ought to be given to them in exchange for this.... Do not let them sacrifice animals to the devil, but let them slaughter animals for their own food to the praise of God, and let them give thanks to the Giver of all things for his bountiful provision.... It is doubtless impossible to cut out everything at once from their stubborn minds just as the man who is attempting to climb the highest places rises by steps and degrees and not by leaps.[30]

Along the way Christian tradition legitimated political *Absolutism*, meddled in the internal affairs of all European nations, and fueled long-ranging religious wars. It also played a role in the development of European (and consequently American) art, culture, and education. As Europeans moved into the New World, Christianity re-created its staying power in *every single* nation of the Americas, *well into the twenty-first century*. Even Mexico, the most secular of Latin American nations, could not curb the power of popular Christianity. In time, England, Holland, France, Spain, and Portugal re-created in the New World the Christian hold of Western civilization. It has remained a constant through five hundred years of continental American history.

In light of this abbreviated evidence, it is hard to see contemporary perceptions of Christian marginality as true. So, if Christianity has been so successful, if its values, myths, and rituals are so deeply woven into Western culture, if its codes still influence Western law, then why is there such a deep feeling of estrangement running through a large segment of conservative believers today? Why do Christians in the largest and richest religious community, in the most powerful and Christian-oriented nation in the world still feel like outsiders? This book argues that Christian marginality is *never dispelled by temporal success*. It is re-created in every generation, with every Christian group that pushes the Church back to its orthodox origins.

So long as dedicated conservative Christians live in tension with the World,[31] so will marginality remain a vital part of their tradition. Their noncontextual reading of the New Testament will continue to feed a sense of exclusion, guaranteeing the marginal disposition of their religious communities. The more earnest Christians retreat from "worldly temptations," the more estranged they will feel from the larger culture. This world is not their home, so it can seriously compromise their faith. In the meantime, marginality revitalizes the larger faith, since Christianity is renewed in purpose by the marginal, sectarian groups that push it back to its original fervor. As long as American conservative Christians retain a literal interpretation of their Bibles, they will rely on marginality to sustain their sense of mission and identity. And they will continue to see themselves as outsiders in America's mainstream culture.

DIVIDED WE STAND: FUELING RELIGIOUS MARGINALITY

Christian marginality is generated by bifurcating the world into two clear camps—the *chosen* and the *damned*. A quick glance at Luke's Beatitudes confirms this notion: the poor, not the wealthy, inherit the kingdom; the hungry, not the sated, are satisfied; the weeping, not those who laugh, find comfort; and the hated and reviled, not the respectable, are greatly rewarded in heaven. The world fits neatly into two sides. More importantly, these two sides must remain eternally antithetical. Members of the two groups may coexist in the same society, sometimes even in the same denomination, and may share superficial similarities such as nationality, class, education, income, or ethnicity. But their everlasting destinies have set them apart. It is this ultimate sorting makes it hard for religious conservatives to compromise, even in a tolerant society.

The issue is not whether they can be compassionate, broad-minded, or sympathetic toward "sinners." There is a teleological divide that cuts to the quick: the "other" does not share my spiritual essence. Avoiding contact with the damned world preserves psychological and religious congruence, but at the cost of social exclusion. So, bifurcation, by necessity, demands *oppressive* and *oppressed camps* if the message is to retain its potency. And no matter how strong the "reviled" side is, those on Jesus' side must always be the underdogs, even if they control all the key institutions in society. Since the persecuted must have persecutors, the rest of humanity is by definition their enemy, their motives always questionable, their intentions always suspect.

Bifurcation fosters marginality *especially among the most literal readers of the biblical text*. To them, being a Christian means being reviled, suffering in Christ's name. The marginal condition in this world is the blissful lot of the dedicated faithful. In fact, those in the conservative Church do not fear persecution. Persecution only strengthens their resolve. It confirms their righteous status. *What they fear is indifference*. To a literal reader of the Bible, if the faith does not generate persecution it is too weak. So it follows that if the world simply ignores Christians, that becomes a sign of spiritual failure. A faith that requires constant rejection and forsaking cannot stand without a present (though perhaps imaginary) threat.

To put things in perspective, bifurcation was once a useful tool for the nascent Church. It helped a fledgling Christian movement survive harsh conditions. The first Christians were surrounded by competing faiths at a time when they were facing political persecution. Their faith's survival was not assured. Suspecting Christians of sedition or apostasy, the Roman government put a premium on Christian affiliation—one could lose loved ones, or even one's own life, for following only the Messiah. Bifurcation under such a threat made perfect sense. Marginality increased the solidarity among believers, helped them develop a strong Christian identity, and sustained their urgent sense of mission. Persecution and martyrdom only united early converts, driving them into dedicated, self-sacrificing religious work.

The fascinating thing about Christian marginality though is its *staying power*. Two thousand years hence, as Christianity celebrates a monopolist hold on the West, some of its followers still feel persecuted. That sense of persecution still rallies American conservative Christians to battle. In their case, one gets the sense that marginality drives the push to challenge the "dark" side (i.e., secular humanism) in every corner of American society. And in an era of instant gratification, increased consumerism, and extensive scientific intrusion in everyday life, there are plenty of enemies to battle! The widespread sense of religious marginality within American conservatism confirms the notion that feelings of exclusion are crucial to keep believers actively engaged in the promotion of their faith (and of late in the restoration of their society).

There is plenty of sociological data supporting the connection between marginality, increased faith promotion, and subsequent growth. For instance, Laurence Iannaccone finds that churches with a marginal worldview are the fastest growing in America.[32] In a longitudinal study of American Christianity, Roger Finke and Rodney Stark show that denominations *with the strongest sense of marginality* were precisely the ones that became long-term winners in the American religious market.[33] Denominations with the clearest sense of bifurcation, the highest cost of religious membership, and the most demanding, exclusive, and unapologetic faith are the ones that grow the most in American history. As churches lower their marginal standards or weaken their zeal, they stop growing.

Sociological research also explains how marginality is *preserved* within Christianity. Traditionally, feelings of marginality run strongest amidst smaller, fringe Christian groups that continually push the larger faith toward stricter, orthodox practices. Disenfranchised, working-class sects continuously challenge the more established churches toward greater rectitude. However, as their dedicated members work hard and abstain from worldly luxuries, they (and their churches) prosper. Prosperity pushes them away from their original zeal toward a more conciliatory stance within the affluent culture. In other words, churches that do well eventually lose the marginal edge. Once marginal fringe groups accommodate to the more comfortable standards of mainstream society, splinter groups emerge from within, rekindling the original drive, and the cycle starts again.

The classical works of Max Weber, Ernst Troeltsch, and Richard Niebuhr all document this process. The growth of marginal sects led to their religious *mainstreaming*, and to larger cultural compromises. Zealous offshoots then pushed devotees to return to the "true faith," assuring the continuity of the marginal vision within Christianity.[34] As long as fringe groups remind the larger Church of its supposed tension with the World, Christian marginality never goes away, no matter how successful particular marginal groups may become. Offshoots will always recapture the original zeal. So the marginal desire for righteous living, even at the cost of earthly possessions or social status, is a constant source of renewal for the entire faith.

It is fair to assume that the presence of marginal groups within Christianity dates back to the faith's beginnings. Marginality was the hallmark of some congregations in the early Christian community, but it also inspired the privations of sixth and seventh-century monasticism. It informed Saint Benedict's rule and the travails of St. Francis' penitent order. Marginality drove Luther to rebuke Vatican rule and fueled John Wesley's fiery Methodism both in Europe and later on American soil. Marginality brought a certain brand of Christianity to the New World and to the American frontier. It filled the slums of Northern industrial cities and small Southern towns with ample religious fervor. All along, its orthodox practices renewed the established Church, reminding it constantly of worldly tensions that are rarely found in the more established confessions.

Today's Christian Soldiers

As previous sociological research predicted, current conservative groups have enjoyed an unprecedented level of success during the last two and a half decades. Since the 1980s, they have amassed enough members and material resources to quickly become key players in the American religious economy, *and* in the larger public arena. But unlike previous marginal groups, whose marginality was compromised by their newly gained middle-class status, current marginal Christians *insist on retaining their zealous faith.*

Rejection of worldly riches was easier throughout most of the twentieth century, when Christian conservatism was limited to fewer faithful, with lower rates of educational and occupational attainment, who gathered in small, fringe groups. However, as the American religious economy realigned during the second half of the century, Christian conservatism expanded its reach into the more educated and middle-class segments of American Christianity. In time, large nondenominational conservative megachurches sprung up in most American cities. New publishing houses and support services came into being to promote the marginal faith. Now Christian conservatives are confronted with a situation where they hope to sustain an ascetic and otherworldly spirituality, *without* having to sacrifice their middle-class tastes and higher levels of prosperity.

Who, then, are these new Christian soldiers? For the purposes of this survey, they are first and foremost Protestant. Unlike their Roman Catholic counterparts, American Christian conservatives do not entertain an *analogical faith*.[35] They do not see God imbuing material reality with grace.[36] The analogical worldview requires a sacramental understanding of the divine revealed through stories, music, icons, and art. The God of marginal Christianity is utterly transcendent. Separate from creation, He (the marginal Christian God is a patriarchal *He*) is not to be confused with it. Immanence to religious conservatives is akin to idolatry, an unacceptable sin. Thus, marginality seems most acute among highly conservative, fundamentalist, or evangelical Protestant groups[37] in the United States.

What sets these religious conservatives apart from other American Christians is their interpretation of *salvation history*. They see God working through human history to redeem the saved. Salvation is God's utmost intent for humankind, the epicenter of human history. All that came before and will be experienced afterward exist for the explicit purpose of bringing God's plan to fruition. The details of the plan may vary from group to group, but most agree that the ultimate goal of history is the rescue of God's saved. The timeline for human redemption also varies. Some groups are *Dispensationalist*, premillenial activists,[38] others postmillennial. Nevertheless, all groups see God's plan for humanity in similar fashion: all human events lead to the final establishment of God's kingdom as the endpoint of history.

Lately many groups have come to believe that Christ gave his followers dominion over the world and will not return until they *Christianize* it. ("That at the name of Jesus every knee should bow ... and that every tongue should confess that Jesus Christ is Lord.")[39] Their part in God's plan energizes them to restore America, to refashion it as a Christian nation. In that sense, marginality reshapes reality for contemporary Christian conservatives in cosmic ways.[40] First, it provides them with a *history-bound and rational* (in the sociological sense) religious worldview.[41] But it also motivates them to take upon themselves the task of fleshing out God's *salvation history* through the voluntary and disciplined practice of their faith. That call had always formed the basis for their proselytizing work. Nowadays it also informs their push for America's restoration.

Another known characteristic of conservative Christianity is its view of salvation. Christian conservatives argue that no one is born a Christian; each must become so by *choice*. Those to be saved must have a salvific encounter with God and be born again (which explains the proselytizing). The emphasis on individual salvation has two important consequences for the movement. First, much as the larger culture, *conservative Christianity is highly individualistic*. Individual salvation also implies *intentionality*—one has to be old enough to be spiritually accountable to God, to acknowledge his/her need for redemption.

Voluntary salvation also affects the marginal faith's view of the Church. *Conservative Christianity has no unified, corporate profile* akin to the structures of mainline denominations. Mainline churches have a stronger national identity than that of their local congregations.[42] National offices and regional jurisdictions engage in nationwide initiatives that link up local places of worship. Marginal Christianity, on the other hand, is organized around loose coalitions of autonomous congregations. Salvation is an individual experience that must be reproduced time and again in order to create a local church, a community of the saved. Each marginal congregation serves as the training ground for the faithful: they are called to grow in faith, bear witness, and save others. Their joint effort defines the congregational work.

So, conservative congregations work together through decentralized networks that share their individualistic and autonomous worldview to accomplish tasks that are beyond the resources of local groups.[43] As Meredith McGuire describes them:

> The purely voluntary associative basis of religious networks makes them more flexible supports for the modern mobile individual. Similarly, the contemporary religious emphasis on personal experience and the individual's "right to subjectivity" are well suited to personal motivation and decision-making in a societal situation where values and ends are not institutionally "given."[44]

Needless to say, the faith's voluntaristic approach, in a society that prizes individualism, generates a strong degree of loyalty. It is based upon a spirituality of change, whereby a personal, life-transforming event places the believer at the center of human history (all else must dwarf by comparison). The saved become God's vessels and part of his unfolding plan for humankind. It is a calling that generates few defections. For instance, a study of baby boomer spirituality found that 80 percent of those who grew up conservative Protestants remained so through adulthood, compared to 65 percent of mainline Protestants. Moreover, while two-thirds of mainline boomers dropped out during their teens/early twenties, only slightly more than a third of conservatives (36 percent) did so. And of those, 25 percent still consider themselves conservative Protestants (though inactive).[45] It seems that salvation history adds a unique quality to Christian marginality in America.

CREATING A CHRISTIAN ORDER

One of the issues raised by this book is the fact that the recent success of Conservative Christianity presents a challenge to the faith's traditional nature. For most of the last century, marginal groups decidedly rejected modernity. The evolution of conservative Christianity during the last quarter of the twentieth century changed its approach to modernity. Marginal Christian communities no longer shun the modern, but seek to *co-opt* or to *colonize* it. Current Christian conservatives are happy to appropriate modernity's benefits. Unlike their predecessors, they are more educated, have higher-ranking occupations, and the organizational skills/expertise to develop a carefully planned, large-sized, orthodox religious movement. They also have the cultural capital and political clout to push harder for a Christian social order.

Evidence of the change was plentiful by the century's end. The *megachurches* that now dot American suburbia exemplify their talent.[46] As early as the 1980s it was possible to track the appearance of Christian theme parks, contemporary Christian music (CCM), the increase in conservative high schools and colleges, and a number of lifestyle changes (Christian dieting, exercising, and dating are good examples here). Their newly acquired talents and resources made it hard for marginal groups to resist flexing their muscles in the public square. Efforts to bring prayer to public schools, to introduce *Intelligent Design* in the science curricula, to ban abortion and gay marriage, and to multiply Christian (i.e., Protestant) symbols in public spaces grew exponentially in the last two and a half decades.

Ironically, those feeling most marginal nowadays are also the savviest about political action committees and the use of conservative power. Take *Coral Ridge Presbyterian Church*, for example. The 10,000-member Florida congregation has sponsored, for the past ten years, a national conference ("Reclaiming America for Christ") to equip Christian activists in their push to take the country back to its Christian origins. In the words of its senior minister, Rev. D. James Kennedy,

> As the vice-regents of God, we are to bring His truth and His will to bear on every sphere of our world and our society. We are to exercise godly dominion and influence over our neighborhoods, our schools, our government ... our entertainment media, our news media, our scientific endeavors—in short, over every aspect and institution of human society.[47]

One would not expect this kind of agenda from a traditional conservative congregation, nor such religious bifurcation from a mainline Presbyterian minister. Clearly, the American religious landscape has shifted. Nevertheless, *Coral Ridge* is part of a large network of churches and parachurch groups committed to establishing a Christian order in the United States. Kennedy, one of the three best-known leaders among American evangelicals, interacts regularly with powerful politicians and high-ranking government officials. He, along with other conservative leaders, hopes to *Christianize* the country one issue at a time, until their faith represents the nation's predominant worldview.

The rest of the book profiles the transformation of the conservative Church, and its push for America's restoration. Chapter 2 shows how marginal Christianity is co-opting modernity, how marginal believers are *Christianizing* secular, modern activities rather than preserving the detached, ascetic mode of their predecessors. In remaking modernity, they replace the *godly life* of previous Christian eras with the *God-filled life* of today's Christian suburbia. The result is the creation of a Christian cultural ghetto, with exclusive Christian clubs and activities that cater only to the redeemed. The chapter explores how the conservative Church is building a suburbia that parallels its secular counterpart. Middle-class tastes, lifestyles, and amenities have transformed the way conservative Christians experience their faith.

Chapter 3 traces the political organizing undertaken by marginal believers in their effort to *colonize* America's public square. Religious conservatives have adopted a piecemeal approach to the country's restoration, which is aimed at challenging secular America. Using single-issue organizations, they attack modernity from multiple angles with a unified agenda. The single-issue approach hides their ultimate goal: the establishment of a Christian social order. The faith's influence in America's culture wars has guaranteed that issues normally approached on the basis of their practical or technical merits, are now reviewed under the religious prism. The presence of the conservative Church in the American political arena further polarizes our nation. To Christian conservatives, every issue gained brings the ultimate goal of Christian restoration a little closer.

Chapters 4 and 5 describe the conservative agenda for the new millennium. Chapter 4 explores conservative Christian activities related to religious freedom. Here, religious conservatives are working to reduce state intervention in their family life and in their children's education. Defense of the family requires a push for traditional family values and the protection of the nuclear, heterosexual marriage. Defense of schooling led to the creation of homeschooling and Christian schools ranging from kindergarten to college. Chapter 5 examines conservative Christian efforts to promote public morality. Marginal believers are pushing for greater state control of human sexuality, and governmental support for a hegemonic Christian presence in the public arena. Regulation of sexuality places conservatives at odds with more progressive trends brought by the 1960s cultural revolution. The push for a Christian public arena conflates religion and politics in ways that challenge America's traditional separation of Church and State.

The concluding chapter considers the overall impact of this new conservative movement for the faith and for the larger society. Success is reshaping the conservative faith, *and changing its internal dynamics*. The gargantuan task Christian conservatives set out for themselves of restoring America presents quite a challenge. What will happen to the faith if the final result is not a Christian order? Furthermore, what are the implications of the Christian co-optation of modernity for the larger society? Can the balance between Church and State withstand such frontal attack? Will the drive for Christian hegemony challenge our constitutional protections regarding religious freedom? Will the conservative Christian push for a new social order transform American society?

Marginal Christianity is part of a larger neoconservative movement that has evolved into a hybrid of religion, politics, and social control.[48] Given its extensive reach—the institutions, structures, and processes it controls—the movement can deeply affect the way we live for quite a while. Thus the timeliness of this study, and the need for us to understand the full consequences of its evolution.

2

WILL THE CIRCLE BE UNBROKEN? CO-OPTING MODERNITY

"Christians understand that church is not an activity—it's a lifestyle. Being part of the body of Christ is how you live life. It's not Something you do once a week."[1]
—Pastor Buddy George, Saddleback Church, California

The first sign of change in American Christian conservatism is not found in the country's political scene. It is found in the Church's co-optation of modernity. More affluent and educated than their predecessors, current religious conservatives are expanding the borders of their faith to encompass quite secular everyday activities. Too beholden to suburban comforts, they strive to sanctify the profane. Take the *Church on the Move* in Tulsa, Oklahoma, for instance. Every Wednesday night some 800 young congregants gather in a 92,000 square foot, state-of-the-art *community entertainment center* (CEC). The CEC has the ultimate in sanctified entertainment—basketball courts; iPod, computer, and video game stations. Young people listen to MP3 downloads, play ball, shoot pool, or share a video game, after taking part in a hip worship service that includes a ten-member Christian rock band.[2] One wonders how sanctified the video games are, or if what is browsed in cyberspace is exclusively religious in nature. But the wholesomeness of the setting somehow makes it all praiseworthy.

Underneath this conservative version of sanctified entertainment lies an honest desire to lead a holy life, even if amidst fast-paced activity. *The trick is to be simultaneously modern and pious.* That struggle (being in the World but not *of the* World) has been at the heart of Christianity since its inception. Christians of every era have wrestled with the demands of the Kingdom and the practical requirements of an imperfect world. Jesus invited the apostles to leave it all behind and to follow him. Yet they managed to stay in touch with their home communities and visit family regularly. After his death some even returned to the fishing boats to make a living.

That tension has been there ever since: Christians are simultaneously heaven-bound and earth-cast. Decisions that carry eternal consequences are framed within situation-driven, temporal conditions. The quest for utmost holiness has been a constant in Christian history. Church documents from the early days, to the Patristic era, to St. Augustine's and St. Aquinas's writings, to modern creeds like the Westminster Confession or councils such as the Vatican Council II, all register such lofty goals. Holiness inspired creeds, encyclicals and councils all the way to the twenty-first century. It haunted Paul. It dominated the early Church's Zeitgeist. It drove Christian mysticism in the high Middle Ages. It encouraged the rise of monastic orders. It pervaded Luther's and Calvin's Protestant search for justification. Holiness drove Crusades, and led Pilgrims across the ocean to found a city on the hill. All along, mundane demands have followed Christianity's most daring flights of spirituality; the soaring always anchored by our earth-cast condition.

Not surprisingly, American Christian conservatives are just as desirous of a holy life. So much so, they are redefining holy living. In America's Christian suburbia the *holiness* of previous eras is being replaced by the modern notion of the *God-filled life*. What once meant a life of discipline, sacrifice, and obedience to God's universal, timeless standards, is now a life of Christian suburban activities, be they work-related, hobbies, sports, or leisure. The former pointed to Christ's utopian paradigm of human existence, with *real discipleship costs*. The latter affords religious conservatives the means to relish modern living. This is not a subtle switch, but one that is quite effective, since it allows millions of marginal believers to pursue a passionate faith while keeping their traffic with the modern world.

Jesus' standards for holiness were not only hard, but also *impractical*.[3] Followers were asked to give up everything: to forsake marriage and family, to lead a life of mendicancy, to roam the countryside, to survive on itinerant preaching, and to belong to protosocialist communities whose property was shared. Sometimes the Messiah's rules were stricter than the Law of Moses. Disciples were forbidden to lust in their hearts, to divorce, to worship while holding grudges. They were told to work on the Sabbath, to expect persecution and imprisonment, to pray for their enemies, and to bless those who cursed them. Such level of *intentional dedication* demands quite a sacrificial disposition. But the Kingdom of God was at hand and they were making haste to prepare for it. Gone were plans for steady vocations, for the joys of long-lasting friendships in their hometowns, for a lifelong journey with the love of their lives, or the simple pleasures of watching their children come of age.

The *God-filled life*, by comparison, carries a far more convenient price tag. It is possible to remain happily married, to pursue a successful career, to keep a prestigious and well-paying job, and to have a finely appointed home in a plush, gated neighborhood. One is allowed to enjoy the fine things in life, to claim that property taxes are not biblical, and to share in the comfort of like-minded country club friends. The modern version of holiness heaps praise upon the free market, presses for stronger prison laws and the death penalty, cuts welfare to the nation's neediest, and supports a strong defense budget. All that is required is for one to give lip service to Christ, while engaging in those practices.

In all fairness, the original standards of holiness demanded too much perfection, a worldly detachment that could not be met under earthly conditions.[4] Failed Christian communal experiences, like the Shakers, give us plenty of warning about its hardships.[5] An imperfect world requires some degree of accommodation. Even the Amish deal with the constraints of city and county ordinances, and the exacting health standards of the modern market. Well-intended religious practices must eventually compromise with the demands of practical realities. *So every Christian age becomes known for the concessions it makes.* For the early Church, for instance, it meant reexamining worldly detachment when Jesus' Second Coming failed to materialize. Those energized by the *parousia* had to go back to making a living, owning homes, raising children, tending fields, and building local communities.

Other eras forged equally distinct compromises. The Constantinian Church was as power hungry as other Roman institutions. Popes in the Middle Ages begot children, some who grew up to be princes of the Church. Catholic priests had wives and children as well. Bishoprics and parishes were bought by wealthy European families. The Crusades proved a profitable enterprise for Christian knights. The Protestant wars were politically expedient for European kings and princes. The Church hierarchy benefited from the absolute power of kings. Protestant clergy broke with the traditional teachings on usury to legitimate new forms of trade and investment as capitalism reshaped European economies. Iberian Christians slaughtered or imprisoned entire Latin American societies in the name of God. Closer to home, Southern clergy relied on their Bibles to defend slavery on American soil.

Thus, it is not surprising to find the quest for a holy life equally compromised today. In our period of late modernity, with globalization reaching into every corner of the world, there is greater choice, reflexivity, and uncertainty as modern individuals and societies try to colonize the future.[6] Instant communication, integrated worldwide commerce, and rapid technological change create complex demands upon the spiritual world.

If modernity is problematic for Christians in general, it is more so for their conservative peers. Greater individual autonomy may seem good for a highly individualistic faith, but greater social interconnectedness makes it harder for religious conservatives to avoid "pernicious influences." Much like previous generations, today's marginal believers wish to be faithful, and to lead lives of spiritual integrity. But they must do so under very *modern* conditions, having to constantly sort out which parts of the world are essentially evil and therefore unredeemable, and which are co-optable. Such a confusing process yields different standards in different regions of the country, varying from group to group, congregation to congregation, and in many cases from minister to minister. No wonder Christian bookstores have mushroomed across the land, with rows and rows of self-help Christian books.

GOD AND THE INTERNET

Modern living multiplies choices, which multiply spiritual guidelines, as well as dangers. It generates anxieties unknown to Christians in other eras. It requires daily sorting of well meaning, but spiritually threatening practices. Affluence throws conservative Christians into a maelstrom of trends, lifestyles, and niche capitalist markets. Should Christians diet? Should they work in certain industries? Should their children listen to secular music? To co-opt modernity, marginal believers have to reshape their secular practices into sound Christian living. They must constantly review their career choices, friendships, interactions, and decisions, striving for flexible living under rigid orthodox teachings. How to sort? How to choose? How to approach the ancient texts? Which practices to co-opt? Opinions vary and guidelines conflict, turning the quest for holy living into a confusing enterprise.

The struggle to discern God's will for one's life can be quite problematic. Google "God's will" and you will be overwhelmed by more than six million Web sites of page after page of ministries solely dedicated to guide born-again Christians through the pitfalls of modern life. With names like *Christian Answers*, *Deeper Life Family*, *Got Questions? In Touch*, *Into Thy Word*, or *Nehemiah Ministries*, the sites offer short- and long-term plans to cope with modern dilemmas. Sporting up-to-date, psychological language, they carefully anchor their instructions with randomly picked Bible verses. The biblical texts insure the overall promise of discernment of God's mind in all pressing matters.

Ironically, modernity generates a multifaceted form of conservative spirituality, riddled with multiple options. For those of us not used to cyberspace spiritual counseling, the most important skill in seeking God's guidance seems to be the ability to *hyperlink the right biblical passages in the right order*. Little attention is paid to biblical narrative or text criticism, or any other form of biblical exegesis. Once the right verses are lined up the right way, all is revealed. Some sites even provide real life examples to illustrate the process of discernment:

> Jennifer is considering a job offer that seems good from every angle except one: she's uncertain how to reconcile it with a past experience of guidance. When Jennifer was offered her current job as a legal secretary in Sacramento, she was living in Tallahassee. She was a new Christian then, and anxious to be certain about God's will. On a balmy May afternoon, she spent several hours walking on a Gulf beach, praying for God's guidance. After praying for about an hour, she felt a surge of conviction that God wanted her to accept the offer.[7]

If anything, cyberspace ministries only confirm the notion that modern choices increase religious anxiety. Make the wrong decision, take the wrong turn, and you can be faced with stark spiritual consequences. Discernment of God's will is so critical today that even those too young to understand its nuances are taught to seek it. The Google search yielded at least one middle-schooler's home-school assignment on how to find God's will.[8]

Fortunately, the conservative search for divine direction is not restricted to cyberspace. The marginal Church is responding to raised levels of spiritual anxiety by creating workshops and congregation-based ministries related to the *God-filled life* (a life where God is supposedly present in every area of living). Conservative religious communities all over the United States are marketing *discipleship* programs to help members sort out their Christian responsibility in these modern times. Megachurches in large metropolitan areas provide year-round *discipleship* training. Smaller congregations, in more remote areas, offer short-term clinics or weekend workshops.

In fact, entire independent ministries have been built upon *God-filled life* programs. Take Houston's *Lakewood Ministries*, for instance.[9] Founded in 1959 by a former Baptist pastor, *Lakewood* was a large, charismatic congregation at the time of the founder's death. With a "feel good" approach to modernity, in six short years, his son—Pastor Joel Osteen—has put *Lakewood* on the national megachurch map. When Joel succeeded his father in 1999, the church had 6,000 members, a local television program, and a ten million-dollar budget. By 2005 he had turned it into a fifty million-dollar enterprise, with an international television audience, and the 16,000-seat Compaq Center as its headquarters (previously owned by the Houston Rockets—renovations alone cost $92 million). *Lakewood*'s previous sanctuary seated about 8,000 worshipers, and it took 1,200 ushers and 2,800 volunteers to keep its Sunday operations flowing. Some 30,000 visitors stopped by weekly. Osteen's televised services now reach 95 percent of the nation's households and 150 other countries. The church has sixty full-time ministers on its payroll to provide personal counseling and related ministerial duties.

The secret of Osteen's success? The *God-filled life*. His messages focus on the fact that God can make something new of people's lives, regardless of social condition, age, race, or gender. Amidst life's most confusing choices, it is still possible to know God's will. Unlike his father, Pastor Joel does not deliver hellfire-and-brimstone sermons. Despite the size of his congregation, the preaching is cozy, intimate, and chat-like. Messages are delivered in a serene, emotionally neutral style, shaped by a "gospel of hope and self-help—simple Scripture-based motivational messages, notably devoid of politics and hot-button policy issues."[10]

To Osteen, Christian living is about finding the *God-filled life*, about reaching one's potential as a child of God, and about finding higher levels of *fulfilled living*. Services generate the sense that anyone is truly welcome in *Lakewood*. The congregation bills itself as the church for the "unchurched." Hymn lyrics and biblical texts are projected on wide screens, for ease of reading. The inviting, down-home liturgy produces a sense of intimacy and care. Osteen's core message is summed up in his book, *Your Best Life Now: 7 Steps to Living at Your Full Potential* (2004). In less than a year the book sold over 1.5 million copies (a Spanish translation is being quickly produced). Royalties alone allowed Pastor Joel to forgo his $200,000 church salary. Book promotions sent him on a fifteen-city tour in 2005.

Lest we be cynical about his motives, Pastor Joel is not driven by the same crude moneymaking schemes of the 1980s televangelists. There is no direct soliciting in his televised services. No appeal is made for financial support. His out-of-town rallies normally charge a nominal fee to cover the lease on the venue. Tapes of his sermons can be purchased, but are not flaunted on TV. For him, TV ministry is truly an outreach, not simply a fund-raising tool. He sincerely believes his ministry empowers people to live out their faith in an uncertain and modern world.

24/7 Holiness

The pursuit of the *God-filled life* necessitates the creation of a Christian modernity. Only within the safe bounds of the faith can marginal believers address their modern anxieties. So they *Christianize* middle-class lifestyle and activities, creating *exclusive* services, clubs, health care, and even professional associations. Safety at last, within Christian bounds.

Unfortunately, the building of a Christian modernity places the Church in the odd condition of constantly sending mixed messages. For instance, media work is sinful, say in Hollywood or secular TV, but perfectly honorable at the 700 Club. Secular politics are morally bankrupt, but perfectly acceptable if one is a Christian political operative. Work in secular newspapers may be immoral, but completely praiseworthy if one publishes a Christian Webzine. The longer this goes on, the harder it becomes to draw the line. Can a Christian Gospel singer cross-over to Pop? Can a successful 700 Club anchor crossover to Fox News? Where is the ever-changing secular line?

The Church gives equally mixed messages in its public stances. Marriage is indissoluble, but megachurches create large-sized singles' ministries for all the divorced adults who crowd their sanctuaries. Evolution should be banned from public schools, but evolution-based medical technologies are fine in secular hospitals. There should be a Ten Commandments monument in every public square, but is it OK for Pat Robertson to suggest the U.S. government should murder the President of Venezuela (what happened to "Thou Shall Not Kill?"). Premarital sex ought to be forbidden, but those who lose their virginity can "reclaim" it at abstinence youth rallies. Homosexuality is a sin, but "cured" Christian gays can go on to ministry so long as they keep a "normal" heterosexual facade.

If only traditional standards could fix these highly, socially fluid conditions we live in! Faith incongruence stems from the fact that contemporary religious conservatives enjoy higher levels of education, occupation, and prestige. So it is harder for them to completely extricate their lives from the world. They end up neither able to fully reject, nor fully *Christianize* modernity. The more access to schooling, professional jobs, and material resources they have, the more enmeshed they become in secular activities. They live in American suburbs, have white-collar jobs, and share similar hobbies with other Americans.

This level of cultural immersion terribly complicates the Christian conservative effort to sort out the sacred and the profane. In other words, *the God-filled life does not eradicate spiritual anxiety, it exacerbates it.* When secular and Christian versions of modernity align, things are fine. But when they diverge, questions abound about the threshold of holy living. For instance, should a Christian engineer develop a weapon of mass destruction for a defense contractor? Or should a Christian biochemist work on chemical compounds that might later be used for contraceptives? Should a Christian doctor work in a for-profit hospital that puts stockholder interests above sound health care? Should a Christian surgeon in a cancer unit work for a hospital that performs abortions?

As the persistent questions abound, the struggle for holiness affects all kinds of middle-class occupations: Should a Christian accountant take a high-paying job in a corporation that has cigarette, liquor, or pornographic interests? Should a Christian stockbroker recommend highly profitable investments in morally tainted companies? Should a Christian architect design workplaces that increase management control over overworked employees? Should a Christian lawyer represent commercial interests riddled with dubious ethical practices? Should the director of a Christian school or clinic hire the best-qualified help or only Christian workers?

Leading a holy life today can be a complicated and tortuous business. No wonder dedicated Christians require so much guidance. One way to minimize modern contradictions is to *diffuse* holy living. While other Americans practice a segmented form of Christianity, one restricted to Sunday mornings and Wednesday nights; marginal believers spread their faith into every aspect of their lives. Other Christians may know the secular world requires tolerance, so they refrain from bringing religion into their work settings, neighborhoods, clubs, friendships, or hobbies. Life in a modern, multicultural society requires respect for people's private choices, faith included. So, religious differences are not part of expected social intercourse.

Anxious about modernity, conservatives bring their faith into every aspect of living and every social setting. Religion becomes a public affair: there is a Christian way to grow up, enter adolescence, deal with sexuality, find a mate, hold a family together, define school curricula for one's children, choose a career, find the right job, or enjoy leisure time. The irony in this redefinition of holiness is precisely how *modern* it is! Even *traditional values*, a hallmark of the conservative Church, are quite contemporary too. They stem not from ancient biblical prescriptions, but from an idealized version of 1950s America. Think of a religious version of *Ozzie and Harriet*; or better yet, *Pleasantville*: devout people, living in heterosexual families of breadwinning fathers and homemaking mothers. They all dwell in clean, safe, and quiet neighborhoods in a place where every neighbor is God-fearing; every community abhors abortion and homosexuality, and promotes prayer in public schools, and Christian patriotism.

Unfortunately the scenario is as foreboding as the sitcom in its end result. Life in such an artificial and uniform world would be as sterile and unreal as a made-for-TV series. The conservative fixation with the 1950s betrays the marginal Church's degree of *cultural captivity*. What is now considered "biblical" is nothing more than religious nostalgia for a cultural golden age. By comparison, the *godly life* of biblical times was rather stark and uncertain, with wars, pestilence, homicides, fratricides, droughts, and famines. To Abraham, following *El* meant a nomadic life, organized around irregular contacts with horticultural and pastoral societies. Polygamy, incest, jealous murders, infanticide, and intertribal rivalry were a constant in those days. Tribal gods demanded blood sacrifice, revenge, and harsh extended kinship duties. Assuming, of course, that the faithful were not enslaved in Babylon or Egypt, in which case they would have a harder time keeping family and community together.[11]

Close scriptural scrutiny also reveals the lack of biblical support for some of the 1950s' standards. Take the "biblical" Christian, heterosexual, nuclear family, for instance. Biblical families were strikingly different from such modern ideal. They resembled a small polygamous tribe; with a patriarch, his multiple wives, and concubines; married children, their wives and concubines; and grandchildren. This biblical "family" roamed around different lands, sustained by animal herds or farming, sometimes by living in small settlements of related, extended kin. The deity images of those times—shepherd, warlord, ruler, or king—bespeak of the premodern harsh conditions of the biblical world.

The conservative Christian ethos, on the other hand, is quite contemporary *and* quite American. As marginal believers read their King James Bibles, they do so through the ideological lens of an affluent, technological, suburban community. Not surprisingly, their "biblical standards" have an eerie resemblance to their own lifestyle. Their biblical interpretation legitimizes an idealized patriarchal world, based on 1950s cultural norms. As American values of olden days are superimposed to the sacred text, they become divine, universal. This kind of biblical exegesis shows that Christian conservatives take more than the English language for granted when they seek God's guidance. They assign a privileged hermeneutical status to their own culture, whereby American standards become biblical standards—part of the Creator's original plan for a redeemed, harmonious middle-class society.

PURSUING THE CHRISTIAN *QUALITY OF LIFE*

Their sacralization of middle-class values leaves religious conservatives blind to the depth of their cultural indebtedness. It also makes them vulnerable to fads that affect the larger American middle class. To be blunt, *what sells in suburbia sells equally well in Christian suburbia*. When the conservative Church creates a Christian niche/lifestyle within American capitalism, it surrenders the moral high ground to rather secular market trends. Take movie distribution, for example. Secular Hollywood relies on a distribution network of megaplex cinemas to sell its products. Conservative Christians have built their own circuit. In the fall of 2005, when the third installment in the series *Left Behind* was released, producers bypassed the movie chain system for a 3,200 church circuit. One producer reasoned that the church circuit represented "more locations, in more Zip codes, than all the major theater chains combined."[12]

Christian bookselling works the same way. Bill Anderson, president of the 2,200-member Christian Booksellers Association, says that sales of Christian books, CDs, DVDs, apparels, and gifts now exceed $4 billion a year. "More and more, churches have become gathering places that offer a panoply of services," he argued, "and one of them is retail."[13] Anderson's boast was enough to make a seasoned *Washington Post* reporter wonder whether conservative Christians could see the irony of having their own marketplace: "Among evangelical Christians the marketing rush often excites conflicting emotions: pride and excitement about the burgeoning Christian marketplace and how it might influence the wider culture, combined with anxiety about the commercialization of religion and how Hollywood might corrupt unwary churches."[14]

Creating a parallel version of modernity is not without its perils. There is always the danger that Christian marketing will blindly adopt the same shallow logic that drives other American consumer impulses. In a country devoid of violent regional conflicts, disenfranchised ethnic minorities (prone to terrorist acts), or large pockets of famished populations, it is easy to see how church life can become relatively sheltered and unduly influenced by the market. In the process, the marginal Church becomes the official sponsor of the new Christian marketplace.

American marginal believers do not have to face the deep existential crises that their counterparts face in other parts of the world. Third World Christians live in places where babies die of malnutrition every eighteen seconds, where children are sold into lives of slavery or prostitution, where unemployment hovers around 70 percent, and where three-fourths of metropolitan populations live in makeshift shacks. Living in a stable and secure world, American marginal believers develop more pedestrian *theodicies*, focused on personal slights or idiosyncratic upheavals. Spiritual crises involve being embarrassed in front of friends, or losing a client, escaping a car accident, changing jobs in mid-career, surviving a divorce, or missing a loved one. When immediate survival is not at stake, the conservative religious mind wanders toward more trivial matters. We proceed to examine the ways in which conservative Christianity is redefining holy living in America.

The Divine Body

Until 1980, *neither* dieting *nor* exercising ranked very high as a conservative spiritual priority. Winning souls, then, seemed more important than creating well-shaped bodies for the glory of God. The new trend might strike olden days' conservatives as too narcissistic to be part of the Christian agenda. They would be quite surprised by the body-beautiful movement that has grown within Christian circles since then. It all started in the 1980s, with books such as *God and Vitamins* (1980), *"Weight" on the Lord* (1983), *A Life Styled by God: A Women's Workshop on Spiritual Discipline for Weight Control* (1985), and *The Amazing Body Human: God's Design for Personhood* (1987). This first wave had quite modest goals. Authors wished to educate Christians about sound health practices. Book topics included childhood development, human sexuality, brain chemistry, metabolic rates, genetic health factors, and aging-related issues.

The *cosmetic* concern surfaced in the 1990s, with more market-savvy books such as *The Genesis Diet: The Biblical Foundation for Optimum Nutrition* (1996), *Julie Morris' Step Forward! Diet: Learn to Cast Your Cares on God—Not the Refrigerator* (1999), *Creationist Diet: Nutrition and God-Given Foods According to the Bible* (2000), or *The Maker's Diet* (2004). These works were more motivational, with chapters like "Deceptive Foods," "All the Fat Is the Lord's," or "God's Pharmacy," mimicking the secular industry approach. Gregory Jantz's *The Spiritual Path to Weight Loss: Praising God by Living a Healthy Life* (1998), and Gwen Shamblin's *Rise Above: God Can Set You Free from Your Weight Problems Forever* (2000), are good examples of the trend. Shamblin, founder and CEO of the nation's largest Christian diet company, even developed a series of videos, audiotapes, books, conferences, and twelve-week seminars in similar fashion to the secular version. She estimates that God's desired size for a proper Christian woman is a four or a six.[15]

Other niche-targeted works included books dealing with adolescent troubles, unrealistic beauty standards, or the more pathological aspects of dieting. Two examples of the adolescent market would be Andrea Stephens' *God Thinks You're Positively Awesome: Discover Your True Beauty—Inside and Out!* (1997), and Shannon Ethridge and Stephen Arterburn's *Every Young Woman's Battle: Guarding Your Mind, Heart, and Body in a Sex-Saturated World* (2004). Books like Beth Ley's *God Wants You Well* (2001), Danna Demetre's *Scale Down: A Realistic Guide to Balancing Body, Soul, and Spirit* (2003), and Sharon Jaynes' *The Ultimate Makeover: Becoming Spiritually Beautiful in Christ* (2003), deal with unrealistic beauty standards. As diets led to pathological conditions, Christian publishers promoted works such as Christie Pettit's *Starving: A Personal Journey through Anorexia* (2003).

The fascinating aspect of this trend is that most authors automatically accepted the *usual commercial standards of American beauty*. Nothing is wrong with looking like a Barbie doll; what is needed is the *Christian* angle. Beauty guidelines developed by commercial interests are uncritically accepted as if they represent universal standards of physical perfection. No one seriously questioned whether those standards were driven by cynical marketing, or if they were too shallow to bring real happiness. The only thing questioned was *the motivation behind the pursuit of beauty*. As long as conservative Christian women adopted American beauty standards to show their *love for God*, their otherwise skin-deep desire for attractiveness was completely commendable, acceptable, and praiseworthy. As a result, the secular, suburban pursuit of the body beautiful was transmuted into a Christian exercise in holy living and devotion.

Ironically, the topics discussed in these books could have come straight from secular self-help works or popular women's magazines. A sample of chapter titles suffices to make the case: "Frustration and Denial," "Avoidance," "Owning Up and Opening Up," "Changing Habits," "Breaking Through," "Measuring Up," "Insecurity," "Guilt and Gaining Weight," "Guilt and Self Identity," "Emotional Eating," "Confidence Makeover," "Overcoming Inferiority," "Inadequacy," "Pursuing Power," "Changing the Way We Think," "Letting Go of the Past," "Doing a Reality Check," "Myths That Intensify Our Struggle," "Making Friends with the Mirror," and "Breaking the Cycle of Abuse." When it comes to physical beauty, the wisdom of the world has become the wisdom of conservative Christian suburbia.

For the athletically inclined there is a budding series of Christian exercise routines which offer an alternative to secular bodybuilding. Ben Lerner's *Body by God: The Owner's Manual for Maximized Living* (2003) is a top seller in the field. The book highlights the importance of discipline and nutrition, of following proper bodybuilding techniques, and adopting stress-reducing approaches to life as part of its overall program. Chapter titles include themes like "The Way God Designed You to Eat," "Resistance Training Programs," "Peace By God," and "The Owner's Manual for Stress Management." It is hard to see how the physical laws of bodybuilding would be any different for Christians. But Lerner's high sales indicate that Christian bodybuilders prefer a more biblical approach to their pursuit of physical perfection.

For Christian women there are books like La Vita Weaver's *Fit for God: The 8-Week Plan That Kicks the Devil Out and Invites Health and Healing In* (2004). Published by Doubleday, the book is proof that the Christian market has become hot enough to attract a giant secular publishing house. When large New York corporate publishers produce this kind of work, it is clear that the Christian conservative lifestyle has become quite trendy. Weaver, an ordained minister and fitness trainer, appears regularly on the *Trinity Broadcast Network*'s "TotaLee Fit," a popular program of "aerobics and praise." Her exercise routines include reciting Bible verses and hymn singing for the full-impact effect of "praise, prayer, and inspiration." She also markets her video series *Hallelujah! Aerobics*.[16] Her exercise ministry probably finds echo in the exercise programs supported by megachurches to aid members in their pursuit of the God-filled life.

Nevertheless, the Christian diet/exercise trend is quite a recent development in Christian spirituality. One is hard-pressed to find beauty concerns of this sort in previous Christian eras. The early Christian attitude toward the body reflected the Greek duality of body and soul. The body stood for humankind's sullen, corruptible nature, always threatening to defile the purity of the soul. Previous Christian generations assumed the body warred against the spirit. In fact, in the Middle Ages they mortified their bodies through fasting, prayer, and corporal penances.

The Christian diet/exercise movement rejects the old duality by *respiritualizing* the body. In the words of a student of the movement, "During the past few decades of this industry's explosion, millions of American Christians have made a religious duty out of diet, theologizing about food and fat as never before. Disregard what goes into your body, they say, and you will not only gain weight, look ugly, and feel awful, but you will also doom yourself to a lifetime and likely an eternity of divine disfavor. The body is a hazard to the soul, able to demolish the hardest-won spiritual gains merely through ingesting the wrong material."[17]

Preoccupation with body beauty is a recent Christian concern. Ancient Christian spiritual practices paid little attention to the development of a well-sculpted, tanned body. There were no Patristic handbooks on bodybuilding. Augustine left no reflection on praise and aerobics. There is little indication that previous generations of believers were as deeply concerned with fashionable standards of beauty. In a sense, Christian dieting and exercising seem more grounded on the recent American middle-class obsession with a healthy and long life. It may reflect more the desire of aging baby boomers to remain physically fit and attractive over a longer lifespan, than St. Paul's concern for fit spiritual living. That members of the marginal Church entertain such concern only proves their degree of cultural captivity. The "spiritual" pursuit of beauty may have more to do with *being attractive in the here and now*, than preparing for the hereafter.

Finding a Soul Mate

In a time when religious conservatives are so concerned with beauty, it is not surprising to find them also looking for love. Previous generations of marginal believers may have relied upon propinquity and the congregational grapevine to find their soul mates. But this savvy, more socially and geographically mobile cohort deals with mate selection in more sophisticated ways. In matters of the heart, today's faithful cast their fate upon the vagaries of an impersonal, Internet process.

For instance, *Christian Soulmates* (CS),[18] the most popular Christian dating site, bills itself as "the best online dating site for Christian singles." With a sophisticated design, CS offers live chat, e-mail accounts, voice intros, instant messaging, "1 click matching," "Soul mate SMART-search," personalized profiles, and unlimited browsing. On-site testimonials attest to its effectiveness. Those in need of specific "pointers" can take advantage of its on-line bookstore. *Adam Meets Eve Christian Singles Dating* (AME) promises that "God, the best Matchmaker of all, created your perfect soul mate, your personal Adam or Eve." The site exhorts future clients to "pray for [their] soul mate daily before you ever meet, start dating or become pen pals."[19] It counsels singles never to lose hope, no matter the circumstances. To help things along, AME sponsors matchmaking cruises. Christian Cinderellas can find their charming Princes in exclusive Christian ocean liner vacations.

Clients of the site also rely on the exclusive wisdom of the credentialed matchmaking team of Pastor Jim Reeves and Dawn DuBois:

> With a Doctor of Ministry degree, Jim Rives (Reeves) had a passion to create a ministry to provide insights for Christian Singles into finding and building better relationships. Centered in God, it is a desire to help others find the right "balance" in their lives. Christians often think that this balance is just spiritual—it is NOT! It involves all of us—spiritual, physical, psychological, emotional, and financial. Each week Pastor Jim covers topics relating to issues and situations that Christian Singles face as they relate to others, topics like dating, sex, divorce, marriage, re-marriage, relationships, romance, and more. If you have a topic or question that you would like Pastor Jim to consider for future articles, please visit our Christian Singles Help pages: featuring Articles; Books; and Dating, Courtship and Relationship Advice by Pastor Jim. You will also find Professional Christian Counseling by Dawn BuBois, a registered therapist with a Masters degree in Social Work and over twenty years of experience.[20]

Another site, the *King's Singles Christian Dating Club*, is "designed to help Christian singles find a Christian date ... in the hopes of creating more families who live for and glorify God."[21] According to it, Christians find it difficult to find a soul mate because they have fewer places to congregate. So the site sponsors matchmaking events. For non-Christians the site explains what it takes to become one, and warns that membership is exclusively for Christians.

Even Christian senior citizens have a dating site, the *Christian Single Seniors* (CSS). The site offers guidelines on writing the "Perfect Christian Bio," and warns browsers against "picture window-shopping, casual dating, and sexual advances via e-mails." It considers itself a safe space for those seeking other "marriage-minded members," who want to build "a friendship leading to a 'serious relationship' in the Lord's timing."[22] For senior citizens in search of true love CSS features silver (free listing only) and gold memberships (unlimited e-mailing to other members), proving that with a little cash incentive, senior Christians all over the United States can find a match truly made in heaven.

Christian Paradise,[23] a Christian entertainment directory, lists at least eighty-five Christian dating services in the United States. Some are geographically based (*Mid-Atlantic Christian Singles, Bay Area Christian Singles Alliance, Upstate Christian Singles, Central Jersey Christian Singles, The Single Scene in Colorado*), some gender-specific (*Christian Women and Singles Ministries and Resources*), and some work-specific (*The Single Pastor's Connection*), or faith-specific (*Apostolic Singles* for "Christian singles in the Apostolic faith only!"). Some are exclusively dedicated to staging of matchmaking events (*Christian Activities Online*).

The fascinating thing about this popular trend is that secular dating services have discovered this growing matchmaking market. They now offer "For Christians Only" matchmaking areas in their Web sites. *American Singles*,[24] one of the largest Internet dating services in the nation, pioneered the "Christian Personals" section. Other services, such as *Perfect Match*, *Single C*, *Love and Seek*, *Match Dating*, and *All Personals* quickly followed suit. The interest of secular, money-making enterprises on exclusive Christian dating shows how profitable this slice of Christian modernity has become. When paired with the body beautiful trend it offers quite a glimpse into the suburban Christian conservative psyche.

Making a Joyful Noise

If dieting, exercising, or matchmaking are part of the contemporary religious lifestyle, so is modern music. In the era of CDs, DVDs, iPods, and MP3s it was only a matter of time before one could find contemporary Christian sounds in Christian festivals, radio stations, cable channels, and Web casting. In the spirit of suburban co-optation, and moving beyond the quaint nineteenth-century melodies of their predecessors, marginal believers are *spiritualizing* modern secular genres by adding Christian lyrics to them. Contemporary Christian music (CCM) blends a fresh, provocative Christian message with more modern musical tastes. Its spiritual appeal may come from the lyrics, but the suburban audience is attracted to "safer" versions of secular genres/lifestyles that until recently had very little to do with faith.

The wholesale adoption of every genre available in the larger music scene makes it possible to have Christian versions of Alternative Music, Contemporary Music, Dance/Techno, Ska, Punk, Pop, R&B, Rap/Hip-Hop, Rock, and Heavy Metal.[25] It is precisely this approach that makes CCM more controversial than Christian dieting or dating in conservative circles. Its "worldly" rhythms expose the fault lines between the older Christian conservatism and the more current one. The first shuns CCM and the latter adopts it wholeheartedly. It is a debate that has been going on since CCM came into the musical scene in the late 1970s.

For old school conservatives contemporary musical genres do not lend themselves to Christian co-optation. They are so essentially wicked and can only corrupt inexperienced young Christians. CCM is in fact a "Satanic ploy" to exploit the younger generation. For trendier versions of the conservative Christianity any music format can be praiseworthy, any genre can be "redeemed" for Christ.[26] For this generation of young Christians it is possible to "make a joyful noise unto the Lord" in any music styles they love. God can use CCM to convert young people and to inspire them toward Christian service. The music preserves

Christ's core message in a language that speaks to young people, that resonates with their cultural tastes.

If the battle seems gratuitous to outsiders, it is quite serious within religious conservative circles. CCM is qualitatively different from previous church music. For the first time in Church history, Christian artists are writing songs for mass entertainment, not cultic practices. To more traditional church musicians the trend is "foreign to the Bible."[27] Traditionalists have set up Web sites to alert young Christians about the dangers of contemporary Christian music. Testimony from a teenager highlights the issue of safe boundaries within Christian suburbia: "'Christian rock' had made me a shallow, rebellious young Christian. It made it easy for me to get into regular rock music. When I finally submitted to God and got the rock music out of my life, I was able to see the double standard that is lived out by "Christian rock" musicians."[28]

In truth, the liturgical use of secular music is not new to Christianity. The Church has co-opted its fair share of melodies, transforming bar songs and folk ballads into worshipful, sacred renditions. Martin Luther is well-known among sacred composers for his use of German folk songs in the Lutheran Psalter. Many inspired nineteenth-century compositions in America's hymnody, including the "Battle Hymn of the Republic," had secular origins as well. The difference is that CCM is not created for liturgical purposes. It is marketed to *compete* with secular music in the larger society. CCM is music for live stage performances, for widespread broadcasting, and for televised shows. For the first time in Christian music history, entire secular genres—not just simply songs—are being *Christianized* for entertainment's sake.

The debate is further complicated by the fact that CCM has the explicit goal of inspiring young Christians, but its commercial side completely mimics the secular marketing strategies of the larger music industry. CCM songs are mass-marketed in music stores, radio, television, the Internet, and live music festivals. Its artists are showcased through national booking agencies (one agency lists 118 CCM acts),[29] or Webzines (the *Christian Rock Connoisseur* lists 132 CCM artists, sponsored by twenty-seven different recording labels). The United States has thirteen CCM-dedicated radio stations and a television station (TVU) that claims to be the Christian MTV ("a music video format with a teenaged taste that rawks!").[30] The industry music magazines promote acts, track ratings, and merchandise Christian apparel (see CCM *Magazine*, *Christian Rock Net*, *Christian Music*, and *CC Music*).[31]

Specialized CCM Web sites promote trendy bands and in-depth news. *Jesus Freak Hideout* offers previews/reviews of albums, movies, and video clips; music news, and CCM merchandise. Its database has detailed information on CCM artists and upcoming events. *Worship Circus*, the official Web site for the CCM band, features press releases, diaries, interviews, bios, photos, and related merchandise.[32] Since sales depend on the regular interaction between artists and the fan base, there is a national network of Christian festivals that provides CCM artists with a regular live-performance circuit. The *Christian Concert Authority* in Atlanta oversees ticketing for Christian concerts nationwide. There are more than seventy festivals staged year-round in the United States (see Table 2.1). Some have been running for more than a decade.[33]

In sum, all the marketing strategies developed by the secular music business have been smoothly adopted by its Christian counterpart. Again, one is hard-pressed to find an equivalent pattern in two thousand years of Church history. Christian musicians were not popular entertainers in Galilee, Thessalonica, or Rome. The Church's Middle Ages festivals were darkened by public displays of heretical burnings. If Christianity can claim the likes of Palestrina, Bach, or Mozart as sacred composers, their sacred music followed strict standards of exclusive liturgical celebrations. CCM represents the religious co-optation of a larger cultural enterprise. Despite the divisive reactions it causes, it is clear that contemporary Christian music has developed, marketed, and sold enough products to become commercially viable. Its loyal audience has carved a niche in the secular entertainment industry for a distinctively contemporary Christian sound. In other words, another slice of suburbia has been *Christianized*.

Taking God to Work

Not all conservative efforts to *Christianize* modernity are related to leisure and entertainment. The next two sections explore the Christian co-optation of work and health care, two areas of postindustrial societies that are normally strictly secular in character. Despite the odds against the introduction of religion into those two arenas, the pressures have increased during the last twenty-five years, on the part of conservative Christians for the co-optation of those secular spaces.

Late industrialization splintered the world of modernity into public and private spheres. Whereas the private was defined by an array of personal choices, a veritable collage of styles, eras, and tastes; the public was built upon a highly regimented, bureaucratic organization of work life, based on interdependent, structured processes of production, organized around impersonal rules and regulations. No world could be further from the religious than that of public life.[34] Modern societies, with multicultural populations and diversified economies, circumscribed the world of work to the secular arena. One cannot refuse service to a customer or discriminate against a supplier on the basis of race, class, gender, *or* religion. Commercial firms do not restrict business to those of similar faith. The free market imposes its own logic upon the business world.

From the time they enter the job market to the time they retire, modern workers are surrounded by networks of individuals and firms—suppliers, buyers, loan officers, inspectors, coworkers, supervisors, clients, and competitors—linked through a series of interactive business processes. They deal with people from all walks of life, who hold different levels of education, job training, income, occupation, class, status, age, ethnicity, gender, sexual orientation, and yes, religious

Table 2.1 CCM Music Festivals in the United States

Arkansas
Brumley Gospel Sing, Fayetteville

California
Beyond Sunday Festival, Camarillo
Future Quest, San Diego
Joshua Fest, Quincy
Joy Fest, Santa Clara
Spirit West Coast, Del Mar
Spirit West Coast, Monterey
Spring Celebration, Santa Clara
Tom Festival, Anaheim

Colorado
Christian Artists Seminar, Estes Park
Rocky Mountain Winterfest, Estes Park

Florida
Night of Joy at Walt Disney World
Rock the Universe, Orlando

Georgia
Atlantafest

Idaho
Rock the Canyon, Twin Falls

Illinois
Agape Music Festival, Greenville
Cornerstone Festival, Bushnell
Edan Concert, Chicago
Godstock, Fairfield
Powerlight Fest, Springfield
Central Illinois Christian Concerts

Kentucky
Crabb Fest, Owensboro
Ichtus Festival, Wilmore
National Quartet Convention, Louisville
Newsong Fest, Leitchfield

Louisiana
Greater New Orleans Christian Concert

Minnesota
Higher Ground Music Festival, Winsted
Minnesota Christian Chronicle Festivals
Sunshine Festival, Willmar
Spirit Fest Midwest, Detroit Lakes

Missouri
Crossover Festival, Lake of the Ozarks

Nebraska
Solid Rock Festival, Gering

New Hampshire
Soulfest, Gilford

New York
Kingdom Bound Ministries, Six Flags, Darian Lake

North Carolina
Singing in the Smokies, Bryson City
Son Fest, Charlotte
Youth Fest, Zebulon

Ohio
Alive Festival, Canal Fulton

Pennsylvania
Blue Mountain Gospel Festival, Kempton
Creation Festival, Agape Farm, Mount Union
Purple Door Music Festival, Lebanon
Witness Festival, Quarryville

South Dakota
Hills Alive Festival, Rapid City
Oy Fest, Stickney

Tennessee
Great Smokies Praise Fest, Pigeon Forge
Southern Gospel Music Fan Fair, Chattanooga

Texas
Christian Concerts, Dallas/Fort Worth
Legacy Arts and Music Festival, Huntsville
The Texas Youth Evangelism Conference, Dallas

Virginia
King's Fest, Paramount Kings Dominion, Doswell

Washington
Creation Festival, Gorge Amphitheater, Gorge
Tom Festival, Stevenson

West Virginia
Gospel Jamboree in the Hills, Mineral Wells

Wisconsin
Fisherman's Festival, Milwaukee
Lifest, Oshkosh
Powerfest, Porterfield
Rainbow Valley Christian Music Festival, Wausau

Source: http://musicmoz.org/Religious/Christian/Concerts_and_Events and http://mmiworld.com/tip.htm.

background. Given the economic calculations of the marketplace, workers are expected to treat others and be treated with secular professional demeanor and respect. Modern economies require a smooth flow of goods and services based on the laws of supply and demand. Those laws are built upon the premises of rational, calculating economic actors; actors who are driven by the desire to maximize their profits and minimize their losses as they engage in business transactions. So workers are expected to focus on the utilitarian aspect of their trade, not on their religious mission.

Traditionally Christianity has recognized the autonomous, if ambiguous, nature of work. Work is theologically defined as both *sharing in God's creative energy*, and as *punishment for our fallen nature*. When equated with God's co-creative impulses, work is portrayed as a blessing, a gift equally bestowed upon all, and the means for us to express our talents. When framed as paradise lost, work is defined as toil and hardship, the earning of one's keep by the sweat of one's brow. This theological ambivalence has pervaded the Church's approach to labor in all Christian eras. Work can be a joy or a curse, and sometimes both. However, as Church labor became more specialized, its leaders developed clearer demarcations between *sacred* and *secular* work. The rise of a professional clergy greatly contributed to that distinction.[35] In time, Christians refined their work-related theology, developing ancillary concepts such as *calling, steadfastness*, and *faithfulness* in the discharge of one's secular vocation.

Saint Augustine differentiated the duties to the City of God (sacred labor) from those owed to earthly kingdoms (secular labor). Saint Aquinas had an elaborate list of Christian duties, including work-related ones, in his *Summa Theologica*. Martin Luther spoke of two Kingdoms and stipulated that followers of Christ had clear obligations to both, being expected to live out their *calling* (beruf) in the secular world.[36] In similar fashion, in his *Institutes*, Calvin emphasized the importance of faithfulness to one's calling as a sign of a redeemed nature.[37] Prior to the Reformation, the Church framed the world of work through corporate gilds and trades, clearly defining the obligations appertaining to making a living.[38]

The Industrial Revolution pushed the Church beyond feudal gilds and European corporatist economies. Urban factories drained the countryside of laborers, creating large, industrial centers. Mining expanded to supply the energy needs of manufacturing. Transportation systems created national markets, greatly expanding individual mobility. Immigration brought waves of newcomers and new faiths to our nation's shore. City life loosened the moral code of an agrarian era, adding pressure to family life. Small town religious mores were broken down. Caught in the maelstrom of change, American Christianity had to develop Christian guidelines to deal with the industrial era. Mainline Protestant denominations and the Catholic Church drew up codes of social ethics in response to industrialization. Urban missions were created; the plight of the urban poor (including crime, hunger, squalid settlements, and child labor) addressed; and labor representation defended.

Slowly a programmatic approach to industrial work developed within mainstream Christianity, providing the first initiatives in what later would become welfare state provisions. Denominations that pioneered this work took a prophetic stand as they addressed captains of industry. But even here churches were reluctant to challenge the secular nature of work. They offered guidance to secular leaders, but never presumed to dictate the nation's labor policies.[39] Unlike its progressive counterparts, the conservative Church did not produce a set of teachings regarding the nature of work, nor did it challenge its alienating conditions in the modern marketplace. Christian conservatives take the nature of work for granted. Work cannot be redeemed, only workers can be saved.

To *Christianize* the workplace, then, marginal believers brought the saved together in Christian trade associations, and matched Christian employers to Christian employees. Christian associations give redeemed workers the opportunity to meet like-minded peers, enabling them to promote their faith through their particular trades. The matching of Christian employers and employees allowed the marginal Church to minimize worker exposure to the vagaries and temptations of the secular marketplace. All in all, the *Christianization* of work co-opts another important aspect of modern life.

The number and reach of conservative Christian professional associations is considerable. Take the *Christian Medical and Dental Associations* (CMDA), for example. One of the oldest professional associations in America, the CMDA boasts a 17,000-member roll. It sponsors overseas medical mission projects, provides members with a network for fellowship and professional growth, finances student campus ministries in medical and dental schools, publishes educational/inspirational materials, hosts marriage and family conferences, offers continuing education for missionary doctors, and develops overseas academic exchange programs. For those seeking a Christian physician, the CMDA offers a "Christian doctor search engine."[40]

The *Christian Legal Society* (CLS) provides similar services for Christian lawyers and law students. The association welcomes members who are "committed to proclaiming, loving and serving Jesus Christ, through all we do and say in the practice of law, and advocating biblical conflict reconciliation, public justice, religious freedom and the sanctity of human life."[41] It exists to sponsors fellowship activities for its members. Its goal is to transform "the legal profession . . . one heart and mind at a time by enlisting lawyers and law students everywhere to faithfully serve Jesus Christ in the diligent study and ethical practice of law by ministering to the poor, reconciling people in conflict, defending life and protecting the religious liberties of all people."[42] CLS also offers a "Christian lawyer search engine" to the public.

While Christian doctors and lawyers may enjoy the most resource-rich associations in our country, there is a Christian association for almost every career or trade imaginable. There are Christian associations for nurses, pharmacists, entrepreneurs, accountants, managers, engineers, sociologists, economists, biologists, geologists, writers, periodical publishers, booksellers, broadcasters, real estate agents, farmers, firefighters, police officers, military officers, airplane pilots, and airline personnel, to name only a few![43] Looking at the list and size of these associations' memberships it is hard to believe that any religious conservative could imagine their faith under threat in America.

Matching Christian employers and employees is another matter of great import for the conservative Church these days. Internet Christian job ad sites abound. Some operate on a membership basis, where users sign up for a monthly fee and gain access to multiple job listings, a job search engine, resume posting, business training, or specialized trade certification. Others are sponsored by Christian businesses. Most job ads seek people with a secular expertise, but Christian orientation. Jobs are available in several industries, including manufacturing, business, communications, publishing, Web design, and health care.

Sites that operate as extensions of larger Christian holdings include *Christian Jobs*, a division of the *Salem Network* (a communications corporation that includes radio, Web site, and marketing interests);[44] The *Christian Career Center*, sponsored by *Gospel.Com Net* (the center offers free consultation sessions, a career checkup inventory, career guidance, and a career resource bookstore. It also sponsors a Christian job fair); and *Christian Employments*, operated by *EnterGlobe Enterprises* (which bills itself as "the fastest growing Christian Networking site on the Internet... with interests in construction, holiday rentals, management consulting, and investments").[45]

Independent job ad services concentrate on job postings and employer databases. The *Christian Employment* site showcases a mentoring page, a bookstore, a self-employment section, and a resource center. *Christia Net*, "the Worldwide Christian Marketplace," operates as a straightforward classified jobs page. *Christian Find It* specializes in individual entrepreneurship, listing business opportunities, dealerships, franchises, investment partnerships, multilevel marketing, and home-based businesses. *Praize Jobs* offers job ads in business and ministry. So does *Jobs 4 Jesus*.

Three sites focus exclusively on church-related positions. *America's Christian Job Source*[46] provides listings for pastors. *InterCristo* is operated by *CRISTA Ministries*, a religious holding that includes broadcast stations, camps, schools, adoption services, senior care, troubled youth, women's ministries, Christian veterinary mission, and international missions.[47] *Christian Placements*, operated by *Church Staffing*, claims to provide "the largest freely searchable database of Christian and Ministry jobs on the Internet."[48] Needless to say, most job ads are limited to conservative churches and denominations.

A quick analysis of the industry leader, *Christian Jobs*, indicates that there is a wide spectrum of jobs available for Christian job seekers these days; just as there is a widely trained Christian workforce seeking placement. The site lists 27,388 resumes, along with job ads ranging from plumbers, to carpenters, to insurance agents, to loan officers, to executive directors. Its employer clientele includes respected business names, such as Anderson Consulting, the Continental Trust Bank, Farmers Insurance, Adecco, Pre-Paid Legal Services, RCO Engineering, and Follett Higher Education Booksellers.

Some 32 percent of *Christian Jobs'* employers are in the business sector, including human resources, recruiting, financial services, banking, insurance, accounting, advertising, and IT consulting. Almost 10 percent are in the heavy industry/manufacturing sectors. Eight percent are in education, including eleven Christian schools and four colleges. Another 8 percent are in Christian broadcasting and communications, including five cable companies, four radio stations, and two newspapers. Finally, 3 percent are in the publishing and bookselling business and 2 percent are in health care.

Godly Health

The newest trend in health care insurance is not an insurance plan, nor is it sponsored by the insurance industry. No board of health care providers or insurers supervises the new program either. In fact, the *National Association of Insurance Commissioners* questions its legitimacy and fights its operation in the United States. And yet, these new health plans thrive to the tune of thousands of subscribers who contribute hundreds of millions of dollars toward their health care coverage. Moreover, their members' medical bills are getting paid, hospital care is being covered, and the whole enterprise is succeeding through a voluntary, mutual-aid system of bill-sharing plans that is organized by unlicensed conservative Christian organizations.

The new plans are described as "voluntary arrangements between like-minded people to share medical expenses...in fulfillment of the New Testament exhortation that Christians should bear each other's burdens."[49] And born-again Christians all over the United States are trading regular health insurance coverage for these affordable "church plans." The three leading Christian organizations in the field have enrolled enough members now to sustain large and viable operations. *Medi-Share* has 60,000 subscribers; *Samaritan Ministries International* reaches 35,000 members; and the *Christian Brotherhood Newsletter* also claims membership in the thousands.[50] One site claims that it has paid to date more than $400 million in claims.[51] Another puts its tally at $150 million.[52] For monthly contributions ranging from $150 to $300, born-again Christians can bypass the entire health insurance industry and have their health care needs covered.

The plans cost less than the average insurance fees because they are *restricted to born-again Christians* so they do not subsidize "high risk, sinful lifestyles"[53] (participants must be certified by their ministers to be regular churchgoers). They forbid smoking, immoderate drinking, homosexuality, and extramarital sex. Plans also do not pay for abortion or adulterous sexually transmitted diseases. Other restrictions may include heart disease, obesity, or psychiatric disorders. Educational materials and Web-based seminars from the three leading organizations help members assess their lifestyle and set health-related goals. The groups also offer personal health education consultants,[54] with at least one site providing "telephone-based coaching."

The plans also cost less because the sponsoring organizations are not bound by the same regulations as the insurance industry. Which is to say, their coverage is *not actually guaranteed.* Web site disclaimers notify future clients that the groups are not insurance programs and are not subject to insurance rules. In fact, these Christian groups do not have any financial reserves set aside to cover medical costs. Monthly contributions from the pooled membership are used to pay all outstanding bills. Cost sharing across a broad membership cuts the odds that any client will be burdened with a large bill. Along with the money, participants are encouraged to send cards and letters to the families being helped, to let them know they are being held in prayer. Services include medication discounts and "Christian Disability Sharing," whereby believers facing income loss due to illness or injury are supported by their brothers and sisters in the faith in a similarly pooled fashion.

State insurance regulators are concerned with the spread of unregulated church plans precisely because cost-sharing plans provide no guarantee of coverage. Since church health care groups do not operate under public scrutiny, there is no form of accountability. Lack of independent audits or financial controls could create problems. Professor Mila Koffman, from Georgetown University's *Health Policy Institute* argues that church plans take advantage of religious people who cannot afford regular health insurance. "Insurance companies have to file financial reports to regulators every year—these plans don't," he says. "Who knows how much money they're taking in or paying out?"[55]

In fact, lack of accountability has created problems for the plans. Ohio regulators forced the *Christian Brotherhood Newsletter* into a court-order receivership after a jury found that its president, Rev. Bruce Hawthorne, and other group officials had absconded with $15 million, which they spent on luxury houses, expensive items, and even a stripper's salary. Kentucky officials took *Medi-Share* to court to halt its operations in the state. They issued a consumer alert warning residents that church plans did not provide protection similar to health insurance. Maryland and Wisconsin temporarily halted church plans, but their respective legislatures reinstated the plans.[56]

The three leading organizations are quick to point out that they have annual audits, and to provide a clear tally of their expenses. According to *Medi-Share* its administrative expenses cover from 18 to 22 percent of the money it collects. The rest, some $43 million in 2005, is used to pay claims. Moreover, testimonials on their Web sites "document" the efficacy of the plans. A pastor with colon cancer had his $57,000 bill paid in full. A woman with bronchitis and maternity-related needs received $12,000. A man with eight broken vertebrae had his $150,000 treatment cost completely matched. Another woman with congestive heart failure received $200,000 to pay her bill. One man who has contributed to his church plan for ten years, despite never using it, says he enjoys supporting the larger Christian community in a very concrete way.

The New Testament-style mutual aid coverage seems to be delivering results, and perhaps opening up new potential services for the religious conservative market. Tomorrow there could be Christian home or car insurance programs, or perhaps a network of nursing homes or church clinics supported by born-again Christian money. But of all the co-opting trends discussed so far, the mutual aid care is perhaps the only one with a precedent in Church history. Early Christianity was known for its communal sharing and living. The Middle Ages Church had its confraternities and mutual aid societies. Through history, church associations helped less affluent members to cope with financial hardships, including job loss, medical expenses, funeral costs, or disaster recovery efforts.[57] Church gilds protected the trade rights of its members, assuring fair trade practices. In some cases, confraternities made civic contributions, commissioning painters, sculptors, and architects to build and beautify local towns, churches, or commercial centers.

So, there is, in fact, a long tradition of mutual aid in the larger Christian heritage. However those confraternities were created out of necessity, at a time when no other form of relief was available. Prior to the advent of the modern state and its administrative bureaucracy, there were no equivalent secular services in European societies. Confraternities provided the much-needed social infrastructure and welfare support for large European communities. Which is to say, those societies were not created out of a need to exclude the "non-saved." They were not concocted to insulate European Christians from other members of their societies. In fact, they preceded the social welfare system and the modern health care industry by centuries. What is striking in the conservative Christian health plans is precisely the desire to leave out the rest of the United States. It is by far the most exclusive conservative institution reviewed in this chapter. Unless a minister is willing to vouch that someone is a regular churchgoer, no service is provided.

NOVUS ORDO CHRISTIANORUM

The contemporary conservative quest for *holy living* is quite impressive. By co-opting modern practices marginal believers minimize their exposure to the outside world, while expanding their faith's influence into larger areas of our society. The quest is marked by the conservative Church's dualistic, bifurcated impulses; driven by spiritual anxieties brought on by the modern age. Co-optation of modernity presents conservative Christians (or so they think) with the means to keep the world at bay. As McGuire argues,

> Dualism enables believers to name the sources of their anxieties, fears, and problems. This identification is in itself an important source of believers' sense of order and control. Identifying certain difficulties as caused by evil forces also implies a clear-cut

course of action. Believers locate their personal courses of action within a cosmic struggle, a continual battle between the forces of Good and the forces of Evil. This identification provides explanations of all events—good and bad—that occur in their lives, and it gives meaning to everyday existence. Even trivial aspects of daily life become part of the order implied in the dualistic worldview.[58]

The problem with this sanctified version of modernity is that it creates a veritable, voluntary religious ghetto; one whose borders keep expanding. The idea is not simply to *Christianize* rock and roll, or to follow a Christian diet, or to find an evangelical date, or to work for a born-again employer. The ultimate goal is to enlarge the net, so as to spread "redeemed" spaces until they encompass the whole nation. In other words, to create a *Novus Ordo Christianorum*. This effective wholesale diffusion of conservative Christianity into every area of society is guided (as other chapters will demonstrate) by a larger vision, one of creating a holy and righteous country, with little tolerance for religious diversity. This may not be a conspiratorial effort, or involve a push for holy theocracy, but the co-optation of modernity does shrink America's secular arena, presenting theological, political, and social challenges.

Theologically, the conservative push for such social order represents an effort to prematurely sift the *wheat* from the *tare*, sort the *saved* and the *damned* before harvest day. Their desire to minimize, if not eliminate, any long-term contact with *unsaved* Americans lead Christian conservatives to create exclusive clubs, services, work associations, and health care plans. The resulting order is *distinctly* and *exclusively* Christian. Their lofty goal is understandable, since religious networks do provide meaningful support for believers:

> Like other social institutions, religious groups are network-driven.... Participation in church-related activities brings individuals together with others who have a similar status characteristics as well as common religious beliefs. For church members, regular interaction with these like-minded others may reinforce basic role identities and expectations. Through formal and informal involvement in their church communities, these persons may gain affirmation that their personal conduct and emotions with regard to daily events, experiences, and community affairs are reasonable and appropriate.[59]

The creation of a Christian order reflects to some extent that all-American sense of optimism we share toward life: the notion that life is *perfectible*, and that it can be bettered given the right amount of effort, ingenuity, and good luck. Our optimistic culture must give pause to other nations, especially those still smarting from past internecine religious wars and failed religiopolitical experiments. But it pushes us to constantly strive to improve ourselves, our families, our communities, and our country.[60] Even our founding documents betray this optimistic American "can-do" approach. No other country shares our Constitutional preamble: "We the People of the United States, in order to form a *more perfect* Union."

Judging by those standards, the contemporary conservative redefinition of *holy living* is not only quite *modern*, but also very *American*. It represents a *Christian twist on the old notion of American exceptionalism*. Marginal believers are working toward their own version of a more perfect Union: in this case, a *Christian* Union. But the approach carries social and political consequences because it affects all of us, all Americans—Christians and non-Christians, religious and secular. Picture this: from home to work to school to courthouse to city hall, their Christian way of life influencing every aspect of society, winning every heart, binding every law.

The Christian conservative "more perfect Union" requires nothing short of America becoming the country of the *saved*, with every citizen a bona fide born-again member of the Christian Kingdom of God. The dangers here are the same that plagued previous American utopias, starting with John Winthrope's "city upon the hill." To be precise, religious conservatives run the risk of *spiritual hubris*, of *national idolatry*. This very American conservative Christian project equates our earthly home with God's perfect abode, our earthly culture with God's perfect holy community. In doing so, marginal believers seek to build God's New Jerusalem, *the one only the Messiah could build*, by their own means. Instead they raise a temporal New Jerusalem, one akin to that city dreamt by the Pilgrims, and by every generation of American Christians since then who have tried to establish God's Kingdom on earth.

The conservative Christian version of a more perfect Union has precedents—it has been nourished by like-minded colonial preachers, frontier revivalists, and *Dispensationalists* in the industrial age.[61] Incidentally, it is a dream that also haunted the Apostles. In their patriotic zeal, they too longed for a temporal, righteous kingdom. They fought over who should sit at the right or left side of their king once he ascended to the throne. At every occasion, Jesus rebuked their political aspirations. He either confused them by claiming the Kingdom was already with them, or informed that the time and place for the Kingdom (and appertaining honors) was God's alone to decide, on God's own terms. In the meantime, Jesus commanded his followers to live out their faith humbly on this earth, amidst both the *saved* AND the *damned*.

So, the New Jerusalem dreamed by contemporary conservative Christians is not too different from the one hoped for by the Apostles. Much like them, American marginal believers desire their country to be the paragon of human perfection. The problem is that *the Bible promises no earthly perfection*, especially the perfection of an entire social order. Millennia of Church History should warn us against such ambitious goal. It drove the dedicated faithful of previous eras into never-ending religious wars. By excluding significant populations of other Christian countries, the quest for a Christian theocracy led to civil wars, dissensions, and religious persecutions in places like England, Germany, Spain, and Italy. Utopias, even heavenly ones, tend to be destroyed by their internal contradictions, and eventually by the practical demands of an imperfect people, living in an imperfect world.

3

GOD SHED HIS GRACE ON THEE: COLONIZING THE PUBLIC SQUARE

"If they don't vote our way, we'll change their view one way or another. We're going to take back what we lost in the last half of the 20th century."[1]
—Gary Grass, California Pastor and Executive Director, the Center for Reclaiming America

Suburbia affords this generation of conservative Christians the organizing skills to dream beyond religious borders. If the first moment in America's *Christianization* comes from bringing modernity into the Church; the second results from spreading the faith throughout society. As marginal believers build large networks of megachurches and create goods and services for a growing conservative market in the United States, they also muster the resources to make their voice heard in our public arena. The education, managerial savvy, and business acumen that come with middle-class careers afford Christian conservatives the possibility to establish their version of the faith as the sole foundation for America's social order. Once set in motion, this work of America's *Christianization* has only grown.

The co-optation of modernity transforms secular practices into holy living, while the colonization of the social order expands the reach of the conservative message. The first moment is relatively invisible to other Americans, since it takes place within the confines of exclusive born-again clubs and activities. But the second is hard to miss, since it presents a public threat to the separation of Church and State. It is an effort that challenges the most fundamental premises of American collective life, including the nature of our government and our pluralist culture. Given the Constitutional check on the establishment of religion, a religious takeover of the American public square must be carefully orchestrated. The most direct strategy, of course, is to *boost the perception that Christianity is a faith under siege*. That can prompt public opinion to support clearer and more visible *public expressions* of the faith. If prayer is being banned, or Christmas is under attack, or the Ten Commandments are no longer publicly displayed, or Jesus' name is no longer used in public invocations, people must rise up and defend their religious heritage. Staged events, large-scale demonstrations, and boycotts spring up in the name of religious freedom.

A variant strategy involves *the symbolic mixing of faith and official government business*. On June 5, 2005, facing a tough primary challenge, Texas Governor Rick Perry staged a bill-signing ceremony on church grounds. The legislation being signed restricted abortion and prohibited same-sex marriage, two very public causes of the religious conservative community. When pressed by the media Perry argued that though "on the grounds of a Christian church, we all believe in standing up for the unborn."[2] Meanwhile, his campaign drummed up support for the event among conservative Christian groups by urging churches and individuals to "fill this location with pro-family Christian friends who can celebrate with us."

Sometimes the public promotion of Christianity turns legislative chambers into veritable places of worship. Recently, a U.S. District Judge had to order members of the Indiana State House of Representatives to stop mentioning Christ or making sectarian prayers in their formal benedictions, after complaints from several legislators led to a civil liberties suit. His review of fifty-three invocations given during the 2005 legislative session showed that fifty were clearly identified as sectarian Christian. It is hard to see where the State ends and the Church begins. The prayer that prompted the suit was offered by Clarence Brown, a lay Christian, who thanked God "for our lord and savior Jesus Christ, who died that we might have the right to come together in love."[3] He then proceeded to lead the chamber in song, in an enthusiastic rendition of "Just a Little Talk with Jesus."

A few lawmakers were so distraught by the event that they walked out. At least four, all Christians, voiced dismay that a public building, maintained by the taxes of all Indiana residents, could be used for Christian worship. The suit represented their effort to stop the practice. The judge found other prayers were equally sectarian. One used Paul's injunction to the Colossians to "Whatever you do, do all in the name of the Lord Jesus." Another called for worldwide Christian conversion: "We look forward to the day when all nations and all people of the earth will have the opportunity to hear and respond to messages of love of the Almighty God who has revealed himself in the saving power of Jesus Christ." It is hard to ascertain the *public* purpose of such invocations.

A more ideological approach to the colonization of the public square involves the *use of Christian principle to guide public policy*. Prior to the 1980s, Congressional policymaking was more driven by technical or political factors. Religious reasoning was avoided in respect of Congress' diverse constituencies, and policymaking revolved around pragmatic and bipartisan interests.[4] That pattern held even as the country faced a calamitous war (Vietnam) and race-related riots. During the last twenty-five years, however, sectarian reasoning and political divisiveness have consistently increased in both chambers of Congress. From faith-based initiatives, to abstinence education programs, to congressional meddling in the Terri Schiavo case, elected officials now use religious motives to set national policy, in a *de facto*, back-door establishment of conservative Christianity.

Faith-based legislation carries serious political consequences: first, because it privileges a particular moral worldview while pretending to represent the interests of all Americans; second, because it is based on *belief* rather than *empirical evidence*. Since faith-based laws do not require technical or scientific assessment of their results, those subjected to them do not enjoy the usual safeguards that are found in more traditional policymaking. As religion trumps scientific fact, it imposes considerable risk to all affected constituencies. One thinks here of areas like stem cell research, or the environment, or human sexuality.

A faith-based health bill could have deleterious effects that are hard to detect and address up-front. Take, for instance, sex education policy. When guided by the premarital abstinence values of conservative Christians, the policy ignores important medical guidelines that are crucial to the issue. The secular, valid need of American families to protect children from unsafe sex, unwanted pregnancies, or sexually transmitted diseases (STDs) is outweighed by religious wishful thinking that abstinence will take care of everything. Public funding that otherwise could be employed for medically sound educational programs is instead diverted to unproven abstinence projects, sponsored by quasireligious educational companies. The results are the kind of unenlightened health care that opens doors to serious health threats.

Thankfully, national data is still collected on the topic. The *National Longitudinal Study of Adolescent Health* tracked 12,000 teens from high school to young adulthood. The study found that 20 percent of them had signed Christian virginity pledges. Those teens did delay sexual activity, marry younger, and have fewer sexual partners. But they also engaged in riskier sexual behavior, since they were less likely to use condoms and more likely to engage in oral and anal sex. Not surprisingly, the rates of sexually transmitted disease among teens who signed virginity pledges were similar to those of the larger sample. Moreover, 88 percent of them ended up engaging in premarital sex anyway.[5] In other words, faith-based policymaking wishes for a world that does not operate under the same empirical rules of everyday reality—in the process it creates health risks for which it has no pragmatic or scientific provisions.

The most dramatic strategy to colonize our social order is *the election of stealth conservative believers to public office*. Since the 1980s, conservative Christians have placed a good number of candidates on ballots. Here their education, occupation, and wealth have amplified the power of the conservative message. The aid of a few wealthy donors has guaranteed that born-again candidacies prosper. Stealth, of course, is a premium. The *Christian Coalition* instructions to political operatives in a 1992 *County Action Plan* for Pennsylvania urged them to "never mention the name Christian Coalition in Republican circles." The Coalition goal was for each member to become "directly involved in the local Republican Central Committee so that you are an insider. This way you can get a copy of the local committee rules and a feel for who is the current Republican Committee."

The next step included recruiting religious conservatives to take over the committee, so as to run born-again Christians against moderates who "put the Republican Party ahead of principle."[6] That strategy worked rather well in California. Back in 1980 the Christian Right decided to take over the state senate. With the aid of State Senator H. L. Richardson and the financial backing of wealthy Christian donors like Howard Ahmanson and Rob Hurtt, the group began targeting open seats. By 1983 the number of state senators sponsored by the Christian Right had grown from four to twenty-seven. By 1994, now with the support of State Senator Rob Hurtt, who was also the chairman of the Republican Campaign Committee for the state legislature, conservative Christians were only four seats away from majority senate control.[7]

"EATING AN APPLE ONE BITE AT A TIME"

This is no longer the conservative Church of previous eras, with its appalling low rates of political participation or public visibility. It is a Church triumphant, with clear goals for the colonization of political power. Scarier still, this is a Church triumphant that has the structure and resources to make impressive inroads into America's public square. Nevertheless, religious strategies are not enough to colonize the secular order. To do so those strategies must be backed up by a disciplined and well-funded network of workers, of conservative Christians involved in single-issue grassroots organizations (see Table 3.1). It is perhaps this single-issue approach and the regimented grassroots' efforts that most distinguish this late effort of conservative Christians to leave a solid imprint on public matters.

The single-issue approach is critical for at least two important reasons. First, single-theme campaigns rally the faithful into *targeted* political action, allowing for broad-based recruiting and long-term fund-raising capabilities. Second, single-issue campaigns disguise the ultimate and broader agenda. When conservative Christian organizations attack America's secular arena from multiple directions, they *mask the coordinated nature of the attack*. The long-term goal may be the *Christianization* of the country, but the only thing visible are multiple groups rallying against different issues—abortion, same-sex marriage, stem-cell research, or evolution. Such ingenious strategy advances a Christian social order in piecemeal fashion, in a stealthy, decentralized way. As Richard Land, of the *Southern Baptist Convention*, explained so well: "You eat an apple one bite at a time."[8]

In the long run it is not about any particular issue, it is about the creation of a Christian nation. The best possible scenario for culture warriors would be the establishment of a born-again America, run by a Christian White House,

Table 3.1 A Sample of Conservative Christian Groups in America

Advance USA
Alliance Defense Fund
Alliance for Marriage
Alliance for the Separation of Schools and State
American Center for Law & Justice
American Christian Liberty Society
American Coalition for Traditional Values
American Family Association
American Policy Roundtable
American Values
American Vision
Americans for Constitutional Truths
Arlington Group
Becker Fund for Religious Liberty
Belcher Foundation
Blackstone Institute of Public Law and Policy
Campus Alliance
Capital Christian Center
Care Net
Center for Christian Statesmanship
Center for Law and Policy
Center for Law and Religious Freedom
Center for Public Justice
Center for Reclaiming America
Chalcedon Foundation
Child and Family Protection Institute
Christian Action Network
Christian Citizen, USA
Christian Coalition of America
Christian Defense League
Christian Defense Coalition
Christian Educators Association
Christian Exodus
Christian Family Coalition
Christian Freedom Foundation
Christians for Justice
Christian Law Association
Christian Legal Reformation Club
Christian Legal Society
Christian Policy Network
Christian Research Institute
Citizens for Excellence in Education
Coalition of Public School Ministries
Coalition on Revival
Concerned Women for America
Council for National Policy
Creation Research Society
Culture and Family Institute
Discovery Institute
Eagle Cross Alliance
Exodus International
Faith and Action
Faith and Values Coalition
Families Across America
Family.Com
Family Policy Network
Family Research Council
Fieldstead
First Priority Ministry
Focus on the Family
Foundation for American Christian Education
Foundation for Moral Law
Foundations of Law PAC
Free Congress Foundation
Gateways to Better Education
Graybrook Institute
Home School Legal Defense Association
Howard Center for Family, Religion, and Society
Intercessors for America
Institute for Creation Research
Institute of Christian Economics
Institute on Religion and Democracy
Judeo-Christian Council for Constitutional Restoration
The Liberty Counsel
Life Decisions
Life Dynamics
Life Education and Resources Network
Mayflower Institute
Mission America
Movement for Christian Democracy
National Alliance Against Christian Discrimination
National Association of Evangelicals
National Christian Foundation
National Christian Leadership Conference for Israel
National Clergy Council
National Coalition for the Protection of Children and Families
National Council on Bible Curriculum in Public Schools
National Legal Foundation
National Ministry Center
National Pro-Life Action Center on Capitol Hill
National Reform Association
Operation Rescue
Parents' Right Coalition
Plymouth Rock Foundation
ProLife Political Action Committee
Prolife America
Renew America
RSVP America Campaign
Rutherford Institute
Science Ministries
Society for the Practical Establishment and Perpetuation of the Ten Commandments
Vision America
Wake Up America
Wall Builders
Wilberforce Forum

Source: Internet survey, including cross-reference links from the listed organizations' pages (Summer 2005). (The list does not include regional or state-level organizations, or Christian professional associations).

supported by a Christian Congress, and endorsed by a Christian Supreme Court. Surprisingly, we may not be too far from that reality. When President George W. Bush took office, Pat Robertson symbolically resigned from the presidency of the *Christian Coalition*, signaling that Bush's ascendance would place the President in "his rightful place as the head of the true American Holy Christian Church."[9]

The approach seeks to preserve the nation's democratic appearance, while seriously transforming the nature of the government. Its vision is driven by *Dominionism*,[10] a theocratic ideology whose tenets have deeply influenced the conservative religious community. The ideology supplies the "Biblical Blueprint" for the establishment of a Christian society, one whose basis stems from a peculiar reading of the Old Testament (Hebrew Bible). *Dominionism* argues Christ has already given American Christian conservatives dominion over the nation's political institutions until his return.[11] All that remains is for marginal believers to implement his command, to take over public life. Pat Robertson puts it best,

> God's plan is for His people, ladies and gentlemen to take dominion.... What is dominion? Well, dominion is Lordship. He wants His people to reign and rule with Him.... But He's waiting for us to... extend His dominion.... And the Lord says, "I'm going to let you redeem society. There'll be a reformation.... We are not going to stand for those coercive utopians in the Supreme Court and in Washington ruling over us any more. We're not going to stand for it. We are going to say, 'we want freedom in this country, and we want power...'"[12]

Success then, requires multiple single-issue organizations that continuously push for the *Christianization* of different aspects of American life. This "plurality" of voices offers the impression of a broad and diverse array of conservative interests. But its leadership is constantly *networked*, much in the fashion of interlocking directorates in the business world. Conservative religious leaders communicate regularly, taking active part in advancing each other's causes. The "splintered" approach may hide the whole agenda from outsiders, but there are plenty of footprints to be found.[13] The impression of a large grassroots movement betrays efforts too choreographed to be spontaneous. Nevertheless, it is an approach that works well with the current political conditions in our country. It multiplied conservative constituencies at a time when Republicans controlled both houses of Congress.

The single-issue approach starts with a push for *fairer representation*. Picking a particular cause, the conservative Church presses for the inclusion of a "Christian voice," charging that the topic lacks "balance." Under protests for fair representation, conservative organizers get a seat at the table. Once they gain access, however, the push for the primacy of the Christian worldview intensifies, until balance is gone in their favor. For those familiar with the conservative takeover of the *Southern Baptist Convention* (SBC), the strategy is strikingly familiar. Starting in the late 1970s, conservative Baptists realized that control of the entire denomination rested upon the Committee on Committees. By taking hold of it, they could then nominate board members for all the SBC agencies.

Arguing for greater representation, the conservative group eventually gained majority control on the committee. After they gained majority control, however, conservative Baptists put a stop to all nonconservative representation. As a result, board member by board member were carefully replaced, so that every slot in the boards of all SBC agencies were filled with their own representatives. One by one all seminaries fell under conservative control, along with the publishing house, and the home and foreign missions boards.[14]

Conservative Christianity is employing the same tried and true approach, this time not for the taking of a denomination, but for the colonizing of an entire social order. Under the guise of challenging the overrepresentation of "secular humanists" in our culture, marginal believers are staging a well-orchestrated attack on the public square. Their push is backed by an impressive array of resources. Religious media keeps issues alive for its broad-based constituency. Religious colleges train the next generation of culture warriors. Religious law schools and business schools refine the skills of future leaders. Religious donors fund think tanks. Religious organizations support political campaigns. This is not a single-generation fight. It is a methodical, long-term, and drawn out process. One the conservative Church is patiently playing out. The righteousness of the cause justifies all the investment in resources, talents, and infrastructure. All are needed to see the effort through.

COLONIZATION AS A RECENT STRATEGY

The disciplined effort to take over America is something quite new in conservative Christianity. Since the "modernist" battles of the 1920s (the Scopes monkey trial, prohibition), marginal believers have done little in the larger public arena to slow or revert America's secularization. The early battles garnered considerable attention, but science eventually became a tool to fight Communism, and prohibition was repealed by FDR. It would take another sixty years before the surge in membership and resources would lead Christian conservatives back toward the sponsoring of a broad public agenda.[15] This time the mission is fueled by conservative dismay over the cultural revolution of the 1960s. Marginal believers saw in it the country's downward spiral into indecency and self-absorption. The freedoms gained in the 1960s, and the ensuing politics of identity generated by the women's movement and the gay movement, deeply alarmed the conservative Church.

A shocked Francis Schaeffer, eminent conservative theologian, described his moral outrage in a 1982 televised interview:

> Today we live in a humanist society. They control the schools. They control public television. They control the media in general. And what we have to say is we live

in a humanist society... the courts are not subject to the will of the people through elections or re-election... all the great changes in the last forty years have come through the courts. And what we must get in our mind is the government as a whole, but especially the courts, has become the vehicle to force this view on the total population, even if the total population doesn't hold the view.[16]

For religious conservatives who grew up in the placid 1950s, Americans had strayed too far from their moral foundations. Thankfully, Reagan rallied them back by holding up the 1950s as the cultural paradigm for the nation. By then the Church's resources allowed it to step boldly onto the larger stage. The freedoms of the 1960s became part of its cultural battlefield. The goal was to push back the clock. College-educated, politically savvy leaders[17] led the religious movement, piecing together, issue by issue, a conservative grassroots reaction that is still reshaping America.

According to some scholars, the rise of the "new" Church was *class-based*; a result of the clash between the "*old*" and "*new*" middle class in postwar America. Postwar social transformations pushed out the old middle class of farmers and small-business owners. Those groups were replaced by a new middle class of white-collar knowledge workers. The "new" Church resulted from a coalition between the old middle class, threatened with downward mobility and political irrelevance, and the working-class that was already part of conservative Christianity. The coalition was created to preserve a fading way of life. While there is much truth to that process, as the movement grew, marginal Christianity mutated into a different community. Knowledge workers from mainline churches started switching to conservative groups in the early 1980s. The newcomers left their churches of origin seeking more traditional religious homes.[18]

The influx of new talent allowed organizations like the *Christian Voice*, *Moral Majority*, the *Roundtable*, and the *Christian Coalition* to put the conservative Church in the political driver's seat. The Reagan era opened the door for a symbiotic relationship between Republicans and religious conservatives. But in the last two decades the composition of religious conservatism turned it into a more sophisticated movement. The spread of *Dominionism* (mentioned below as Reconstruction) within conservative circles aided in the rise of a well-funded, doctrine-driven form of religious activism:

> Traditionally, groups like Jerry Falwell's *Moral Majority* were "premillennial": They believed that humanity was inevitably headed for Armageddon, which would most likely arrive with a nuclear blast, whereupon Christ would appear in the Second Coming and set things right.... Reconstruction's alternative was "postmillennialism": Christ would not return until the church had claimed dominion over government, and most of the world's population had accepted the Reconstruction brand of Christianity. The postmillennial twist offered hope to the pious that they could change things—as long as they got organized.... For premillennialists, Reconstruction's revolutionary philosophy offered an opportunity to turbocharge the religious right.... This not only emboldened activists, it gave Reconstructionists a chance

to spread their organizing message: If you want to do God's work, this needs to be God's nation.[19]

The continuous influx of talented newcomers assured the growth of like-minded activist groups. Dedicated religious organizing raised enough funds to fuel a large-scale right-wing program. Conservative political action committees (PACs) raised $6.4 million in 1977–1978, compared to the $1.2 million of liberal PACs. By 1979–1980 conservative PACs were amassing $11.3 million to $2.1 million of liberal PACs.[20] Broadcasting power followed the conservative growth. By 1987 the Christian Right had 1,370 religious radio stations and 221 television stations in the United States, far more than any other religious group.[21] Today the *National Religious Broadcasters Association* boasts a media network capable of reaching an audience of 141 million.[22]

The discipline needed by the movement was ensured by the careful restructuring of the typical conservative congregation: "Key to the growth of evangelicalism during the last twenty years has been a social structure of 'cell groups' that allows churches to grow endlessly while maintaining orthodoxy in their ranks.... Most evangelicals attribute [the strategy] to Pastor Paul Cho, of South Korea, who has built a congregation of 750,000 using the cell-groups structure."[23] The Church's efforts dovetailed nicely with the conservative turn in American politics. With support from the Republican Party, religious causes sprung up during the last two and a half decades. In return, the marginal Church shored up the Republican lock on government. Christian cultural warriors worked tirelessly for Newt Gingrich's revolution. They campaigned just as hard for Bush's presidential elections. As Congress opened its doors to seasoned religious organizers, they proceeded to roll back thirty years of bipartisan secular freedoms.

The United States entered the twenty-first century with a two-term Bush White House, Republican control of both chambers of Congress, and a steady appointment of conservative judges to the bench (including the Supreme Court). It is a level of interdependence that would have been unimaginable at mid-twentieth century America. The end result, so far, has been a shift in American politics from the loftier goals of the Great Society at midcentury—space exploration, civil rights, the war on poverty, equal rights for women, international cooperation, the Peace Corps—to the private morality of conservative Christianity at century's end. Matters of great import for government these days include the fighting of abortion, the promotion of abstinence, the push for *Intelligent Design*, the placement of conservative judges in the courts, and keeping Terri Schiavo alive.[24] As the national agenda got narrower, more resources and regulatory powers shifted toward oversight of private moral issues.

In an insightful book, Alan Wolfe argues that America traded the pursuit of *greatness* for the pursuit of *goodness* (in the most self-righteous meaning of the word).[25] The most powerful nation on earth, the one that could single-handedly lead other nations in the pursuit of peace, a clean environment, a battle against world hunger, poverty, or curable epidemics, is instead caught up in a moralizing war over the private lives of its citizens. The religious push to colonize the secular public square has become so intense by century's end that President George W. Bush had to go on record to defend *the right of all Americans to express their views*! No one could have ever imagined Presidents Eisenhower, Kennedy, Johnson, or Nixon having to remind us that,

> The great thing about America... is that you should be allowed to worship any way you want, and if you choose not to worship, you're equally as patriotic as somebody who does worship. And if you choose to worship, you're equally American if you're a Christian, a Jew, a Muslim. That's the wonderful thing about our country, and that's the way it should be.[26]

While the President defended religious freedom in the national media, a fact-finding review by the Yale Divinity School uncovered widespread religious intolerance at the Air Force Academy in Colorado Springs. Born-again faculty, coaches, and cadets were using strong proselytizing tactics on the other cadets. Second-generation Jewish cadets, whose families had an impeccable record of military service to the country felt ostracized, pressured to convert. Yale's findings prompted an internal military review that confirmed the intolerance. In response, the school pushed the whistle-blowing chaplain out of her post.

When Democrats introduced an amendment to the Defense Appropriation Bill requiring the Academy to develop a preventive plan to end such proselytizing, Representative John N. Hostettler (R-IN) rose to defend Christianity: "... the long war on Christianity in America continues today on the floor of the House of Representatives and continues unabated with aid and comfort to those who would eradicate any vestige of our Christian heritage being supplied by the usual suspects, the Democrats. Like a moth to a flame, Democrats can't help themselves when it comes to denigrating and demonizing Christians."[27]

It was a simple equation: Democrats were "Christian-hating atheists"; Republicans, defenders of the faith. Not surprisingly, Hostettler's words were stricken from the record after he faced strong protests and the threat of rebuke for violating House rules. The event, however, signaled the extent to which religious conservatism had influenced the highest lawmaking body in our land. When an elected official publicly defends the right of Christian faculty to proselytize in a military institution, and dares to suggest that Christianity is under attack by the *democratic process*, we are no longer holding up the wall between the Church and the State. The Air Force Academy is funded by taxpayers of *all* faiths.[28] Its mission is to train soldiers to defend *all* America's freedoms. What would Rep. Hostettler say if the academy was promoting Islam, Judaism, or Buddhism?

The Christian State

Given the decentralized approach to America's restoration, it is hard to find a single document describing the overall conservative strategy. It is possible to collect mission statements from different organizations, but they represent at best slices of the larger plan. *Dominionism* has certainly contributed to the movement's blueprint, but coalitions require more than a single theocratic ideology. The groups under review are too diverse to neatly line up behind a single expressed theory of religiopolitical governance. Fortunately, the action plan can be tracked by other means. Conservative religious groups come together in large coalitions to coordinate common interests. An example of that is the *Arlington Group*.[29] Founded in the mid-1990s, it has served as a forum for conservative Christian leaders from all over the United States, a space where they can develop broad initiatives and long-term strategies. Unfortunately those meetings are off the record and by invitation only.

But a more public network, the *Coalition on Revival* (COR), also serves a similar function. It connects conservative religious groups that work for the "reformation in Church and society in America."[30] Sixty well-known conservative religious leaders make up its National Steering Committee (see Table 3.2). Together with another 300 theologians, pastors, lawyers, doctors, and businessmen they have created seventeen working groups that produced COR's ambitious outline for America's *Christianization*.

The COR plan is described in seventeen "Worldview Documents,"[31] perhaps the most thorough treatment of the entire conservative agenda. One document in particular, *The Christian Worldview of Government*, offers a rare glimpse into the conservative approach for recreating our social order. The tone of the document is fascinating for students of conservative Christianity, because it represents a 180-degree turn in its view of government. For most of the twentieth century, Christian conservatives viewed the State with deep suspicion, refraining from political participation.[32] Now they see it as a tool for divine control of society.

In fact, the document starts with God's authority over the State: "When a ruler decrees either by words or by deeds that he is independent of God's government or that justice is defined according to his self-made laws, then God acts in judgment."[33] Self-rule per se is not being questioned, but rather *self-rule not guided by a higher power*. That allows COR to support the current structure of government, while affirming the need to place it under divine control. Divine authority over a secular State is a standard that challenges the entire corpus of Western political theory, a body of knowledge painstakingly gained over millennia. It challenges the political wisdom of self-rule, gained under great cost in human life from the Renaissance, to the Enlightenment, to the revolutions that gave birth to the modern state. Both the French and the American revolutions were fought on that basis, on the idea that the governed alone are the sole basis for the legitimacy of the ruling systems they set up for themselves.

COR's document brushes the whole political edifice aside, and it is easy to see why. Western political theory challenged the Church's authority when it offered a secular basis for government. In that sense, COR's thesis of a higher authority for human ruling sounds strikingly more similar to Iran's fundamentalist view of political power than to any political philosophy adopted in the Western world:

Table 3.2 The Coalition on Revival's National Steering Committee

Dr. Joseph Aldrich, *Multinomah School*	W. Wellington Boone, *Manna Chrst. Fellowship*	Laury Eck, J.D. *Christian Mediation*	Dick Hillis, D.D., *Overseas Crusades*
Rev. Ray Allen, *ACT Ministries*	Harold Brown, Ph.D., *Trinity E. Divinity School*	Dr. Ted Engstrom, *World Vision*	Dr. Steven Hotze, *Physician*
Dr. Gary Amos, *Regent University*	Dr. E. Cannistraci, *Evangel Chrst. Fellowship*	Michael Farris, *Home School Legal Defense*	David Howard, L.H.D., *World Evangelical Fellowship*
Rev. Francis Anfuso, *Christian Equippers*	Rev. Jack Carter, *CFNI*	Roger Flemming, *The Navigators*	Rev. Dick Iverson, *Portland Bible College*
Gleason Archer, Ph.D., *Trinity E. Divinity School*	Rev. David Chilton, *Church of the Redeemer*	Marshall Foster, *Mayflower Institute*	Ron Jenson, D. Min., *International Leadership*
Virginia Armstrong, Ph.D., *Blackstone Institute*	Evelyn Christenson, *E. C. Ministries*	Rev. Gerald Fry, *Calvary Community Church*	Dee Jepsen, *Regent University*
Theodore Baehr, J.D., *Good News Communications*	Glenn Cole, D.D., *Capital Christian Center*	Bill Garaway, *Business with a Purpose*	Col. Glen Jones, *Military Ministry/ CampusCrusade*
David Balsiger, L.H.D., *Biblical News Service*	Dr. Robert Coleman, *Trinity E. Divinity School*	Arthur Gay, D. Min., *South Park Church;* Petter Gemma, *National ProLife PAC*	Roy Jones, *Republican Senatorial Committee*
William Barker, Th.D., *Presbyterian Journal*	Lawrence Crabb, Ph.D., *Grace Seminary*	Duane Gish, Ph.D., *Inst. for Creation Research*	Rev. R. P. Joseph, *Southfield Presbyterian Church*
Rev. Ern Baxter, *Ern Baxter Ministries*	Art Cunningham, *Hughes Aircraft*	Jose Gonzales, *Semilla*	D. James Kennedy, Ph.D., *Coral Ridge Presbyterian Church*
John Beckett, *Intercessors for America*	Gary DeMar, *American Vision*	Dr. Charles Green, *Network of Christian Ministries*	Joseph Kickasola, *Regent University*
Dick Bernal, *Jubilee Christian Center*	Ted DeMoss, *Christian Business Men Committee*	Rev. Dan Greenlee, *Calvary Cathedral*	Dr. David Kiteley, *Shiloh Christian Fellowship*
E. Calvin Beisner, *Author*	Gladys Dickelman, *National Day of Prayer*	Col. Robert Grete, *Rocky Bayou Christian School*	Paul Kienel, Ed.D., *Association of Christian Schools International*
Dick Benjamin, *Abbotts Loop Christian Center*	Colonel Doner *Christian Action Network*	Jay Grimstead, D. Min., *Coalition on Revival*	Henry Krabbendam, Ph.D., *Covenant College*
Charles Blair, D.D., *Calvary Temple*	Rev. Jeff Donnan *Christians for Justice*	Rev. Ronald Haus, *1st Century Broadcasting*	Tim LaHaye, D. Min., *American Coalition for Traditional Values*
Richard Bliss, Ed.D., *Inst. for Creation Research*	Dr. Robert Dugan, *National Association of Evangelicals*	Dr. Lewis Hicks, *Physician*	
Rohn Boehm, *Youth with a Mission/Revive America*			

Table 3.2 (cont.)

Richard Lappert, Ph.D., *Connecticut State Department of Education*

Harold Lindsell, Ph.D., *Christianity Today*

Dr. Paul Lindstrom, *Chrst. Liberty Academy*

Allan MacRae, Ph.D., *Biblical Theological Seminary*

Rev. Ronald Marr, Editor, *Christian Enquirer*

Dr. Peter Marshall, Author

Connaught Marshner, *Child & Family Protection Inst.*

Rev. Bob Martin, *Maranatha Christian Churches*

Robert Martin, *Fieldstead & Company*

Ted McAteer, *Religious Roundtable*

Josh McDowell, D.D., *J. M. Ministries*

R. E. McMaster, Jr., *The Reaper*

Robert McQuilkin, D.D., *Columbia Bible College*

Bishop John L. Meares, *Evangel Temple*

Mr. Robert Metcalf, *Christian Studies Center*

Rev. Lou Montecalvo, *Redeemer Temple*

Rev. Joseph Morecraft, *Chalcedon Presb. Church*

Rev. Bob Mumford, *Lifechangers*

Gary North, Ph.D., *Inst. for Christian Economics*

Raymond Ortlund, D.D., *Renewal Ministries*

J. I. Packer, Ph.D., *Regent College*

Dr. Luis Palau, *Luis Palau Evangelistic Team*

Ed Payne, M.D., *Medical College of Georgia*

Rev. Dennis Peacocke, *Strategic Christian Services*

John Perkins, D.D., *Voice of Calvary Ministries*

William Reed, M.D., *Christian Medical Foundation*

Jerry Regier, *Family Research Council*

George Rekers, Ph.D., *USC School of Medicine*

Dr. Adrian Rogers, *Bellevue Baptist Church*

R. J. Rushdoony, Ph.D., *Chalcedon Foundation*

Michael Rusten, Ph.D., *Business Consultant*

Rev. Ron Sadlow, *Second Presbyterian Church*

Robert Saucy, Th.D., *Talbot Seminary*

Edith Schaeffer, Author

George Scipione, *Chrst. Counseling & Education*

Rev. Owen Shackett, *The People's Church*

H. Schlossberg, Author

Shelby Sharp, J.D.

Mark Siljander, Former Member, *United States Congress*

Robert Simonds, Th.D., *National Association of Christian Education*

Rev. Charles Simpson, *Gulf Coast Cov. Church*

John Sparks, J.D., *Grove City College*

Carolyn Sundseth, *White House, Office of Public Liaison*

Bob Thoburn, *Fairfax Christian School*

Lary Tomczak, *The People of Destiny Mag.*

Paul Toms, D.D. *Park Street Church*

Joseph Tson, D.D., *Romanian Missionary Society*

Bro. Andrew van der Bijl, *Open Doors*

Jack Van Impe, Ph.D., *Jack Van Impe Ministries*

Dr. Peter Wagner, *Fuller Theological Seminary*

Larry Walker, Ph.D., *Mid-America Baptist Seminary*

Dr. Robert Walker, *Christian Life Magazine*

Russ Walton, *Plymouth Rock Foundation*

Bob Weiner, *Maranatha Campus Ministries*

Dr. Luder Whitlock, *Reformed Theological Seminary*

Rev. Al Whittinghill, *Ambassadors for Christ*

Rev. Donald Wildmon, *American Family Association*

Rev. Jerry Wiles, *Bible Pathway Ministries*

Rev. Mike Williams, *Hillside Church*

Ralph Winter, Ph.D., *U.S. Center for World Missions*

Dr. Don Zoller, *McLean Bible Church*

Source: Gary DeMar and Colonel Doner (eds.), *The Christian Worldview of Government* (1989).

from God alone comes the authority to rule. The whole document, in fact, is about divine authority. God, not the people, sets the conditions for political rule: "At stake in each area of dispute in the culture wars is the question of authority: Who is responsible for the care of the family, and how much the state and other institutions shall intervene? Who can define the role of women in society, and how much authority should men retain in the family? Who defines the ethical boundaries of business, public culture, education, and other issues of public policy? Who can determine when life begins and when it should end?"[34]

On those terms, self-rule is contrary to God's law. It is a sign of human arrogance and a threat to human freedom. God alone rules individuals and nations. Our fallen condition renders us incapable of *justly governing ourselves, by our own means.* COR denies that true government stems from the people. True government comes from obedience to biblical laws ("and laws soundly deduced therefrom");[35] thus, from God stems all political power, and from the Bible his guidance for human rule. Similarly, God grants the state authority to protect its citizens. Transgressions are met by God's wrath as dispensed by the police force.

Justice in the Christian State exists to assure that lawbreakers receive their fair punishment. Since justice is defined by God, the State cannot redefine it. Its principles do not evolve with society. Based on biblical revelation, justice cannot be changed; which explains why conservative Christians have worked so hard to appoint strictly constructionist judges to our courts, judges who are also God-fearing Christians. Fully versed in the Bible and the law, they will not "update" justice, but apply its wisdom based upon precedence and biblical standards. Along those lines, since civil government cannot operate without divine guidance, there should be no separation between Church and State. In fact, one of the civil government's foremost duties is the protection of the true "Church of our Lord Jesus Christ."

The State should never "be neutral toward Christianity and treat it as equal with all other so-called religions."[36] "Man-made" religions, the document argues, do not have the same rights as the true faith. So there is no need for tolerance or equanimity in spiritual matters. The Church's primacy is the very foundation of the Christian State: "We deny that it is moral for earthly governments to establish laws that run counter to God's Biblical principles, and that it is moral for earthly governors to govern independently of those principles."[37]

Incidentally, there is no such thing as social welfare in the Christian State. Welfare is a misguided notion, a dangerous form of social engineering. Its programs keep the needy from taking charge of their lives and that goes against God's natural order. People should rise up on their own initiative, under the aegis of the free enterprise system. Honesty, hard work, and discipline alone are the means to better one's condition. It follows then that those who do not apply themselves ought not to expect governmental handouts. God may have granted the State authority to collect taxes, but he does not desire to have them squandered on the poor. That is not the biblically mandated way. The approach here is more Pauline: those who do not work, should not eat.

The document ends with a call for action. It invites all born-again Americans to aid in the implementation of this vision. They should influence "those in the field of government who agree with our affirmations and denials to implement these proposals in their work." Religious activists should mobilize and network "[their] Christian resources and [work] in concert with the other professional spheres both inside and outside COR, to see the behavior of the Body of Christ and our nation changed more closely to the view of reality and morality presented to us in the Holy Scriptures."[38] To that end, the coalition has established a nationwide prayer network with volunteers who pray regularly for every public official whose office has a bearing on American citizens. The full colonization of the secular is just a matter of time. The process is already running its course and true Christians are rallying up to aid in *Christianizing* the public square.

Were we to take COR's proposal seriously, the implications would be quite revolutionary. The document advocates nothing short of sedition. Democratic rule would be replaced by Christian theocracy. America's restoration would go beyond acknowledging the country's Judeo-Christian roots. It would require a reconstruction of our society. It is a logic that betrays the Founders' most basic assumptions about self-government, *especially* Thomas Jefferson's views of religious freedom. Taken as a whole, the document advocates a wholesale negation of the American political heritage. Such an approach can be only explained as a result of conservative Christian zeal, since COR leaders are rather patriotic and law-abiding citizens otherwise. But it shows the dangers of crossing the wall of separation of the Church and the State. It assumes religious homogeneity in society where there should be none, especially established by government.

Nevertheless, it is easy to see how the COR program would rally the average marginal believer. For those with a deep sense of alienation, of estrangement from their own culture, who live in a society far more secular than they can stand, a Christian takeover sounds extremely appealing. The notion of a Christian theocracy must stir the imagination of the estranged believer, with its promises of realignment of the nation's ethos with Christian beliefs and practices. The complete refashioning of government agencies, courts, schools, clinics, and every aspect of the public square would be paradise for the marginal believer. Moreover, it would assure God's continuous blessings upon his/her country, since religious conservatives believe that the basis for America's predominance in the world is not our *humanly built* economy, technology, or military prowess. Our power comes from God's choosing us as his shining beacon for the world.[39]

If well meaning, this line of thinking would have horrifying consequences. Its logic makes timely Robert Ingersoll's centenary warnings:

> For many years priests have attempted to give to our Government a religious form.... All this is contrary to the genius of the Republic, contrary to the Declaration of Independence, and contrary really to the Constitution of the United States. We have taken the ground that the people can govern themselves without the assistance of any supernatural power. We have taken the position that the

people are the real and only rightful source of authority. We have solemnly declared that the people must determine what is politically right and what is wrong, and that their legally expressed will is the supreme law. This leaves no room for national superstition—no room for patriotic gods or supernatural beings—and this does away with the necessity for political prayers.[40]

Christian Civic Responsibility

Compared to COR's militant views, the manifesto of the *National Association of Evangelicals* (NAE), "For the Health of the Nations: An Evangelical Call to Civic Responsibility," seems milder.[41] It calls born-again Christians to political action, but its tone is more cautious, more diplomatic. That is not surprising, given the NAE's broader confessional representation. Its current membership is estimated at 45,000 churches and more than thirty million believers. The plan suggests a more limited presence, more limited religious participation in public life; one that even seeks to strike a balance between right and left-wing political positions. Its preamble praises the media for noticing NAE's pro-life and family work, but also points out the organization's involvement in disaster relief, refugee resettlement, the fight against AIDS, human rights abuse, slavery, sexual trafficking, and prison rape.

If the NAE tries to straddle the political spectrum these days, its origins are clearly conservative. The organization was founded in 1942, as a network for evangelical denominations, congregations, and individuals. It had a simple mission: to demonstrate "the unity of the body of Christ by standing for biblical truth, speaking with a representative voice, and serving the evangelical community through united action, cooperative ministry, and strategic planning." To that end, the NAE seeks to "confront society with the relevance of the gospel,"[42] a charge NAE officers take very seriously.

The organization boasts one of the most powerful religious lobbies on Capitol Hill. Its recent past president, Ted Haggard (former pastor of the 12,000-member *New Life* megachurch in Colorado Springs), conferred with President Bush or White House officials *every Monday*. When the President signed the Partial-Birth Abortion Bill in 2003, Pastor Ted was one of the eight ministers flown to DC for the Oval Office ceremony.[43] That is a remarkable level of access to the most powerful office in the world.

The NAE manifesto starts out by calling the evangelicals' attention to their unique opportunity. At the dawn of the twenty-first century, they comprise one quarter of the electorate. They have a real chance to influence important political developments in the "most powerful nation in history." The manifesto admonishes NAE members not to take the current opportunity for granted (by its own estimates only half of all evangelicals vote). They should participate in public life because "Jesus is Lord over every area of life" (a *Dominionist* tenet). Evangelicals should engage in political action because "God created our first parents in his image and gave them dominion over the earth" (another *Dominionist* claim). Increased evangelical participation could provide "key" American political leaders with the means to fight "the forces of authoritarianism [and] radical secularism." The battle cry could not be more direct, nor more urgent.

Since dominion in a modern society is diffused through various institutions—the state, the family, the school, the churches, the businesses, and the labor unions—the NAE expects born-again Christians to take the burden of promoting "just governance" wherever they can. They should be active in the public arena because giving it up would mean leaving it to "the Evil One" (yet another *Dominionist* tenet). In his own timeline God will "bring about the fullness of the kingdom," but in the meantime Christians should "speak prophetically to society," and "work for the renewal and reform of its structures."

While such a goal may seem laudable, it could be turned on its head, by simply replacing the word "Christian" for that of any other faith (Muslim, Jewish, Buddhist, or Hindu). Doing so would reveal the danger in this line of thinking. Imagine a similar manifesto, issued by a national Islamic association. Suppose the group claimed Allah gave them political dominion over every area of life, and invited faithful American Muslims to rise up and install "just governance wherever they can." Assume, further, that the organization asked every dedicated American Muslim to "speak prophetically to society" and work for the Islamic "renewal and reform of the nation's social structures." The reaction would be earth-shattering. Yet, NAE leaders can hold a national press conference in Washington, DC to launch their manifesto and go on the national media advertising its merits, without a ripple being made by other groups in civil society. It shows how far the secular arena has been colonized.

Similar to COR's worldview document, the NAE manifesto concerns itself with justice. Evangelical civic engagement should "bless our neighbors by making good laws." The assumption, of course, is that an evangelical-based justice would suit all Americans, or that it would be a better alternative to our current system. Evangelical courts, laws, and judicial decisions should provide us with greater justice and equanimity. But how would such a system be different from other religious-based courts like Iran or Nigeria? Why should a literal interpretation of the Bible replace self-rule in the American compact? The authors of the manifesto are not bothered by those questions, since Jesus' authority overrules the authority of the State.

In fact, evangelicals should obey civil authorities only when they "act in accord with God's justice and his laws." Authorities ought to preserve "the God-ordained responsibilities of society's other institutions, such as churches, other faith-centered organizations, schools, families, labor unions, and businesses." But no mention is made as to who decides when authorities are acting in accordance to God's justice or not. Who determines when civil resistance is justified? Fortunately, the document acknowledges that evangelicals might differ from other

Christians and non-Christians over the policies they defend. So it suggests that they approach political engagement with "humility and cooperation" if they hope to achieve "modest and attainable goals for the good of society."

Since the Bible does not directly address all the complex processes that affect a modern society, the document welcomes the wisdom of "social, economic, historical, jurisprudential and political analysis" in aiding born-again Christians to chart their public engagement. Social problems have *individual* and *structural* causes, and therefore cannot be solved without a more sophisticated understanding of society. That is why evangelicals are grateful for democracy: it allows Americans to sort out issues as they "hold government responsible for fulfilling its responsibilities to God and abiding by the norms of justice."

The problem with that view of democracy is that it assumes that all Americans have a similar definition of what God expects from their country. What happens if people of good conscience disagree as to the right path? Who determines the godly way? What if God provides a different plan for the faithful of different American religious traditions? Why would the Christian plan be better than the Jewish plan or the Buddhist plan? Such simple questions spell out the problems of a faith-based government.

The manifesto warns Christians to beware of "the potentially self-destructive tendencies of our society and our government," but it does not specify those tendencies. Is it self-destructive to go to war? Is it self-destructive to develop massive nuclear arsenals? Is it self-destructive to poison the environment? Is it self-destructive to maintain huge national deficits? And is it self-destructive to let the bottom strata of the wealthiest nation in the world fall into homelessness? None of it is made clear. Instead, the document offers a list of worthy causes, deserving of evangelical political engagement. It pledges to work for *religious freedom* and *liberty of conscience*, the nurturing of *family life* and children, *the sanctity of human life*, the promotion of *justice and compassion for the poor and vulnerable*, *human rights*, *peacemaking*, and *environmental care*. While most Americans agree with the worthiness of the seven causes, they might not agree with the way the NAE defines them.

For instance, the NAE supports religious freedom, but only for "rich traditions of ultimate belief and practice." For the NAE " . . . the First Amendment protects religiously informed conscience, [but] it does not protect *all matters of sincere concern*." In other words, new religious movements, new age beliefs, or even a secular lifestyle would not fall under the equal protection clause. It is a rather limited notion of religious freedom after all. In the same vein, the NAE defends the nurturing of family life and children, but it adopts a narrow definition of family, specifically the traditional heterosexual nuclear family. In fact, to defend the family, the NAE proposes that the U.S. government stop treating "other kinds of households as the family's social and legal equivalent." By those standards, gay and lesbian couples in long-term, committed relationships would not be a family, nor would they provide a good setting for adoption.

So, unfortunately, what starts out as a broad, worthy cause—one that all Americans could support—ends up being a narrowly defined one, guided by a particular lifestyle. It is a vision that would clearly divide traditional American Christians from other segments of our secular society. One wonders if that's the evangelical way to "bless our neighbors by making good laws."

The narrow definitions are extended to the other topics. Strangely, protection of "the sanctity of human life" includes abortion, but not capital punishment. It seems that the "life" of the unborn is holy, but not so the lives of convicted criminals, people for whom—in theory—Jesus also died. How do evangelicals determine, in the name of Christ, when someone is beyond redemption? Did Christ die only for the worthy, the well-behaved, and the churchgoer? What about the thief on the cross right next to Christ's? It is hard to imagine a God whose son was a victim of the death penalty actually supporting such institution.

Concern for the poor is not framed as caring for "the least of these," or "feeding the hungry." For the NAE, concern for the poor entails diminishing "gross disparities in opportunity and outcome." The underlying assumption, of course, is that social inequality is part of God's natural plan. Some are always more deserving than others, particularly if they are blessed with talent and industry. All that is needed is to narrow the gap between the powerful and the powerless. That might also explain why the manifesto is against taxing private property. Despite its advice that evangelicals use historical, political, or sociological tools to address social ills, the document fails to question why postindustrial conditions in America make it impossible for certain segments of the population to ever rise above poverty level.[44] It also fails theologically when it ignores Jesus' admonition against amassing treasures on earth; or his instructions to Zaccheus and the rich young man to divest themselves of wealth for the sake of the Kingdom.

The manifesto favors the protection of human rights, but proposes that there are *inappropriate* rights too, such as "same-sex marriage" or "the right to die." One wonders—if the rights of minorities are not legitimate, why protect anyone else's rights in the first place? Are not the rights of dominant groups by definition already safeguarded? If the majority of Americans are heterosexual, how will same-sex marriage threaten their "right" to heterosexuality? If the majority of Americans do not suffer from terminal illnesses, how does death with dignity threaten their right to life? Once again, the issue of authority plagues the manifesto. Or rather it grants conservative Christians the authority to make all the judgment calls. When people of good conscience disagree as to what rights should be protected, who decides which ones are appropriate and which are not?

The section on peacemaking is guided by the classical theological argument about the just war. But in a modern, high-tech age, do Christian principles really affect decisions to go to war or the means by which to wage it? Has any American war ever been labeled "unjust" by Christians? And if so have any of them been preempted by such labeling? Has any American war ever been justified as not self-defense? Does not the strength of one's army and ability to stage a successful campaign ultimately justify all wars *post facto*? The futility of it raises questions about the usefulness of a just war theory. What are Christian standards for an *acceptable* war? Is going to war for the sake of oil acceptable? How about a war driven by desire for regime change? Is it Christian to treat the death of thousands of noncombatants "collateral damage?" Is it Christian to ignore international law in matters of war and peace? Moreover, what happens if the evangelical parameters for a just war are not unanimously agreed upon by all American citizens? The document does not explain.

The section on the environment is perhaps the most agreeable for the majority of Americans. The document urges the nation to be mindful of nature and to recycle. Governments should encourage fuel efficiency, reduce pollution, and support sustainable use of natural resources. But even here the recommendations do not easily translate into operational directives. How should government encourage fuel efficiency? By increasing gas mileage requirements for American cars, or by giving bigger tax breaks to the energy industry? Is it really moral to explore, extract, and market fossil fuels at a time of global warming, or should we be investing in green, renewable sources of energy? Since America has the worst environmental record of all industrialized societies, should we repent by giving up comfort and wealth? Or should we settle for "manageable" standards of environmental pollution? No clear answers are forthcoming.

The document ends with a pledge to foster more civic engagement. It calls upon Christian leaders in public office to "deepen our perspective on public policy and political life." It calls upon born-again Christians to become informed and vote. It calls upon churches and religious agencies to foster civic responsibility. Unfortunately the logic behind the manifesto is similar to the COR document: Christians ought to lead, never follow. The goal is for Christians to control America's public arena and set the priorities for the rest of the nation. The promise is that sectarian Christian dominion will surely lead to our national prosperity. The justification is that Christ has already given his followers earthly dominion. This infusion of conservative Christianity into all political institutions and civil society requires, of course, the shrinking of our secular public square. It is a beatific vision that might inspire evangelicals. But it offers no solace for those who wish to preserve religious pluralism in our country.

RELIGION AND THE MODERN STATE

The current push to establish a Christian order in the United States betrays the conservative Church's new Constantinian impulse. It is a desire akin to the one that pervaded Western history from the fourth to the sixteenth century of the Common Era. That desire created the pre-modern European *cosmos*, bringing together the sword and the cross, faith and empire. The Roman Catholic Pope and the Holy Roman Emperor (Kaiser) bound the continent's vast landmass into a single Christian realm. Christendom was the closest thing Christians ever had to universal dominion, a rule that extended to the far ends of the known world.

There is, however, a set of historical pitfalls associated with the desire for Christendom. Under that arrangement, Emperor and Pontiff worked *in tandem* to preserve an oppressive feudal system. *Christendom* meant that Church and State united to sponsor the Inquisition, to launch the Crusades, to redivide kingdoms, to support absolutism, and to set up a worldwide, asymmetrical system of trade between Europe and other continents.

If Christendom regimented Europe's political and religious centers and controlled its diverse population, the Reformation fractured the continent. The development of multiple confessions within Christianity led to a thirty-year war that put an end to the ancient status quo. For three decades of horrendous carnage, Christian fought Christian in the heart of Europe, with both sides claiming divine guidance and support. At the war's end, the European population had been decimated by 40 percent,[45] and its most fertile regions had been utterly destroyed by Christian zeal and political greed. The Peace of Westphalia ended Christendom as a political experiment. Drafted in Münster and Osnabrück, signed by the Spanish and the Dutch on January 30, 1648, and by the Holy Roman Emperor, German princes, France, and Sweden on October 24, 1648, the treaty became a milestone in Western history.

Politically, it marked the birth of the modern state. Religiously, it put a stop to the temporal control of religious leaders. Politically, Westphalia inaugurated the modern period of international law and diplomacy, as it acknowledged the *sovereignty* of European states. Under Westphalia, European nations were granted equal rights of self-determination: rights sustained by mutually established international treaties. Westphalia recognized the sovereignty of the German states, and the independence of Netherlands and Switzerland. From them on, nations in common agreement, not God's commands, would determine the content and nature of international treaties. The era of secular politics was born.

Religiously, Westphalia ended Christendom: the idea that a Holy Roman Empire and the Catholic Church could exercise dominion over the secular world. Westphalia sanctioned Calvinism as a legitimate form of Christianity, and established *de juris* religious tolerance. Rulers could still choose the official religion of their domains ("*cuius regio eius religio*"), but subjects gained freedom of worship.[46] That freedom of worship set the tone for the ecumenical toleration that now is common practice in industrialized, European nations. Westphalia ended religious warfare in Europe.[47] Churches would no longer equip armies to do their bidding in the battlefield. Religious questions would no longer be settled by bellicose means but by mutual agreements between Christian confessions. With Westphalia, Western civilization acknowledged *that even within a single faith there can be dissension and conflict.*

Westphalia was not the product of political expediency. It was not cobbled out of military exhaustion. There is a reason the modern state does not rule on religious matters, nor is it ruled by faith. In Westphalia, Europe recognized that Christendom *failed* as a political experiment; and that the struggle within Western civilization to keep all its multicultural and religious strands under a single sacred canopy resulted in chaos, oppression and destruction. When splinter groups claim absolute religious truth and political polarization follows, the arm of the state can be used to unleash civil war and wanton destruction upon both camps of *the saved*. What started as a holy endeavor, ended in division, carnage, and bloodshed.

At Westphalia the Western world realized that *religious governance* was neither sustainable, nor desirable. That same lesson was learned at great cost by the religious wars visited upon the English people. The alignment of a single faith with the arm of the state inevitably resulted in censorship, political persecution, and religious wars. Now fast forward to the twenty-first century, and imagine the horrifying devastation that could be unleashed by an alliance between a single sectarian religious faction (conservative Christianity) and the most powerful government on earth: the only military superpower around. America's *secular order* is critical to our internal balance of power and to our foreign affairs.

The lesson of Westphalia was not lost on our Founders. It inspired Thomas Jefferson's *Virginia Act for Establishing Religious Freedom* (1786), and eventually Article VI and the First Amendment of the United States Constitution. Jefferson knew that religious governance presented a threat to the young Republic. In the *Virginia Act* he argued that:

> proscribing any citizen as unworthy of the public confidence by laying upon him an incapacity of being called to the offices of trust and emolument, unless he profess or renounce this or that religious opinion, is depriving him injuriously of those privileges and advantages to which in common with his fellow citizens he has a natural right; that it tends also to corrupt the principles of that very religion it is meant to encourage, by bribing, with a monopoly of worldly honors and emoluments, those who will externally profess and conform to it.[48]

The Virginia legislature wisely responded to Jefferson's argument by upholding religious tolerance:

> Be it therefore enacted by the General Assembly, that no man shall be compelled to frequent or support any religious worship, place, or ministry whatsoever, nor shall be enforced, restrained, molested, or burdened in his body or goods, nor shall otherwise suffer on account of his religious opinions or belief; but that all men shall be free to profess, and by argument to maintain, their opinions in matters of religion, and that the same shall in nowise diminish, enlarge, or affect their civil capacities.[49]

All his life, Jefferson considered the *Virginia Act* one of his most important contributions to the new nation. To him religious freedom was a crucial pillar of a modern, enlightened, democratic society. His opinion so impressed his peers in Philadelphia that it found a place in our Constitution. The Article VI of our magna carta stipulates that "no religious test shall ever be required as a qualification to any office or public trust under the United States."[50]

For obvious reasons, *Dominionists* either ignore or struggle with Article VI. In *The Nature of the American System* (1965), R. J. Rushdoony, founder of *Dominionism*, put forth the theory that the Constitution was designed to perpetuate a Christian order. But he did so by avoiding Article VI altogether. Gary DeMar, in his *America's Christian History* (1993), argues that Article VI simply forbade government-mandated religious tests. But he fails to explain why tests that were so prevalent during colonial days were so quickly abandoned afterwards. Nearly all colonies required Christian allegiance from public officeholders. Yet the practice was relinquished henceforth.[51]

Echoes of the *Virginia Act* can also be found in the First Amendment of the Constitution, when it forbids Congress from making laws "respecting an establishment of religion, or prohibiting the free exercise thereof."[52] The amendment echoes the wisdom of Westphalia when it separates Church and State.

Those who adopt a *nonpreferential* interpretation of the First Amendment hold that the Constitution does not forbid the practice of religion, but rather the preferential support of one religious faction above others. The Republic, they say, was filled with public religion: public assemblies opened with prayers, public officials asked God's blessings upon the country, and the founding documents invoked the Creator. Still, the threat of a nation run by a cadre of single-minded, sectarian religious rulers was real to the Founders, especially those who penned the following passage in the *Federalist Papers*:

> Direct representation of the innumerable interests of the people, many of them passionate and extreme in their partisan ambitions, was neither desirable nor possible... The combination of large electoral districts and a relatively small House of Representatives would necessarily lead to the selection of moderate representatives agreeable to many factions and cross sections of the population. Further, the institutional complexity of the national government would tend to neutralize conflicts among factions as they attempted to work through the government, and draw them together into moderate coalitions. But beyond all of that, the system would lead to the selection as representatives of those who would be likely to stand above special interests and pursue the true interests of all their constituents, as well as the common good of society.[53]

At the risk of belaboring the obvious, the American State limited itself constitutionally in two clear ways: in the *establishment clause* by "making no law respecting an establishment of religion;" and in the *free exercise clause* by "prohibiting the free exercise thereof." The first clause may indeed forbid state-sponsored religious favoritism, but the second goes beyond that—it guarantees freedom of conscience. Even assuming that the separation of Church and State simply prevented governmental support for *one religion above others* (the first clause), the *free exercise clause* guarantees that as Americans we are free *from having others' faith imposed upon us.*[54] Every citizen is granted the freedom to follow the dictates of her/his conscience. Public religion undermines that freedom when it is imposed upon all.

The point of this review is simple: *without religious freedom, there is no modern state*. A Christian order would take us back to Christian feudalism, to perhaps a modern Inquisition, and possibly corollary religious wars. The secular public square guarantees that multiple forms of Christianity, or any other faith for that matter, can flourish within the same nation. Take away the secular, and you take away some of the most sacred freedoms ever granted by a state to its citizenry. The *secular state* was Westphalia's greatest political invention, one fully sanctioned by our founding documents. It offers a neutral space, where citizens of different backgrounds can coexist and transact their business in peace, without being subjected to religious tests. Our ancestors came to the New World fleeing Europe's bloody religious wars. That memory was not as fresh when they deliberated our independence but fresh enough to mark our political beginnings as a nation.

The Enlightenment notion of the modern, secular state, framed early by Westphalia, guided their thoughts as they composed our founding documents. They knew that without religious freedom we could not blossom, our country would likely face the same scenario encountered by European states after the Reformation. A *secular*, pluralistic, tolerant vision of individual freedom ("E Pluribus Unum") is perhaps the greatest legacy our Founders granted us. It was not easily achieved, but its wisdom has kept us in good stead:

> The left and the right in early America disagreed on the extent to which the United States was even to be viewed as a Christian nation. Thus, not only did the Jeffersonians seek to eliminate all forms of state support for the established churches; they went so far on the national level as to insist that the State was obligated to provide services for its citizens seven days a week—that, for instance, it could not deprive non-Christians of their right to receive mail on Sundays.... In 1830—twenty years after the passage of the Sunday mails bill—a Senate committee report, authored by a future Vice-President and endorsed by a majority of that House, stated explicitly that in the United States religion and irreligion had equal rights, and that laws proclaiming that the government should not provide services on Sunday would work an injustice to irreligious people or non-Christians, and would constitute a special favor for Christians as a group. The report, written by a deeply religious active Baptist, stated these principles in unequivocal terms: The Constitution regards the conscience of the Jew as sacred as that of the Christian, and gives no more authority to adopt a measure affecting the conscience of a solitary individual than that of a whole community.... It is the duty of this government to affirm to *all*—to the Jew or Gentile, Pagan, or Christian—the protection and advantages of our benignant institutions on *Sunday*, as well as every day of the week.[55]

The Founders knew that our strength as a new nation could only come from the freedom to disagree, *even on matters of faith*. In fact, when we unite as citizens in our desire to protect each other's religious freedom, we keep anyone from imposing one system of thought upon all. Christendom was not the answer then, and it is certainly not the answer now. It is not the solution to prospering together in peace. Our country became the first new nation by setting a different pattern of Church and State relations, by disestablishing religion, by moving beyond the European experiment. Building upon that founding wisdom, we chose to embark on a different political program. One of government of the people, by the people, and for the people: The wisdom of our Founders, gained at the cost of so many lives and such wanton destruction in Europe, should never be forgotten on American soil.

4

BLEST BE THE TIE THAT BINDS: DEFENDING RELIGIOUS LIBERTY

> "[To protect] religious liberty and America's Christian heritage by encouraging the application of biblical principles to all spheres of our culture and to all of life."[1]
> —3rd Purpose of Ministry, Coral Ridge Presbyterian Church, FL

Suburbia also affects the conservative Christian mission in the larger society. Their values and causes reflect both a sectarian stance and their new level of affluence. That includes a certain middle-class zeal for the preservation of a 1950s suburban moral order. That suburban vision organizes their efforts to *Christianize* society. To achieve it, they approach the task with a two-pronged, well-defined agenda: some areas of American life need less state regulation, while others require more. Government should meddle less in matters of *religious liberty*, and more on issues of *public morality*. Since the conservative Church cannot effect those changes without the aid of the State, it stands to reason that it will rely upon an array of conservative groups and its overall *Dominionist* blueprint to guide its presence in the public square.

The previous chapter examined the conservative vision for a Christian social order. This chapter and the next explore the actual content of the conservative agenda, the plan for the Christianization of our society. Together, they detail what drives the current religious movement. We start with the vision of a particular conservative group, the *Christian Exodus* (CE). Having decided that the nation is not turning to Christianity fast enough, CE's founding members have developed a unique plan to speed its restoration. Rather than a focusing on a national takeover (an obviously impossible task, given "the abject failure of the Christian Right to accomplish [it] from Washington, DC"), CE members have decided to change America *one state at a time*.

It is a simple rationale: born-again Christians are too scattered to bring the much-needed change. Meanwhile, federal law are still protecting "immoral aberrations": abortion is still a constitutional right, prayers are still banned in schools, a Texas sodomy case was rejected by the Supreme Court, and gay marriage is just around the corner. Upset by these conditions, CE members argue that only by concentrating enough Christians in a geographical area will it be possible for Christians to take over the government. If they can create a Christian social order at the local and state levels first, then it will be easier to move on to the national scene.

As long as the *saved* are geographically scattered, their efforts will be counteracted by secular forces (the group suspects of creeping secular humanism even in the Republican Congress and the Bush administration). To speed America's restoration, CE members developed rigorous criteria for selecting a target state, including voter turnout in primary and general elections, the "moral nature of the [local] electorate," the cost of living and of housing, job availability for out-of-state families, school availability (including homeschooling and Christian schools), and church availability. Based upon these criteria, they have picked their first target—the state of South Carolina. They believe it will be easier to create a Christian social order by taking over county and eventually state government in South Carolina, before moving to the national scene.

To that end, they have invited dedicated Christian families from other parts of the country to relocate to South Carolina. After a careful review they chose a two-city/county area to serve as their beachhead. Phase one will involve bringing enough "Bible-believing" families to the area[2] (about 2,500 volunteers), to create a solid "Christian electorate" at the county level. With those numbers they could control "the city council, the county council, elected law enforcement positions, and elected judgeships." Further emigrations would facilitate taking over the state's General Assembly by 2014, placing it "squarely in the hands of Christian Constitutionalists."[3]

Once in control of the state, CE members would change its constitution "returning proper autonomy to the State by 2016 regardless of illegal edicts from Washington, DC."[4] The group has determined that the federal government has exceeded its constitutional mandate in a number of areas. So, their constitutional change would return to state control matters of education, religion, abortion, domestic behavior, intrastate communication, intrastate commerce, taxation, welfare, health care, and gun regulation. Reclaiming those areas would remedy "overextended federal tyranny." As soon as South Carolina is safely ensconced in conservative Christian hands, the movement would pick the next state and begin anew. The plan is to eventually restore all fifty states to Christ's lordship.

Obviously, one wonders how South Carolinians or citizens of any other state, for that matter, would take to the notion of an out-of-state Christian "occupation." It does not seem to cross the minds of CE members that even South Carolinian religious conservatives might not take kindly to having their born-again brethren from Texas, Arizona, Kansas, Indiana, Iowa, Alabama, or North Carolina telling them how to run their business. The hubris in the notion that a small group of Texas Christians could launch such large-scale political operation, without consulting targeted "constituencies," is consternating. Such large-scale social engineering would never be envisioned by previous generations of marginal believers.

But for the well-educated, legally trained, white-collar Christian conservatives[5] behind CE, accustomed to organizing grassroots movements, the plan makes perfect sense in logic and program. It shows how affluence affects and reshapes the conservative Church's sense of mission. For our purposes, CE provides a *conservative bill of grievances*. Their list parallels the broader agenda of other groups working within the conservative Church. It speaks to what *the country needs saving from*, since the current policies of our government seem to present a threat to the group leaders. In their eyes, redeeming American politics is the precondition for protecting the true practice of Christianity in this country. In that spirit the group contends that:

> Christians have actively tried to return the United States to their moral foundations for more than 30 years. We now have a professing Christian president, a Republican Congress and a Republican Supreme Court. Yet consider this:
> - Abortion continues against the wishes of many States
> - Sodomite and lesbian "marriage" is now legal in Massachusetts (and coming soon to a neighborhood near you)
> - Children who pray in public schools are subject to prosecution
> - Our schools continue to teach the discredited theory of Darwinian evolution
> - The Bible is still not welcome in schools except under unconstitutional FEDERAL guidelines
> - The 10 Commandments remain banned from public display
> - Sodomy is now legal AND celebrated as "diversity" rather than condemned as perversion
> - Preaching Christianity will soon be outlawed as "hate speech"
> - Fathers are denied equal rights under law in cases of child custody
> - Our right to keep and bear arms continues to be INFRINGED
> - Private homes are now subject to arbitrary government seizure
>
> Attempts at reform have proven futile. Future elections will not stop the above atrocities, but rather will lead us down an even more deadly path because both national parties routinely disobey the U.S. Constitution.[6]

The CE's bill of grievances lists four major areas in which America needs saving: *family life*, *education*, *human sexuality*, and *Church and State relations*. The four areas can easily be subsumed under two banners: *religious liberty* and *public morality*. Under religious liberty CE members would place the sheltering of Christian families from state intervention and the shielding of their children from a godless education. Under the rubric of public morality they would include curtailing public tolerance for immoral sexual behavior, and pushing the country toward publicly proclaiming its Christian heritage.

The argument is pretty straightforward. For the sake of religious liberty Christians of good conscience cannot allow government to curb their faith practices. At the same time, for the sake of public morality, the government must push for biblically based sexual mores, and a public square where Christ is honored. That captures, in a nutshell, the two moments of America's restoration: the co-optation of modernity and the colonization of the public square.

The CE laundry list would grow if we were to review all the many conservative groups that are part of the larger conservative movement. Take family life, for instance. Related issues might be the ease of American divorce, the need for "covenant" marriages, the importance of wifely submission, or the creation of a pro-family agenda in the public square. Under education we might find the need for Christian witnessing in public schools, the importance of teaching of Intelligent Design, or the freedom to homeschool. Public morality would attract an equal number of issues. Groups fighting the sale of contraceptives or pushing for abstinence would add grievances to the area of human sexuality. Electing born-again Christians to public office, creating Bible-based legislation, promoting Christian symbols publicly, or appointing Christian judges would fall in the area of Church and State relations. But the issues are still within the same four broad categories.

A careful read of the CE bill of grievances brings something immediately to light. *Religious conservatives wish for less government intervention in their own affairs, and more state regulation of other people's business.* They seek freedom to pursue their own religious obligations at home and schools, unburdened by state oversight. But they wish to burden other people's practices and lifestyles with their own sectarian norms. In other words, the state has a negative obligation toward them, but a positive one toward the general public—it ought to restrain from regulating their communities, but intervene in public affairs when conservative Christians determine that society is losing its moral bearings. Stricter standards of decency are righteously demanded, and more sectarian Christian displays are needed to set the patriotic tone for a Christian spiritual revival among those who live within American borders.

REDEMPTION AS PERSONAL CONVERSION

How did Christian conservatives ever reach the point of wishing to take over South Carolina (or the nation) for that matter? What made them decide the country would be better off if ruled by conservative dogma? Who empowered them to pursue such an ambitious public agenda? Given the conservative Church's size and influence, these are not rhetorical questions. They are part of a larger, ongoing national debate. This book argues that the suburban infrastructure created by the conservative Church in the last twenty-five years is precisely what emboldens its political activists to go out into the public arena, sure-footed and serious-minded. Suburbia transformed the Church's original mission, and provided the resources for its current crusade.

The result is an activist form of conservatism unlike any other Americans have witnessed, and one with the educational, financial, and legal resources, with the ideology and the organizational infrastructure to seek a Christian theocracy in the here and now. Ironically, the present conservative approach toward the state is a reversal of the faith's original modus operandi. Students of conservative Christianity are puzzled by this bold push for earthly dominion. Somewhere in the last twenty-five years, religious conservatives gained enough footing in middle class culture to redesign their Church, and in the process, to dream of redesigning America as well.

For most of its history, conservative Christianity has played a peripheral, fragmented role in the larger American religious scene. Traditionally, the colonial churches—Episcopal, Congregational, and Presbyterian—made up the core of our Christianity. Founded first, along with the Society of Friends, they shaped the social order from colonial days—not only in our form of government, but providing the leadership for the country's religious, political, and economic arenas.[7] Leaders of the colonial churches have rubbed elbows with the most powerful Americans of every generation. Their rules of civility still mark the public square. Our civil religion—national speeches, civic shrines, and symbols—is still tinged with a liberal Protestant patina. Our political structures, with their multiple jurisdictions and checks and balances still resemble the polity of colonial churches. To this day, the American Protestant Establishment is overrepresented in our halls of power, their numbers proportionally much higher than their overall percentage of the American population.[8]

Seymour Lipset argues that the separation of Church and State was critical for our political development, although greatly contributing to this social stratification of American religion:

> The fact that American religion is denominational has facilitated the development of religious groups which tend to serve only those parishioners who are roughly on the same social level in society. And the absence of multi-class religions (such as exist in countries where the church is established or represents the sole religion of the country) has meant that each "class" or ethnic religion could adapt its practices and specific beliefs to suit the needs of the group which it serves. . . . No major social group has long been excluded from, or caused to be disaffected from the "normal" religious life of the nation. Thus, denominationalism may have served to stabilize the polity.[9]

Denominationalism may have stabilized the polity, but it relegated conservative Christian denominations to ministering to the powerless and the dispossessed in culturally isolated sectors of our society. The conservative faith became the creed of the common American; the religious expression of the nation's working poor.

Its prayers and hymns have echoed from the hills of Appalachia, the small farms of the Midwest, and the sharecropping fields of the Mississippi delta. As the nation entered the industrial age, conservative Christianity sustained the hopes of Kentucky miners, migrant factory workers in the industrial belt, day laborers, maids, janitors, and tenant farmers all over the United States.

Historically, Christian conservatives lacked the material and cultural means to transform their society or dictate its public agenda. In addition, their religious worldview and corresponding small-town morality did not predispose them toward political action, much less the intentional, disciplined, large-scale campaign of social redemption we witness today. The best hope of previous conservative generations was simply to be faithful to a simple faith, to live out their religious calling within the confines of their station. For most of their history, they have had but one cause: the spiritual conversion of their peers. They were called to spread the good news of the Gospel, to tell others of God's infinite love.

For most of their existence, autonomous, small conservative congregations have staged local revivals and pooled their money to send hardworking missionaries on disciple-making journeys at home and abroad. Jonathan Edwards contended "that the conversion of one soul... is a more glorious work of God than the creation of the whole material universe."[10] Previous generations of conservative Christians would agree with him. Their missions focused on redeeming the lost who populated the margins of American life. Camp meetings, tent revivals, and door-to-door proselytizing were not meant to take over the country but to save immortal souls.

Previous generations of Christian conservatives knew "this world was not [their] home, [they were] just passing through."[11] The mission was simpler, but sounded an important theological truth about spiritual matters: *the World was not fixable, nor perfectible*. Their faith was not about the *here and now*, but the *hereafter*. They were not called to remake society, but to go forth and make disciples who were heaven-bound. A survey of conservative Christian literature prior to 1980 attests to that single-minded spiritual focus. Bible tracts, church newsletters, mission reports, Sunday school magazines, and women's auxiliary training booklets all sound the same note: being a faithful Christian means reaching others for Christ. The faith was a strictly religious enterprise.

Even as late as 1964, a certain Virginia preacher named Jerry Falwell was still speaking out against religious ministers getting involved into politics: "Preachers are not called to be politicians, but soul winners. If as much effort could be put into winning people to Jesus across the land as is being exerted in the present civil rights movement, America would be turned upside down for God."[12] Thus, it is not surprising that earlier versions of the conservative faith did not elicit intense social activism.[13] To previous generations of religious conservatives the social order was corrupted, tainted by sin. One should not expect much from its fallible laws and power structures. Politics was a horribly sinful enterprise. People had to sell their souls to become good politicians.

In fact, as recently as the 1970s, there was a widespread sense of dread among conservative Christians when a saintly Sunday School teacher from Georgia decided to run for office, first at the state level, then for the White House. Marginal believers, who recognized in Jimmy Carter one of their own, found it hard to believe that someone like him would want to "mess with politics." They were dismayed that a Southern, Bible-believing, born-again Christian could aspire to political office! Throughout President Carter's tenure in the White House many religious conservatives still vacillated to support his effort, or to see the wisdom in such endeavor. Their struggle shows how previous conservative generations viewed a political career as a serious theological risk.

The original conservative faith was built upon *free will*. Taking over the country or imposing a top-to-bottom morality on society went against the deeply ingrained conservative belief *that salvation results from individual choice*. The previous generations of marginal believers respected people's ability to choose. God gave individuals the freedom to accept Jesus' sacrifice *or not*. One could not save them by force, or by exposing them to the Ten Commandments, or by making their children pray in public school, or by banning science from the school curriculum, or by stopping the sale of contraceptives, or by sending homosexuals to jail.

Free will meant that the faithful could only witness. *The Holy Spirit alone had to convince people of their need to change.* This kind of thinking did not make for High Church theology. No seminary-smarts, sophisticated hermeneutics, or historical-critical analysis were required to comprehend it. Its view of *metanoia* was not the currency of trade in the best divinity schools. Its preaching did not charm the elegant pulpits of our great American cathedrals. Put simply, the conservative Christian understanding of conversion betrayed the social location of the faithful. Their view of salvation reflected their little independent rural congregations, their Sunday School teachers with only a Saturday night to prepare lessons, and their old gospel hymns ("Amazing Grace," "In the Garden," "The Old Rugged Cross," or "Just as I Am"). Conservative Christian preachers had no seminary training; their working class church folks had mostly a grade school education.[14] So the faith was built on freedom, *including freedom from this world.*

There is something very *blue collar* about the old conservative plan of salvation. It forsakes worldly riches.[15] There is an implicit disdain for the wealth of elites, those who lorded over the faithful. Conservative Christian hymns exalt Jesus above "all riches of the world." Previous generations of religious conservatives knew their lot in this world was suffering, hardship, trials, and tribulations. *They knew that salvation did not change their material conditions.* Come Monday, the weary jobs and the harsh living would still be there waiting for them. Weekday life was about moonlighting jobs, praying for things not to break around the house, and for the kids not to get sick. It was about living from paycheck to paycheck. Sunday was truly the Balm in Gilead. Church was the respite from a lifelong cycle of hard work and frustration. Church pointed them onward, to the better living of heavenly shores. That was the message that had to be shared with friends and neighbors.

In his study of religion Max Weber describes the relationship between doctrine and social class as an *elective affinity*.[16] He argues that the faithful of different social ranks tend to gravitate toward the religious doctrines that are more likely to suit their milieu. He illustrates *elective affinities* by showing how capitalism was closely related to the *Calvinistic* doctrine of predestination: those successful in this world found predestination not only plausible, but intrinsically satisfying, since it assured them of their chosenness. Their success could be reasonably explained by the fact that God bestowed upon them the ability to lead, and to take on important matters in this world.

By the same token, one could make the case that the downtrodden might take a greater liking to *Arminianism* instead. After all, who needs to be predestined to suffering? For the working class *free will*, not predestination, was the critical elective affinity.[17] The faithful of simpler means found greater comfort in the egalitarian notion that *all* humans were precious in God's eyes, all equally given the same chance of salvation; than on the fact that God preferred the rich. *Radical grace in the hereafter has an elective affinity with the harsh living in the here and now.* The poor may be more moved by the thought that we are all endowed with free will and share in the possibility of being loved by God, than by the idea that the Almighty has loved some more than others, and set them apart to rule over their spiritual underlings.

If Christ died for "the least of these," reasoned the Christian conservatives of old, *then worldly success has nothing to do with redemption*. The message was simple and comforting: worldly success could not be equated with spiritual well-being. The rich young ruler in the Gospels goes away empty-handed for loving money more than Christ. Zaccheus gives half of his riches to the poor, after his encounter with the Savior.[18] Previous generations of Christian conservatives knew that salvation was *the spiritual process of being touched by an egalitarian God*, a process equally bestowed upon the rich and the poor (in the same fashion that God sends the sun to shine and the rain to fall upon the just and the unjust).[19] That *Arminian* approach to the spiritual life drove their mission work.

The point of this theological review is to simply argue that *marginal believers have not always shared a theology of earthly dominion*. It was not part of their doctrinal repertoire prior to the 1980s. They did not see themselves in charge of the political, economic, or social restructuring of America. Nor did God call them to take over the nation and remake it after their own image. If nothing else, earlier generations of marginal believers knew (at a very pragmatic level) that other Americans would not understand their motives, and that they would doubt their ability to undertake the project. More than likely, other Americans would ridicule their faith. They knew that the "wisdom of the saved would be folly to the learned."

Somewhere in the last twenty-five years, the conservative elective affinity with an egalitarian plan of salvation began to change. It migrated from the simple *metanoia*, the personal, salvific encounter with Christ, toward a more structural redemption—the redemption of the whole nation. Step by step, as membership grew and demographics changed, the conservative faith moved away from its humble Arminian roots, its democratic understanding of the way God operates in this world and its emphasis on free will, toward a militant Christian practice. As resources expanded and educated leaders came on board, the early notions of a strictly *spiritual* mission transmuted into a more complex vision.

REDEMPTION AS EARTHLY DOMINION

Saving individuals is still very much a part of the conservative Church's agenda, but it no longer subsumes its entire mission. Now one is also asked to save the nation as well. What started out as individual salvation has evolved into a collective vision of *dominion* over the world. The mixing of conservative doctrine and middle-class living has changed the marginal Church's stance toward modernity. Current religious conservatives see *this world and the next* as their home. Old Arminian truths are being stretched to fit a new lifestyle, a new outlook, and its suburban needs. The faith is still exclusivist, dogmatic, and driven by proselytizing. But now it is also fueled by a *middle class sense of entitlement*, of ownership in America's social, political, and economic arenas.

Redemption is moving away from its homespun origins, toward a broader agenda of national restoration. To the early strands of *Arminianism* are being added *Calvinist* notions of earthly lordship. Lording over the world makes more sense when one has the material and cultural means to make it happen. Larry Ross, president of a Dallas public relations firm that represents megachurches, calculates that "330,000 churches in America [represent] potentially the largest distribution network in the country and probably in the world."[20]

Previous sociological research indicates that affluence affects church doctrine. All things being equal, economic prosperity leads religious groups toward a more accommodating stance vis-à-vis the larger society. Niebuhr documents that process in American Methodism.[21] The social mobility of nineteenth-century Methodists turned the frontier faith into a middle-class religion. As Methodism grew in numbers and resources, its congregations began recruiting seminary-trained ministers and replacing storefront churches with spacious cathedrals. Eventually American Methodism developed a corporate structure akin to the bureaucratic hierarchies found in the business world. By the 1950s it had a corporate identity, with multiple denominational pay ranks and deadline-driven "corporate" targets. Its network of schools and seminaries trained the next generations into the comforts of middle-class.

More importantly, once the denomination became more affluent, Methodist doctrine evolved, showing greater theological sophistication and tolerance toward society's cultural practices. Unlike their Methodist brethren, conservative Christians of today have not parlayed their prosperity into a middle-class religious outlook. Rather, greater membership and resources are empowering an intransigent religious militancy, one that spills over into the public square. No longer at the edge of society, conservative believers are stakeholders of the American dream. They comprise a hefty voting bloc and a powerful economic stratum. They run their own businesses and civic associations, and take full part in American politics, with the savvy of careful consumers. In other words, they are part and parcel of America's social, *if not cultural*, mainstream.[22]

Their current faith is still haunted by its previous marginal ethos. It remains a simplistic religious worldview, with little room for diversity or compromise. The strong bifurcation of the world and marginality still explain why current religious conservatives see themselves as a minority in their own country; why they are still at odds with the main culture and still feel powerless. Unlike Niebuhr's Methodists, who found it relatively easy to step into the middle-class cultural mind-set, marginal believers are still precluded by their faith from feeling at home in their middle-class world (which perhaps explains their need to create exclusive born-again clubs and services).

What is fascinating is that Christian conservatives no longer lack the skills or resources to act upon those feelings of powerlessness. They can organize, push those in power to respond to their demands, *and actually expect results*. Gone is the working-class fatalism of previous eras. Their lot is to manage, lead, and rule as they redouble efforts to impose their worldview upon society. Ironically, the newly gained middle-class skills of religious conservatives only enable them to further promote their faith. Their political influence assures immediate media attention. Their views are object of intense lobbying and cultural clashes. Whatever policy Washington is considering these days, there is always a conservative religious angle to explore. Whatever cultural issue, there is always the expectation that the Religious Right will have a stand on it.

This crusade-like zeal is a far cry from the middle-class approach of other Christian denominations (and even from the working-class disposition of previous marginal generations). Most middle-class denominations shy away from public controversy. Catholics, Lutherans, Methodists, Disciples of Christ, or American Baptists are not fond of seeing denominational struggles paraded in the secular media. By the same token, previous generations of working-class churches—the Assemblies of God, the Church of Christ, or the Church of the Nazarene—are not fond of public attention either. Those groups live out their religious work within the sacred spaces of their sanctuaries. Underlying their practices is the overall American sense that in a *denominational society* one does not make public ultimate claims at the expense of other faiths.[23]

In fact, most middle-class Americans practice a more private form of religion. Their faith is important, but it does not rule their lives. The practical concerns of their social strata lead other middle-class Americans to approach religion with the same commonsensical way they approach other matters. Religion is balanced against other equally important concerns. Alan Wolfe, documenting the *elective affinities* of the American middle class, describes their religion as a "quiet faith"; one that blends two seemingly contradictory tendencies: middle-class Americans believe in the absolute truth of their faith, but welcome the truth of other faiths as well. They hold these contradictory tendencies together by a sense that "however strongly one applies principles of right and wrong to oneself, one ought to hesitate before applying them to others."[24]

Wolfe argues that the commitment of middle-class Americans to individual freedom overrides any possible religious intransigence:

> Clearly, most middle-class Americans take their religion seriously. But very few of them take it so seriously that they believe that religion should be the sole, or even the most important, guide for establishing rules about how *other* people should live. And some, if even fewer, also would distrust such rules for providing guidelines about how they personally should live. Despite the attention that conservative Christians have commanded in the political realm, there is not much support out there in middle-class America, at least among our respondents, for the notion that religion can play an official and didactic role in guiding public morality.[25]

Perhaps middle-class tolerance stems from the fact that middle-class Americans deal in everyday life with a diversity of opinions and attitudes. They realize from experience that to succeed in this world they must forgo dogmatic stances. Wolfe finds in the American middle class a tendency toward "modest virtues," where religion matters, but it should not be preached nor dictated to others.[26] By comparison, contemporary conservative Christianity is all about public claims. There is a right way to live in society, to enjoy family life, to raise children, to teach science, and so forth. It is a faith that must be forcefully shared, a faith that must convince others of the errors of their ways.

The sense of righteousness in that approach belies an unquestioned belief in its privileged hermeneutical condition: if the conservative faith must be at the center of its followers' lives, then it follows that it must be placed at the center of American life as well. So, a newly gained affluence affords today's religious conservatives with the opportunity to restore their entire nation. They boast the largest network of single-cause lobbying organizations in this country. Their leaders consult regularly with the President of the United States, and members of Congress. Their preachers head universities, law schools, business schools, and other large-scale enterprises. The simple faith of olden days has become America's self-appointed source of religious guidance. Redemption has become earthly dominion.

RELIGIOUS LIBERTY: CURTAILING STATE INTERFERENCE

This section reviews two issues of Christian concern regarding religious liberty: family life and public education. The review is not exhaustive, but illustrative of the conservative approach to those issues. Whenever possible, the issues are placed in the category chosen by the groups that advocate them. Data for the chapters were obtained from materials published by the conservative religious organizations. Where appropriate, a particular view on an issue is matched to the originating organization. For each issue, the position of the conservative Church is presented, and then a brief analysis of its cultural indebtedness is put forth.

It is important to highlight beforehand that marginal causes do overlap, so these divisions of the conservative agenda are not mutually excluding—abortion, for instance, may fall in the area of family life for certain organizations, but also under human sexuality for other groups. Issues discussed in one area by a particular denomination might be framed under another by different churches. Nevertheless the formal division allows us to review the conservative Church agenda in a succinct manner.

The Family

Contemporary conservative Christians see the nuclear family as ordained by God. To them, that social unit—the *nuclear family*, a monogamous, lifelong marriage between two people of opposite sex, blessed with offspring—is *the* foundation of a godly society. Also described as the *natural* family,[27] the institution is God's timeless and universal standard for a "normal" adult life. Its heterosexual, life-lasting nature is divinely ordained for all societies and all times, with no room for change or alteration. On this narrow definition of family, all marginal Christian groups seem to agree. No other family forms should be contemplated, lest we invalidate the institution's sacred nature. Since God created marriage and family, we are not allowed to tinker with it.

For the marginal faith, marriage is the most important thing in the life of a Christian couple, second only to their devotion to God. Marriage is the basis for one of God's three foreordained institutions: the family, the church, and the government. It allows the Christian family to create an "altruistic domestic economy," by providing spouses with mutual emotional support and children with a safe environment where to grow. Without such domestic economy, churches and governments cannot fulfill their divinely appointed roles, since the family is the fundamental social unit, the foundation of human society. Societies that abandon the *nuclear family* invite chaos into their midst.[28]

Given the family's crucial importance, marriage should be treated as a *permanent covenant*. Divorce is a human creation, an indictment on our moral decay. Committed Christian couples should see marital struggles as the divinely appointed means toward greater spiritual maturity. The reason modern society faces so many problems today is because of the ease and prevalence of divorce.[29] Since the family is the natural place for child development, marriage should be permanent. "Intact homes" are fundamental for identity formation, and for the children's security and sense of belonging. Through the family, children acquire moral standards and the means to become contributing members of our society. No other social institution offers the same kind of spiritual, physical, psychological, and moral care.

The social importance of the family leads conservative groups to argue that "intact homes" require clearly defined *gender roles*. Healthy and well-adjusted children cannot be raised without the nurturing presence of their mothers. Therefore women should find fulfillment first and foremost in their roles as wives and mothers, not in professional careers:

> Do everything possible to have Mom stay at home with the children. This is a great sacrifice for many women who have already established themselves in a career or families who have great financial difficulty on one income. Pray to God to find the way if this is a difficult situation for you. God will provide, if you believe he will. There is no greater duty on this earth than raising your children.[30]

Similarly, husbands are the family's financial providers. So they should be ambitious and entrepreneurial in their drive to succeed, but not at the expense of their families:

> If your world is so fast that you do not have time to spend with your mate to pray and read the Bible, you may find yourself eventually going down a road that is very unpleasant. We encourage you to examine your priorities! By keeping God first, your whole life will come together. The wisdom of the Bible will never let you down! That is one thing you can count on in these very uncertain days![31]

Such "intact homes" would greatly benefit its members.[32] In "intact homes," children learn from the *complementary roles of their parents*, so they are less likely to be involved in risky behavior. Their families protect them from "premarital sex, substance abuse, delinquency, and suicide." They also provide them with a healthy *template* for their own marriage. In fact, "intact homes" offer clear *safety benefits* as well: children are less likely to be aborted, abused, or neglected; and enjoy better health, financial status, and higher rates of academic achievement.

In "pro-family" societies adults would also benefit from "intact homes." Using a much-cited source (the 2004 *National Center for Health Statistics*), religious conservatives explain that married people are happier and healthier regardless of race, age, sex, education, nationality, or income. They also have the lowest levels of psychological distress, drinking or smoking, and suicide. Married adults enjoy a longer lifespan, greater wealth, and higher incomes. Furthermore, married adults enjoy greater *safety* benefits as well, since women in cohabiting relationships report physical aggression three times higher than those who are married.

Society too benefits from intact families. "Intact homes" mean less abortion, safer homes in the community, and safer communities (the idea being that "intact homes" would translate into lower rates of substance abuse and juvenile delinquency). More nuclear families would mean lower levels of poverty and lower rates of divorce (again, the notion being that married parents would raise children who would be less likely to end their marriages frivolously). Finally, intact families mean lower taxes, since the absence of youth or single-adult related problems means less need for governmental intervention. Intact families also promote higher civic engagement, since married people are more likely to vote, volunteer for projects, and get involved in churches and schools.

Such a rosy scenario betrays the suburban outlook of the new conservative Church. It assumes a situation where people are free from overwhelming debts or highly stressful sixty-hour-a-week menial jobs. It assumes parents who do not struggle against substance abuse, or from the tensions that come from blocked social mobility. Members of this rosy family do not carry scars of cash-strapped alcoholic/abusive parents, or a myriad of dysfunctional social conditions associated with poverty. They live in an imaginary suburb, where everything works just the way it is supposed to.

All that it would take to challenge such scenario would be a visit to any local office of Health and Human Services, or Family and Children Services. People would realize that family life, even when created by a loving heterosexual marriage, where both spouses are born-again Christians, can be dysfunctional and complicated. That would question the rosy scenario's conclusion that pro-family policies would represent a lighter tax burden or fewer social service programs.[33] There is no acknowledgment in the rosy scenario of the struggles associated with modern family living, especially for those not buoyed by the security of a middle-class lifestyle. It is easier instead to argue that lack of pro-family policies translates into an array of social ills.

Conservative Christian groups blame "feminism [and] the sexual revolution"[34] for the troubles facing the American family, suggesting that the current push for "diversity, multiculturalism, and situational ethics"[35] is further weakening family life, and therefore the nation. The result is a laundry list of social ills. Weakened family life results in increased abortion, absentee fathers/mothers, adultery, below-replacement fertility, devaluation of parenting, declining family time, domestic violence, child abuse, child molesting, cohabitation, early sexual experimentation by teenagers, homosexuality, human trafficking, incest, isolation of the elderly, low marriage rates, morally relativistic public education, no-fault divorce, out-of-wedlock childbearing, pornography, poverty, premarital sex, promiscuity, sexual identity confusion, sexually transmitted diseases, teen pregnancy, and violence against women.

How should America react to this moral decay? Christian groups recommend urgent steps to strengthen traditional family bonds,[36] steps requiring a joint effort by State and civil society. The government should pass a federal amendment defining marriage as strictly the union between a man and a woman. It should reduce the tax burden on married families with children, along with tax incentives to married families seeking adoption.[37] *Covenant marriages* should become the law of the land, and the no-fault divorce should be abolished. Moreover, abstinence educational programs should be federally funded.[38] Mandatory reconciliation should precede the granting of divorce for couples with children. Welfare penalties for married recipients should be eliminated. There should be public education campaigns promoting marriage and fatherhood. And communities should encourage fathers to remain committed to families through marriage.[39]

Civil society also plays a role here. The culture should promote a more positive image of the nuclear family. The media should praise marriage and family, extolling its benefits far and wide. Public schools should adopt curricula emphasizing the positive side of fatherhood, and the importance of marriage. Local area clergy should require longer premarital counseling prior to weddings. Businesses should adopt more-family friendly policies, such as flextime, job sharing, home-based work options, compensatory time off, paid leave and financial assistance for adoption, work-based marriage education, and marriage counseling.[40]

While such pro-family approach is laudable, it is also misinformed. It fails to take into account important social research regarding the American family. Social scientists who have studied it since the mid-twentieth century would warn against uplifting a single model of family life as the solution to all our social ills. Real life is fluid, changing, and unyielding to preset definitions of how things ought to be. American families are not weakened because our society no longer believes in marriage and family, but because the institution has been under tremendous pressure to survive fast-paced social change. It is hard to make the case that Americans no longer believe in marriage and family when the majority of adults in the United States are still married; and "being married" is touted as the socially expected goal for adult life. There may be greater tolerance for singles, and people may wait longer to marry these days, but most adult Americans are still involved in long-term marriages.

If anything, the multimillion-dollar dating services and wedding industry should suffice to prove that Americans are still obsessed with finding and marrying the right partner. From sitcoms to reality shows to Hollywood, the possibility of finding eternal love is the cultural fuel that keeps the ratings going. Even those who divorce remarry in large numbers, on average within two to three years of the divorce. From taxes to real estate to groceries to leisure, our society is built on the premise of married adults. Single-family units are still the mainstay of the real estate market. The tourism industry still relies heavily on family packages. The sales of vans and SUVs alone should indicate the level of commitment Americans have to being married and ferrying children across town.

If the American family is a bit more fragile these days, it is not for its lack of appeal. Rather, there are larger social forces that are transforming the institution.[41] Our society grew more complex after World War II. With a greater division of labor, and geographic and social mobility, family life began to change. Economic growth and the switch from an industrial to an informational workplace pushed for an expanded, highly adaptable two-gendered job market. If Mom and Dad go to work these days, it does not mean they love family life less. It means it takes two paychecks to make a living.

Economic transformation also led to greater institutional specialization, removing all the family's external "anchors," the aspects of family life that contributed to its stability. Children no longer learn at home, they have school. Toddlers now have daycare. The family is no longer a unit of economic production, but simply consumption. Sick family members are not treated at home, they go to hospitals instead. Senior citizens end up in nursing homes; they are not taken care of by their offspring. All the external "anchors" that once shored up family life have now been delegated to other institutions. Their loss is not a function of lower moral values, but of living in a more complex, specialized society. Alan Wolfe puts it best when he argues that "the real story about America's divorce culture... is not that people no longer believe in marital commitments. It is instead that they take the marriage vow seriously, but that they also take seriously other vows that may come into conflict with it."[42]

The postwar social transformations led to greater individual affluence, and that led to greater choice. Marital vows compete these days with other "vows." Financial independence makes marriage less appealing to some, from a strictly material point of view. The good news is that more of us now marry solely for love. The bad news is that in a consumer-driven culture, picking a mate has become another form of social consumption. Affluence means more choices. One can marry or not, remain married or not, have children or not. If marriage is more fragile, the commitment to find that someone special (even if it takes several marriages and divorces) remains as strong as ever. However, these days, marriage has been commodified in unexpected ways.

The religious conservative dedication to the nuclear family and its promotion of traditional family values are commendable. Such work may seem like the perfect antidote to our fast-paced times. But turning back the clock on the large-scale social changes of the last fifty years requires more than a romanticized view of the 1950s American family. Deep down, many of us may still want the white picket fence house and the Mom-and-Pop nuclear family. But in an era of multitasking, greater social demands, and longer working hours, no matter how determined we are to honor family life, the conditions that supported the placid 1950s family are no longer in place. Americans work more hours now than we did back then. It takes twice as much work to simply maintain a 1950s standard of living. And individuals are less bound by the rigid duties that pervaded the 1950s family life.[43]

Moreover, *commitment to a fixed cultural standard ought not to be confused with commitment to biblical truth*. The nuclear family is by no means the single model in the Scriptures: much as in life, reality is more complex in the biblical text. Many biblical heroes did not live, nor grew up in nuclear families. Most were actually polygamists. Dysfunctional family incidents are striking for their commonality in the sacred text: Noah impregnated his daughters, Joseph was sold into slavery by his own brothers, Jacob married two sisters, Ruth had premarital sex with Boaz, Esther was a concubine of the king prior to marrying him, King David was an adulterer, King Solomon had 1,000 wives and mistresses, and God asked Hosea to marry a promiscuous and adulterous woman.

Even the functional families of the Bible go beyond the nuclear family model. Adopted as a child, Moses was raised by his own mother. Samuel grew up under Prophet Eli's care. The orphan Esther was raised by her uncle. King Saul adopted David, who loved Saul's son, Jonathan. New Testament evidence is equally mixed. Technically, Christ was raised in a stepfamily. Mary and Martha shared a female-led household. The disciples were asked to leave their families to serve Jesus. Paul led an all-male entourage in many trips. Christ himself seemed unconcerned with family preservation: "Let the dead bury the dead," he advised an eager young man who wished to follow him but felt responsible for aging parents. "I have come to set a man against his father, and a daughter against her mother, and a daughter-in-law against her mother-in-law, and a man's foes will be those of his own household" said the Messiah. Christ's second coming did not contribute to family life either. Paul desired that Christians remained single and childless, as they awaited the *parousia*.

Simply put, the biblical evidence does not support the *nuclear* family as the ultimate standard. Such argument is not good theology nor good public policy. When we place the nuclear family as the ultimate solution to our social ills, we risk falling into idolatry. We idolize a temporal, social structure as being the divine standard for human bonding and child-rearing. *But the Scripture argues instead that God's grace honors any form of human household that is life-affirming, life-giving.* When we place the nuclear family as the ultimate solution to social ills we also assume that *only people out of wedlock are sinful*, or put it sociologically that singles are more prone to social deviance. This bifurcating view of human nature promises that married people resist temptation better than single adults. The fact that abortion, adultery, domestic violence, child abuse, incest, and violence against women take place in *both* married and unmarried homes is a good indication that *something else*—perhaps human nature—not the lack of traditional marriage, compels those sorts of human behaviors.

The assumption that being a Christian and being married automatically sanctifies one's behavior or that Christian nuclear families are less dysfunctional begs empirical verification. What a heterosexual-nuclear-family-only policy will do is to force people to marry young, especially those bound by premarital abstinence. Young couples will enter permanent, covenant marriages at a time when they are still unprepared for the demands of married life and parenthood. Creating such families by the millions nationwide will not automatically grant us, as if by magic, a successful and well-adjusted society.

More likely, we could end up with a far greater number of divorces since age is a strong predictor of family breakups: the younger couples are at marriage, the greater the likelihood they will divorce later in life. The burden of an early marriage will also affect those who remain married. A "perfect marriage" could become the ultimate prison instead of the beatific institution it is meant to be, if the inexperience of young couples leads to dysfunctional behavior. A lasting marriage built by pain and immaturity will hurt all the members of even the most earnest and dedicated family.

These are not empty suppositions. Christian social scientists, looking at national trends, have reached similar conclusions. According to researcher George Barna born-again Christians actually divorce at *higher rates* than non-Christians (26 to 22 percent). Moreover, 90 percent of the divorced Christians broke up their marriages *after accepting Christ*. Brad Wilcox, a Princeton-trained sociologist, found that conservative Protestants are *more likely to divorce* than the rest of the American population.[44] Findings are similar in relation to social ills. Steve Gallagher found that *the percentage of Christian men involved in pornography was not much different* from the "unsaved."[45] Yale and Columbia researchers found that Christian teenagers who pledged to abstain from sex had *similar rates of sexual promiscuity and sexually transmitted disease* as other teenagers in the study. In other words, humans seem to be humans, whether they profess Christ or not.

Social science data do not support even the assumption that Christian family members are more caring or more devotional: "Born-again Christians spend seven times more hours each week in front of their televisions than they spend in Bible reading, prayer, and worship."[46] So, the idealized notion that a heterosexual, nuclear Christian family life will solve all of America's problems is quite unfounded. Belief alone does not turn the nuclear family into a social panacea. Unless we restructure society, with the right kind of priorities and economic incentives, family life will continue to change. Simply trying to push back the clock may be well meaning, but it is not theologically sound, or policy wise. Christian cultural captivity to the 1950s family model does not guarantee spiritual success in family matters.

Education

Given its potential to propagate secularism among the Church's most vulnerable members, schooling deeply concerns religious conservatives. They work hard to curtail the effects of a secular education. If the family is divinely ordained, so is the parental responsibility to guide the children's spiritual upbringing. The state may create the educational system, and mandate its pedagogical standards; but it must not monopolize schooling, else it usurps the parental child-rearing prerogative. Parental oversight is crucial to America's restoration, because an ungodly society sets ungodly educational standards. While society dictates learning standards, Christian parents must supervise the content of their children's education. If society sets the curriculum, Christian parents must protect their children's spiritual well-being.

A secular outlook could undermine the children's spiritual upbringing, leading them to question the parents' moral authority or their ability to teach what is best. Moreover, public schools can be recruiting centers for "secular humanism." Constrained by legal requirements, teachers may end up offering a relativistic moral outlook to their pupils. Worse yet, the science curriculum materials could become a source of apostasy. It is no accident that one of the main goals of the Family Research Council is to protect families and schools from "the cultural forces that threaten them, including biased and offensive media, pro-homosexual activism, and attacks on religious liberty."[47]

For Christian conservatives, real education starts at home. Parents are the first teachers, and the home the first school. There children learn the basics of obedient behavior, of respect for elders, love of God, and loyalty to the country. There they should discover the importance of being mindful of others, of curbing selfish impulses, and of personal accountability. Moreover, at home children learn about their everlasting souls, and the importance of the spiritual world. Schools should not replace parental instruction; only add to what families impart. Students should master the technical and practical aspects of their culture in order to become productive members of society. But schooling should not cloud their moral or spiritual judgment.[48] It is that concern with their children's spiritual welfare that gives Christian parents the right to oversee curricular matters.[49]

But even parental oversight is no guarantee that public schools will be a stable source of spiritual wisdom. Since they are tax-based, schools are subject to the political whims of other interest groups. They serve the interests of those in power. School boards and administrators have to consider the political implications of their policies. Every "improvement" in public schools resulting from Christian political pressure can be undone by the next group that seizes power. The only way Christian parents could control public schools is if they were in "perfect harmony" with society's "political power-brokers."[50] Absent that, the conservative Church adopted a two-pronged approach to education. First, it removed Christian children from secular schools, by placing them in homeschooling or church-based academies. Next, since it could not remove all Christian children, it sought to *Christianize* public education.

The first strategy, by all measures, has been quite successful. The homeschooling movement currently offers professional, standardized materials and training all over the United States. Support services are impressive. Organizations such as *HomeschoolChristian.com* provide educational, financial, and legal information. There are support groups and Christian-sponsored events in all fifty states. Positions papers defend the right of parents to homeschool, and curriculum materials are professionally done. There are also message boards for homeschooling parents.[51]

The Church's second strategy—conservative Christian schools—is also faring well. One of the earliest professional organizations in this area was the *American Association of Christian Schools* (AACS), founded in 1972. AACS currently serves 175,000 students and teachers in 1,050 member schools throughout the United States (and a few foreign countries).[52] The group is a national coalition of "Bible-believing Christian schools" that represent thirty-six locally controlled state associations. Its president, Dr. Keith Wiebe, also pastor of Grace Gospel Church in Huntington, West Virginia, assures visitors to its Web site that,

> The Christian school movement exists for the children. Teachers teach, parents sacrifice, and churches build classrooms for the children. The Christian school's purpose is to guide children to academic maturity and to seek to conform their minds to the image of Christ. The children of today will be the leaders of tomorrow. Sharpening these young minds and building their testimonies to influence the world for Christ is the heartbeat of Christian education. The values taught and modeled in the Christian school shine forth as a ray of light in this modern world. An honest examination of Biblical truth and of the issues facing our society will lead to a clear understanding of the necessity of Christian education and why it is truly for the children.[53]

AACS is not the only group of its kind. There is the *Association of Classical Christian Schools* (ACCS)[54] which offers a strong liberal arts curriculum. And the *Association of Christian Schools International* (ACSI), reaching over 5,440 member schools in 105 countries worldwide, and representing approximately 1,180,000 students.[55] Similar associations are connected to particular Christian confessions. Created in 1920, *Christian Schools International* represents Reformed Christian schools around the globe, serving approximately 500 schools, with a combined enrollment of over 105,000 students.[56] The *Association of Christian Teachers and Schools* (ACTS) supports the Assemblies of God schools.[57] All in all, it is fair to say that the United States has the world's largest network of K-12 Christian schools, with plenty of professional support for faculty and pupils.

The numbers are equally impressive for higher education. Of 1,600 private, nonprofit universities in America today, 900 are religiously affiliated. And of those, 105 claim to be "Christ-centered" institutions. They are supported by the *Council for Christian Colleges and Universities* (CCCU), a higher education association with a $10.5 million budget and member institutions in thirty U.S. states, representing twenty-seven Christian denominations, and offering more than 300 majors to 220,000 students. CCCU also has sixty-nine affiliates in twenty-four other countries that reach another 100,000 students. Christ-centered colleges and universities employ 16,000 faculty and count more than 1.5 million alumni. The council supports them with services such as professional development conferences, research, public relations, collaborative marketing and publications, eight off-campus semester programs, two off-campus summer programs, and two international semester-long partner programs.[58]

The Christian homeschooling movement and the network of Christian schools generate very little controversy, since America has had religious schools dating back to its colonial days. Conservative, moderate, and liberal denominations all have run school systems. In fact, some of the best universities in the United States started as church-related institutions. More contentious is the second half of the conservative Church's strategy: bringing Christ into public schools. That strategy is the single mission of the *Christian Educators Association* (CEA), a professional organization for Christian teachers who work in the public school system. CEA has a clearly sectarian and proselytizing mission. It offers its members practical training and legal advice on how to share their faith in public classrooms.

Testimonials on the association's site make it absolutely clear that teachers know what they are getting when they join the organization. A teacher from Anchorage, Alaska says, "I appreciate being able to belong to a Christian teachers organization. CEA has been a great encouragement and help to my Christian witness in the classroom." Another from Annandale, Virginia writes, "CEA is an alternative choice to the National Education Association, and a professional organization of caring Christians who share a deep desire to touch others with God's love."[59]

CEA encourages its members to move into leadership positions in public schools in order to push for "accurate presentation of historical Judeo-Christian influences on society." The association provides Christian-based materials for the teaching of "moral and spiritual values," and it sponsors a cooperative program with parents and other organizations who "share a similar Christian commitment."[60] Imagine the horror of non-Christian parents once they discover that their children's public school teachers, who are being paid by their tax dollars, are also being professionally trained by a large, well-staffed organization to convert those children! One can only wonder what Christian parents would do, if they found public school teachers being coached on how to proselytize children into Hinduism, Buddhism, or Wicca. Cries of religious liberty would echo all over the country. And yet, these same parents think nothing of having Christian teachers proselytizing in public classrooms.

Teaching the Bible in public schools

One of CEA's top priorities is the reintroduction of Bible teaching in public schools. To that end, the organization sponsors the *Bible Literacy Project*, a nonpartisan, nonprofit project that was founded in 2001 to encourage "the academic study of the Bible in public schools." Its textbook, planned curriculum, and "curriculum adoption kit" make it easy for public schools to adopt the program. A similar effort is being undertaken by the *National Council on Bible Curriculum in Public Schools*. The council's course, "The Bible in History and Literature,"[61] is also a program of study with a sectarian perspective. By the council estimates,

312 school districts in 37 states have adopted the course, with 175,000 students finishing the program.[62]

Apparently the course was not a welcome addition to the public school curriculum of Odessa, Texas. There the council found stiff opposition from Christian parents and civil liberties organizations. The *Texas Freedom Network* commissioned David Newman, an associate professor of English and parent of a public school student, to review course materials. Newman found it "blatantly sectarian." Mark Chancey, a professor of religious studies at Southern Methodist University, found the course "riddled with errors of facts, dates, definitions," and urban legends.[63] Incidentally, a separate review by the *Journal of Law and Education* reached similar conclusions. It found a severe sectarian slant in all course materials, even its supplementary guides. Some 83 percent of the books and articles cited had a sectarian slant.

Another CEA project, the *Coalition for Public School Ministries*, promises to partner Christian parents, churches, and public schools to better equip students. "Using our God-given talents and resources along with faith-based values, we will encourage, support and serve the public school community in a variety of Constitutionally appropriate ways."[64] The coalition encourages Christian parents to seek office on school boards, so they can create (with the support of other Christians in the community) a more lenient outlook toward proselytizing. The constitutional pitfalls of such schemes are considerable. But one gets the sense that CEA is providing an unrelenting push for the *Christianizing* of a public space that should be serving all Americans, without privilege of faith.

School prayer

Until the early 1980s, lower courts adopted a strict interpretation of the *establishment clause*, siding with school districts that forbade religious activities. Concerned with lawsuits, school administrators argued that the ban on religion preserved the separation of Church and State. That approach fueled a number of conservative Christian initiatives, leading eventually to the passage of the *Equal Access Act* (EAA). The EAA protected the right of student-led, noncurricular clubs to assemble in public schools. Since its passage, Conservative Christian clubs have become the most numerous of student-led groups in public schools. According to one estimate, they jumped from 100 in 1980 to 15,000 by 1995.[65] Ironically, the same Christian groups strongly object to the protection of other student-led clubs that endorse atheism, Goth culture, heavy metal, Satanism, Wicca, and Neopagan religion.

Arguments favoring religious activities in public schools are similar to those used to promote Christianity in the public square. Religion, protest the advocates, has always played a central role in our history. The Founders never meant to completely separate Church and State.[66] Some venture further, by saying that school prayer is protected by the *free exercise clause*. Christian students are now prevented from practicing their faith in public. Then there is the "majority rule" argument: Since public opinion supports classroom prayer, forbidding it is downright "undemocratic." Why should a minority of offended individuals stop majority rule? (Never mind the minority's taxes are also supporting the public schools). When all else fails, there is always the tried and true "moral argument": Since prayers were removed from school, the nation has faced a steady moral downturn resulting in all kinds of juvenile delinquency from drug use, to teen pregnancy, to violent crime.

The reality is that freedom of religion does allow churches to create parochial schools, even church-based colleges and universities. But public money and public schooling should not support a particular faith. Public schools are a crucial part of America's secular, public square. Commissioned to educate *all* children, not just Christian children, their inclusiveness and tolerance toward *all* is critical if they are to fulfill their role. Infringing upon the right of nonconservative Christian pupils—even with a generic Christian approach—amounts to state sponsorship of Christianity. As a group that favors banning school prayer argues, "School prayer proponents mistake government neutrality toward religion as hostility. The record shows that religious beliefs have flourished in this country not in spite of but because of the constitutional separation of church and state."[67]

Furthermore, coerced religiosity does not translate into automatic virtuous behavior. Anyone who believes school bullies will stop bullying if they pray is guilty of wishful thinking. Behavior is the result of context and socialization. Dysfunctional Christian families generate as much inappropriate child behavior as other dysfunctional families do. To think that prayer will magically reshape people's actions is to hold a rather simplistic understanding of ritual. If prayer sufficed to correct dysfunctional behavior, the percentage of Christians in U.S. jails would be zero. Regular prayer would keep them out of a life of crime. Unfortunately the empirical evidence suggests otherwise—the majority of convicted jailed criminals, much like the majority of the U.S. population, are Christian. They may read their Bibles, pray regularly, attend prison services, and see a chaplain. But their rates of recidivism indicate that prayer does not result in good behavior. There's more to good behavior than forced religiosity.

Efforts to eliminate sectarianism in public schools date back to the 1800s, to the indefatigable work of Horace Mann, known as the father of public education. As waves of immigrants reached the American soil, the need for secular public schooling became acute. Schools gathered a multicultural, multifaith student population, arriving from different corners of the earth. They were expected to cohere into a single culture and a single nation. Creating that pan-ethnic identity would not be possible if schools required a particular form of religion. Immigrants brought their own churches to our shores. Showing pedagogical foresight, Mann campaigned for the development of a secular, public school system, one that would welcome and educate all Americans. In 1853 a religiously devout State

Superintendent of Schools in New York State defended the practice this way:

> The position was early, distinctly, and almost universally taken by our statesmen, legislators, and prominent friends of education—men of the warmest religious zeal and belonging to every sect—that *religious education must be banished from the common school and consigned to the family and church*.... Accordingly, the instruction in our schools has been limited to that ordinarily included under the head of intellectual culture, and to the propagation of those principles of morality in which all sets, and *good men belonging to no sect*, can equally agree.[68]

Since then, every single American President has supported the nonsectarian nature of public education. The Supreme Court has consistently ruled against religious indoctrination in public schools.[69] For more than a hundred years, the American standard of nonsectarian public education has held strong. One would hope it will continue to do so in the new millennium.

Battling evolution

No topic touches a nerve in the religious conservative psyche quite like the teaching of evolution. Beyond all other scientific matters, the scientific description of life's origins is deeply distressing to marginal believers. Darwin's scientific theory impacts the marginal faith with the same cataclysmic force that Galileo's calculations hit the Thomistic world of Roman Catholicism. The term "heresy" would not be strong enough to define its evil nature. To Christian conservatives, evolution is no less than the devil's work, a tool to derail and undermine biblical authority in modern times. The denial of a six-day creation or that the earth is six thousand years old, completely upends the conservative faith's firm and static view of the universe. The strong reaction is justified by what the conservative Church sees as a frontal attack upon its very foundation. *Evolution threatens the authority of the Bible.*

To marginal believers either the Bible is inerrant and the literal Word of God, authoritative in every aspect of human endeavor, or not. If the Bible is wrong in science, then it cannot be trusted in matters of history, morality, or spirituality. In fact, the literal reading of the biblical text is the very basis for the existence of contemporary Christian conservatism. If scientific evidence can destroy biblical authority on matters of science, so the argument goes, then it can erode its spiritual authority as well.[70] That is why the conservative Church takes a scorched-earth approach to evolution, staging an all-out defense of the Bible as God's scientific truth. If science can present plenty of empirical evidence to contradict biblical interpretation, then its evidence must be denied, discredited, or banned by all means necessary. G. Thomas Sharp, founder and chairman of the *Creation Truth Foundation*, puts it this way: "If we lose Genesis as a legitimate scientific and historical explanation for man, then we lose the validity of Christianity. Period."[71]

The conservative road to stem the floodwaters of evolution in America takes many tortuous turns, far too many for the scope of this book. From flat prohibition in the 1920s Scopes monkey trial, to the push for *Creationism* in the 1980s, to today's insinuations of *Intelligent Design*, the conservative Church has spared no effort to insulate American children from sound biological science. Given its current affluence, it is possible for the marginal faith to invest more heavily on the evolution battle today. Well-funded enterprises like the *Discovery Institute* in Seattle ("the free inquiry and free speech about the issue of biblical origins") are created to promote an antievolution agenda. *Creationist* museums, costing millions of dollars, are being built throughout the nation, representing perhaps the most sophisticated effort ever mounted by Christian conservatives to mystify and blur scientific truth.

The first one, the *Museum of Earth History*, opened in Eureka Springs, Arkansas, in 2005. Its 3,500 square feet of exhibits place humans and dinosaurs coexisting in some primeval garden. The museum also serves as the prototype for similar, but larger regional museums. There is the 50,000-square-foot *Creation Museum* which opened in Kentucky in 2007 (to the tune of a $25-million tab). The museum is fully funded by the *Answers in Genesis* foundation. The Dallas, Texas, *creationist* museum is also scheduled to open its doors in 2007.

Besides promoting scientific misinformation, *creationist* museums provide marginal groups with an important means to bypass the nonsectarian policies of public schools. Field trips can be organized, bringing public school children to those museums for indoctrination. Conferences can be organized to draw local media attention, attracting more visitors to the facilities. It is a twenty-first century, high-tech, Disneyesque marketing strategy for an ancient problem—how to preserve the unpreservable.

A corollary strategy in the battle against evolution involves the concerted effort to "fit" scientific data into the Genesis narrative, so as to "prove" it true. It is a process that yields strange and contorted arguments, bending scientific evidence as best as possible to suit the needs of marginal believers. It also provides a lucrative line of Christian publishing along the way:

> While not all adherents of "creation science" hold all of the following positions, numerous studies have been advanced to show that all the fossil beds were created in a universal flood lasting only a year (Morris 1968, 1982); that the speed of light has changed over time, and might allow the possibility that other celestial bodies (galaxies, the sun, the planets, etc.) may be only a few thousand years old (Setterfield 1983, Whitcomb 1973, Kofahl 1980), and that no new species ("kinds," in the language of Genesis) have been generated since the Creation, which took place only a few thousand years ago (Numbers 1982, Nelkin 1982). By advancing "empirical" evidence, and by calling into question some of the assumptions on which evolutionary biology is based, "scientific creationists" have attempted to use the language, methods, and intellectual prestige of natural science to support a biblical view of earth's origins.[72]

Another tactic involves preventing the general public from viewing any scientific exhibit that might contradict the faith. A dozen Imax theaters connected to science museums in the South cancelled the screening of several documentaries in 2005. Museum directors were afraid that the films might offend local religious conservatives. As a result, entire populations were denied the opportunity to learn more about the world, from a sound, scientific perspective. Documentaries that would be considered innocuous in any other region of the country, such as *Cosmic Voyage* (depicting the universe), or *Galápagos* (about the islands reported by Darwin), or *Volcanoes of the Deep Sea* were discreetly turned away from southern exhibit venues. For the sake of religious certainty, segments of the American public are denied scientific literacy.[73]

The cautionary tale here, much as in Galileo's case, is that scientific discovery cannot be stomped out by church dogma. Barred in one region or country, science migrates to more supportive climes. When the Catholic Church forbade Galileo's endeavors, other scientists continued his calculations in Holland and Germany, proceeding apace with his project. The same can happen to the United States. In fact, some argue that we are losing the scientific edge on a number of areas such as stem cell research.

As technology expands our grip on the natural world, we find overwhelming evidence for the evolution of life on earth. Evolutionary principles can be derived from every level of biological activity in the planet. It cannot be ignored, obscured, or denied, not even by political interference.[74] That a President of the United States would suggest that evolution and Intelligent Design should be presented side by side in a science classroom does not detract from the fact that one is a scientific theory, and the other is not. When President Bush made that suggestion, the reaction from learned quarters was immediate, unanimous, and clear. His own White House science advisor replied that "evolution is the cornerstone of modern biology" and that "intelligent design is not a scientific concept." To defend his boss, he diplomatically suggested that Bush's comment was meant to imply that Intelligent Design should be part of the "social context" of science classes.

The National Center for Science Education spokesperson was more blunt: "Intelligent design is a sectarian religious viewpoint.... It's not fair to privilege one religious viewpoint by calling it the other side of evolution;"[75] an opinion later confirmed by the Dover, Pennsylvania, court case, when a U.S. judge determined that Intelligent Design was an extension of a religious worldview. The head of the government-sponsored human genetic code project, a Christian himself, sadly blamed the evolution battles on the scientific illiteracy of certain Christian groups. He finds "absolutely compelling" similarities between human genes and those of other mammals, tiny worms, and even bacteria: "If Darwin had tried to imagine a way to prove his theory, he could not have come up with something better, except maybe a time machine. Asking somebody to reject all of that [evidence] in order to prove that they really do love God—what a horrible choice."[76] A horrible choice indeed.

5

HIS TRUTH IS MARCHING ON: PUBLIC MORALS AND PUBLIC FAITH

"Believing that America's greatness is linked to America's goodness and believing that God says that righteousness exalts a nation, AdvanceUSA is committed to calling our government to follow traditional, Judeo-Christian values in its lawmaking."[1]

Over the past twenty-five years the Christian conservative community has developed the notion that the best way to protect the faith from secular attacks is to push for a Christian social order. Christian hegemony in the public square is seen as the only antidote to the threat of modernity, a hegemony that starts with restoring public morality. The moral restoration of America is not portrayed as a power grab, but as a push for decency: The 1960s unleashed permissive lifestyles that corroded America's moral fiber. In response, the faithful must take their values to the public square. It is a matter of self-defense:

> The movement is best understood as an essentially defensive struggle by people seeking to sustain their faith and their values.... Presumably, all of us want freedom to practice our religion, to enjoy the rights of free speech guaranteed by the First Amendment, and to fully participate in our duties of citizenship. Yet intolerance towards religion has reached disturbing levels, threatening civility and undermining a basic sense of fairness.[2]

The plan started out simply as a defense of the conservative Christian community. Religious conservatives were unanimous in rebuking the State for meddling in their affairs. State intervention in the areas of family life or schooling was considered intrusive, excessive, and tyrannical. They resented that government could impose secular, permissive guidelines upon their family lifestyle or their children's education. How could godless standards carry higher authority than the stricter biblical injunctions they followed? Religious liberty demanded *less* state intervention. But that was only one side of the conservative agenda. Promoting public morality is clearly the other side. While Christian communities deserved to be left alone, the larger culture needed urgent Christian intervention. To sanitize our culture, the conservative Church has to exercise greater oversight over America's social order. Thus, the public promotion of the conservative faith becomes the strategy to speed America's Christian restoration.

Since the State sets social policy, it stands to reason that the Church has to influence government if it wishes to set moral policies. Moreover, to change the tone of the larger culture, the Church has to influence civil society as well. Thus the double agenda: on one hand, the faithful wish to protect their own communities from outside secular interference; on the other hand, they hope to export their worldview into the larger culture, so as to diminish outside threats to the faith. As theocratic as all of this sounds, religious conservatives do not see their effort as a drive to take over America. To them they are simply bringing the country back to its original state. The problem lies not with our larger institutions, but with the secular humanists who have a grip on our nation. As long as the godless are in charge of tracing America's destinies, secular measures will always impinge upon Christian liberty, and erode the national ethos:

> Believing that America's greatness is linked to America's goodness and believing that God says that righteousness exalts a nation, AdvanceUSA is committed to calling our government to follow traditional, Judeo-Christian values in its lawmaking. We support strong laws against pornography which damages the lives of men, women, and children. We support strong laws upholding community standards so that local citizens can decide what businesses can and cannot exist in their neighborhoods. We support strict laws regarding indecency on the public airwaves.[3]

To religious conservatives, the promotion of a Christian ethos harks back to America's founding as a Christian nation. The Founders, they argue, were devout men of great spiritual depth and moral integrity. They set the tone for a Christian-based form of government and social intercourse. Christianity was so pervasive in the public arena at their time that an official acknowledgment of Christian preeminence was unnecessary. By comparison, America's current secular condition would be abhorred by the Founders. They would be surprised as to how far people have strayed from the founding moral framework. Since our fate as a nation is inextricably tied to faithfulness to God, moving away from the original compact not only threatens the integrity of Christian life in the United States, but also our country's moral health. To the extent that we as a nation are faithful, God blesses us. To the extent that we fail to do so, the country sinks into moral chaos.

So, the promotion of national faithfulness is the very means to drive away sin and apostasy from America's public square; to restore the nation to its Christian beginnings. To that end, marginal believers are willing to flood the culture with their message, to maximize the faith's public presence. They accomplish the task by relying on the grid of conservative groups, organizations, and coalitions they built over the last twenty-five years. Since the State is the most obvious tool for the enforcement of greater social discipline, the Church must pressure government to adopt the conservative Christian worldview. Continuous pressure for an official endorsement of their version of Christianity is to religious conservatives the only way to reestablish a just and moral society. Most Americans would be surprised by that logic, but its self-referential approach suffices to marshal plenty of religious volunteers for the cause.

No conservative religious organization exemplifies it better than the *National Religious Broadcasters Association* (NRB).[4] Founded in 1944, its raison d'étre is the promotion of Christian conservatism by all means of available media. The NRB was created by the conservative Church when the *Federal Council of Churches* gained broadcast access on behalf of mainline, liberal Protestant denominations. Concerned that their message would not reach the mainstream media, evangelical and fundamentalist groups founded the NRB as a combative, unapologetic promoter of the marginal faith. Today, the NRB's 1,600 members are not shy in that role—denunciations, polemics, right wing stances, and rallies are all par for the course when it comes to spreading the good news of Christian conservatism.

The group takes its role quite seriously. When Wayne Pederson, the NRB's newly elected president, gave an interview to the *Minneapolis Star Tribune* in 2002 suggesting that the NRB should move away from the far Christian Right toward more spiritual matters, he immediately lost his job. The association's executive committee quickly replaced Pederson with Frank Wright, the former executive director of the *Center for Christian Statesmanship* in Washington. Wright was chosen precisely because of his right-wing connections.[5] NRB broadcasters had no desire to tone down their participation in the public arena. They are more than willing to engage in heated public debate or opinionated commentary to defend their vision of a Christian America.

That vision, of course, is awash in religious bifurcation and marginality. In fact, it sets the militant tone of all NRB annual conventions. The conventions serve multiple purposes: They showcase the latest in Christian broadcast technology, promote media ministries (some 300 in the 2005 convention), and bring together 5,000 to 6,000 Christian activists. NRB members are driven by their message, but equally obsessed with outreach. NRB affiliates currently control six national television networks and nearly all of the nation's 2,000-plus religious radio stations, with a shared potential audience of 141 million.[6] Despite reaching only a 5 percent share of America's radio broadcasting and less than 20 percent of the television market, NRB members continuously try to expand their audiences by packaging the conservative Gospel in culturally adapted ways. Among 2005 convention seminars/workshops one could find "Marketing: Fresh Innovative Ideas for Driving Traffic to Any Site!" "Sales: Selling Spots with Qualitative Research," and "Finding God in Hollywood."

More importantly, the association works to secure its broadcast reach by cultivating long-term ties with those in power. It is a NRB tradition to invite American presidents to address its annual conventions (Bill Clinton, of course, was the exception). The association also honors Presidential cabinet members and members of Congress. President Reagan's annual address was legendary. President George W. Bush addressed the 2003 convention. Other honored Washington officials included C. Everett Koop, then U.S. General Surgeon, who delivered a lecture at the NRB Convention on the public health implications of the AIDS epidemic. U.S. Attorney General John Ashcroft discussed the war on terror at the 2002 convention. Senator Elizabeth Dole received the association's highest honor for public service. In the past twenty-five years the NRB has steadily courted Washington's conservative political circles. And, of course, since 2000 that courting has been graciously rewarded.

Shortly after his first inauguration, President Bush met in the Roosevelt Room with John Ashcroft and the NRB executive committee. That initial meeting spun regular contacts between senior White House officials and NRB leaders, with the President occasionally dropping in on the conversation. One report suggests that "monthly NRB-White House conference calls were established to give rank-and-file NRB members a direct line to the Oval Office."[7] In similar fashion, once the Republican Party controlled both chambers, the organization found greater access to the U.S. Congress. Its lobbying efforts reached deep into Capitol Hill, with the clear acquiescence of the Republican leadership. NRB affiliates drum up political support within the conservative Christian community, and in return political leaders consult them on policy matters.

NRB members are not your prototypical lonely preacher with a fifteen-minute local radio slot, organized around a minisermon and a few assorted hymns. These new cultural warriors are well-educated, white-collar, entrepreneurial knowledge workers, who are professionally trained in journalism, media design, and broadcasting. They rally up the faithful by regularly selling the image that "real" Christianity is a faith besieged. The goal is to foment a combative Christian response to the perceived attacks by the secular, modern world. Association members and affiliates are a perfect example of what sociologists define as a *particularistic* religious group:

> *Religious particularism* is the viewing of one's own religious group as the only legitimate religion... some religious belief systems include, at their core, tribalistic, particularistic judgments toward nonbelievers... religious particularism seems to *require* a sense of opposition; one's own religion is seen as triumphant over some other. The in-group needs an out-group against which it can compare itself... groups with particularistic worldviews are often able to mobilize the efforts of their members precisely because of this sense of opposition. Particularism enhances militance for one's religious groups.[8]

A report on the 2005 convention finds the group fomenting this sort of particularism. In his opening address, Tony Perkins, president of the *Family Research*

Council, argued that secular humanists had highjacked American culture: "These radicals," he proposed, "[are] doing their best to destroy two centuries of traditional values, and no one seemed to be able to stop them—until now. Will Congress undo 200 years of tradition? Not on our watch."[9] The irony of such a claim, of course, is that this was undoubtedly the friendliest Congress religious conservatives ever had in at least the last fifty years. Congressional support for conservative religious causes reached unprecedented levels during the Bush administration. Yet, Perkins could conveniently set up the Legislative as a straw horse in his fight to restore America.

Perkins' speech was followed by Wright's. The NRB president gladly reported that the U.S. Congress now had 130 *born-again* representatives, before he too launched into an attack on the institution, for its oversight of the *Fairness Doctrine*. To him, conservative proselytizing is too important to abide by the FCC's Fair Doctrine rules: "For the first time in history, representatives and senators may pass hate-crime legislation which is one step to oppose what you do as against the law.... If we had to give equal time to every opposing viewpoint, there would be no time to proclaim the truth that we have been commanded to proclaim.... We will fight the *Fairness Doctrine*, tooth and nail. It could be the end of Christian broadcasting as we know it if we do not."[10]

Summing up the convention, the *Harper's* reporter concluded that the NRB promotes a militant biblicism with a clear restoration agenda. Among other things, NRB members want to reorganize our legal system on the basis of the Ten Commandments. They want to make Creationism (or Intelligent Design) and the teaching of Christian values mandatory in public schools. They think the national media should promote Christian conservatism. They wish to limit federal powers to protecting property rights and the homeland. And they would like to silence all "man-made" religions. That scenario is not a far cry from the one proposed by conservative *Dominionists*:

> The Old Testament—with its 600 or so Mosaic laws—is the inflexible guide for the Society DeMar and other Reconstructionists envision. Government posts would be reserved for the righteous, as long as they are male. There would be thousands of executions a year, with stoning a preferred method because it would turn the deaths into "community projects," as movement theologian North has noted. Sinners in line for the death penalty would include women who commit adultery or lie about their virginity, blasphemers, witches, children who strike their parents, and gay men (lesbians, however, would be spared because no specific reference to them can be found in the Book of Moses). DeMar told me that among Reconstructionists he is considered something of a liberal, because he'd execute gays only if they were caught indulging in sodomy. "I'm happy to just drive them back into the closet," he said.... Besides facilitating evangelism, Reconstructionists believe, governments should largely be limited to building and maintaining roads, enforcing land-use contracts, and ensuring just weights and measures. Unions would not exist, and neither would unemployment benefits, Social Security, and environmental protection laws. Public schools would disappear; one of the movement's great successes has been promoting homeschooling programs and publishing texts used by tens of thousands

of homeschooling families. And, perhaps most importantly, the state is "God's minister," as DeMar puts it in *Liberty at Risk*, "taking vengeance out on those who do evil." A major task for the government key Reconstructionists envision is fielding armies for conquest in the name of Jesus.[11]

PROMOTING A PUBLIC CHRISTIAN ETHOS

The conservative Church has quite an ambitious agenda when it comes to the promotion of a Christian ethos. On matters of public morality, two broad areas concern the Church—the curbing of indecent sexuality and the reclaiming of America's public square for Christ. For many marginal believers the two are closely linked. Were America honoring its Christian heritage, it would not be facing the crisis of immorality that is plaguing our society. This review of the Church's public agenda is by no means exhaustive. Since current religious battles are fluid, changing as Christian conservatives gain footholds in the larger culture, victory in one issue pushes religious groups on to the next. But the review is well within the scope of the chapter.

Curbing Human Sexuality

For the conservative faith sexuality is a gift from God, but it is one that has been vitiated by our sinful nature. Our fall from grace twisted something good and innocent into a perverted source of sin and destruction. Conservatives see sex as a form of spiritual rebellion—against God and human nature; one that harks back to the Garden of Eden. It is only after Adam and Eve eat from the forbidden fruit that they realize they are naked, and become ashamed of their nature. That original shame signals how sexuality was affected by our outcast condition. Other reports of unrestrained libido among biblical characters only provide more ammunition to the conservative argument. Sex is pointed out again and again as the main culprit for the downfall of many godly men and women in the Scriptures.

Because sex can present such a threat to our spiritual health, it is an area where Christians need God's guidance the most. Best to limit it, argue the faithful, to the bonds of marriage. Only within the bonds of holy matrimony, for the strict purpose of procreation, can human sexuality be appropriately redeemed. Any deviation from such model invites moral disorder and even possible spiritual damnation. On this matter, all single-issue groups who work in the area of human sexuality agree. From the *Family Research Council*'s concern with marriage and procreation, to the *Traditional Values Coalition*'s campaign against premarital sex, to the *Christian Answers*' guidance for sanctified sex, to the *Christian Medical and Dental Association*'s (CMDA) clinical sexual proscriptions, the religious push is the same: What the Bible forbids, ought to be forbidden in our society; what it enjoins, should be publicly upheld, no matter the emotional or spiritual cost; and what it fails to address, should still be dealt with under these proscriptions.

So America's twenty-first century sexual practices should follow the mores of pastoral, polygamist, patriarchal tribes, as interpreted by current suburban, middle-class, religious conservatives. What would those mores be? Judging by the groups' literature, the rules are quite simple: God created sex to increase the emotional bond between a husband and a wife, and to help them grow into a larger family through procreation. Therefore sex should be enjoyed only within marriage, for the purpose of family life. It's the typical cul-de-sac, single-family-dwelling neighborhood, middle-class cultural approach to sexuality. Any form of sexuality that deviates from this standard is considered an affront to God's intended purposes. Premarital sex, cohabitation, adultery, prostitution, incest, sexual addiction, pornography, homosexuality, bisexuality, and a transgender orientation are all described as human rebellion against God's established order.

Sexual disobedience brings dire consequences to the perpetrators: sexually transmitted diseases, physical abuse, and emotional scarring. The wages of sexual sins are no less painful or traumatic than sins of a nonsexual nature.[12] Moreover, a nation that tolerates immoral behaviors and practices invites God's rebuke.[13] Conservatives cite biblical examples of entire communities that paid for the sexual sins of their residents. In fact, they point to the Bible as the basis for the stringent sexual morality. Scriptural passages are used to define sexual immorality and appropriate sexual practices. The most popular texts come from the Pentateuch (especially Leviticus and Deuteronomy), along with parts of the synoptic Gospels, and the epistles.

Among the most commonly cited texts against fornication are I Corinthians 7: 2, 36 and Galatians 5: 19. Adultery is condemned in Exodus 20: 14 and Matthew 5: 27. Proscriptions against homosexuality are found in Leviticus 18: 22 and Romans 1: 26–17. Prostitution is forbidden in Leviticus 19: 29, Deuteronomy 23: 17, Proverbs 23: 27 and I Corinthians 6: 15–16. Finally, incest is reproached in Leviticus 18: 6. While not an exhaustive list, these citations provide a good sample of the literal, conservative approach to human sexuality. On the positive side, the Bible also legislates "good" sex. Married Christians should be sexually faithful according to Matthews 19: 4–5 and I Timothy 3: 2 and 12. Wives should submit to their husbands following I Corinthians 7: 3–5. According to Romans 14: 1, 23 spouses should not be asked to engage in sexual practices that go against their spiritual beliefs. Ephesians 5: 29, 33 and I Corinthians 6: 19 remind Christians to respect their partners' need for spiritual purity. Even married Christians should not allow sex to control their lives, according to one interpretation of I Corinthians 6: 12 and 10: 23.[14]

Religious conservatives believe that confining human sexuality to marriage is the moral imperative to create a healthy public square. So, their current culture war on sexuality involves at least three key areas: premarital sex, abortion, and homosexuality. Curbing premarital sex keeps American singles from morally destructive behavior. Stopping abortion and curbing access to contraceptives restricts fornication. "Rescuing" homosexuals from homoerotic tendencies preserves God's "natural" plan for society (the heterosexual family). A nation that reaches this level of sexual purity is one that honors God. These three areas of sexual morality receive a great deal of attention from conservative religious groups, but given their access to power, they also receive a lot of attention from our government. In 2005 the federal government spent $170 million on abstinence school programs, for a total of $900 million over the five years of the Bush administration.[15] Some thirteen states are considering legislation to allow Christian pharmacists to refuse filling contraceptive prescriptions. Four states already have such laws.[16] Twenty-three states have laws defining marriage as strictly heterosexual and seventeen have amendments forbidding same-sex marriages.[17]

The conservative need to defend such stringent morality, based exclusively on a literal reading of the Bible, pushes the Church toward an unrealistic, unscientific, and medically dangerous definition of human sexuality. For instance, a review of federally funded high school abstinence programs, commissioned by Rep. Henry A. Waxman (D-CA), found that these programs frequently provide "medically inaccurate or misleading information, often in direct contradiction to the findings of government"[18] In fact, the report shows that eleven out of the thirteen most commonly used abstinence curricula (adopted by sixty-nine organizations in twenty-five states) contain "unproved claims, subjective conclusions or outright falsehoods regarding reproductive health, gender traits, and when life begins." Among the most common misconceptions were arguments that a forty-three-day-old fetus is a "thinking person," and that HIV spreads via sweat and tears, and that condoms fail to prevent HIV transmission, and that women who abort are more prone to suicide and sterility.[19]

Similarly, a report by the Christian Medical and Dental Associations (CMDA) finds no credible evidence that same-sex attraction is genetically determined. It stipulates that those who act on homosexual attraction do so voluntarily. It argues that claims of genetic or environmental determinism should not excuse individuals from the moral responsibility for their sexual "choice."[20] Other CMDA medical findings include the notions that homosexual acts are physically harmful because they disregard normal human anatomy and function; and that those involved in homosexual acts have higher incidence of drug and/or alcohol dependence, compulsive sexual behavior, anxiety, depression, and suicide; and that homosexual men have a higher incidence of promiscuity, child molestation, and sexually transmitted infections; and that homosexual behavior can be self-propagating.[21]

Such statements from conservative groups would lead one to conclude that sex is the main source of all moral evil, the very cause of humanity's original downfall. If it could, the conservative Church might rewrite the Garden of Eden myth, so as to turn our original sin into sex, rather than *pride* ("Why should God know more than we do?" pondered those primeval ancestors of ours), or *envy* ("Why can't we be more like God?"). Adam and Eve would lose their innocence as a result of loving sex more than God. Current conservative Christian leaders may not be familiar with the broader Church tradition, and therefore unaware of Saint Gregory's list of seven cardinal sins.[22] But of all the seven sins—lust, gluttony, greed (or avarice), sloth, wrath (or anger), envy, and pride—they seem to zero in on *lust* as the prime candidate for an all-out culture war. The problem with America, they argue, is not greed, or pride, or wrath, but sexual fixation.

That explains why one president's sin of hubris (pride)—for staging a war of choice under false intelligence premises and as revenge (wrath) for 9/11—is not a public moral issue. But another president's infidelities with an intern in the Oval Office are cause for outright impeachment. It is a skewed vision of public morality that greatly narrows social Christian ethics. Anything related to sex is wrong. Everything related to the other six moral flaws listed by good St. Gregory is dismissible or not as critical to the nation's spiritual health. The danger with this one-sided view of public morality is that it does not consider the broader stakes involved in governing a country. Moreover, such a narrow view of public morality prevents religious conservatives from mining the rich Hebrew prophetic tradition. Public sins are subsumed into sexual perversion. Yet, all the prophets of old pointed out that the real sins of public life have to do with social ethics: exploiting widows and orphans, amassing immoral amounts of wealth at the expense of the needy, taking political bribes instead of caring for the common wealth, denying the less affluent equal educational opportunities, and withdrawing health care from the poor.[23]

Ironically, the conservative crusade betrays its suburban blind spots. In its effort to clean up the public square, Christian conservatism spends little time *fighting the moral indiscretions of married, heterosexual adults*. On those matters, the Church's efforts are lackluster at best. Take adultery, for instance. There are scarcely any religious groups fighting adultery compared to the multitude fighting abortion or homosexuality. It is simply not seen as a socially dangerous sin. In fact, 13 percent of traditional evangelicals and 19 percent of nontraditional ones think it is OK to have sex with someone other than one's spouse.[24] Similarly, there is no conservative outcry about addiction to pornography. Some 40 million Americans view pornography on the Internet. Web porn is a $2.5 billion slice of the overall $12 billion-dollar industry. About 20 percent of American men and 13 percent of American women admit viewing it at work. At least a quarter of all search engine requests are porn-related.[25] And yet, no outcry is heard from the conservative community.

The truth is that addiction to pornography is one of the best-kept secrets of the conservative Church. A recent *Leadership* survey found "the percentage of Christian men involved [in pornography] not much different from that of the unsaved."[26] Another study reported that 37 percent of pastors struggle with pornography, while 51 percent confess they are tempted by it. Christian addiction to pornography has become so problematic that the conservative religious community held an in-house conference on the topic. Organizations like *Focus on the Family* are setting up toll-free clergy care for porn-related struggles. The group spends thousands of dollars to send pastors to treatment centers.[27]

The diffident approach of religious conservatives toward adultery and pornography shows the conservative mind's captivity to the larger American culture. For most U.S. history, white, middle class, heterosexual married men have set the sexual mores of our society.[28] Those norms, of course, were quite silent about their own peccadilloes—whether incest, adultery, or pornography. To no surprise, we find the same pattern replicated in the conservative religious community: sexual morality is all about restraining the not-yet-married, or sexual minorities. Again, the conservative Church carefully picks and chooses biblical citations to support a larger cultural pattern. Reproach is employed by those in power, who set the standards and have no desire to discuss their own shortcomings as part of that process.

But why the preoccupation with sex? Perhaps because sex presents the human psyche with a bold new way to reframe identity and social relations. Expressing oneself sexually deeply touches a person's identity. It redefines his/her relation to god, to self, and the world. It is hard to be controlled by mystifying religious notions, when one's body awakens to the freedom and mysteries of a sexual identity. Sex also introduces new possibilities and modes of interaction with others in the larger community. Put it differently, *the advent of sexuality complicates social control.* Children's minds are more pliable before hormonal changes interfere with their moral education. They are more passive as well. A middle class, suburban, conservative Christian mother interviewed by CNN admitted hoping that Jesus would return before her daughter reached puberty.[29] She worried that sexuality would affect her child's ability to remain faithful.

The Church suspects (with good reason) that bodily freedom undermines religious control. Thus its concern with sexual repression that dates back to Patristic days. Sexual control played an important role in the development of the medieval rite of *confession* in the Roman Catholic tradition. The medieval Church's obsession with sex resulted in an extensive cataloging of sexual sins, and in the establishment of detailed penances for each of them.[30] That such catalogue even existed is a clear indication of how potent the sexual drive is in human beings; and how assuredly threatening it can be to certain forms of Christian spirituality.

So, *sexual repression enhances religious control over the individual.* Repression of human sexuality is directly related to the Church's promotion of purity and devotion. Part of the conservative preoccupation with sex is connected to the Church's earnest, single-minded concern with spiritual matters to the exclusion of other forms of personal gratification. All faiths, to some extent, seek to control sexuality; but more so those that share an ascetic view of human nature. Ascetic pursuit of worldly detachment is directly related to control of sexual activity. Put in another way, perhaps the conservative Church recognizes in the sex drive the greatest threat to sanctified living. Unfortunately, repressing it does not solve the problem (as shown by the conservative addiction to pornography). Repression contorts and skews real living, forcing honest people to struggle, sometimes over a lifetime, with urges that cannot be framed, accepted, or affirmed by their religious cosmology.

Sexual repression also enhances religious control over the religious community. By confining sex to the bonds of marriage the Church automatically gains an enormous amount of influence over the Christian family, the only institution where libido is now allowed. Tighter sex regulation gives the religious community greater control over the family, the congregation's basic building block. Couples have to rely on the Church for guidance as they deal with complex sexual and medical issues. Singles, forbidden from sex altogether, are at a greater mercy of their Church elders, since their behavior is more carefully monitored. Moreover, by turning procreation into the *télos* of human sexuality, the Church seriously narrows the broad array of sexual experiences available to adults.[31] Emphasis on procreation curbs any form of sexual experimentation. It also offers the conservative mind the means to redeem sexuality from its otherwise lascivious and perverted nature.

Finally, *sexual repression enhances religious control over society*. Under the banner of fighting sexual immorality, marginal believers can challenge every freedom gained in the 1960s and 1970s, by the gay and women's movements. In fact, a good number of conservative groups sprung up as a reaction to the Equal Rights Ammendment's progressive agenda, and groups such as the National Organization for Women. Similarly, the Church's battle against the "homosexual agenda" is a way to challenge the civil rights victories of gay and lesbian organizations, victories won after the Stonewall riot.

Legislating morality, however, is far more complicated than simply regulating the faithful. The marginal Church's irreducible understanding of Scriptures sets it on a collision course with America's secular, evolving standards of morality. The literal reading of the Bible leads conservative groups to interpret all the personal gains brought by the 1960s and 1970s revolutions as an abomination to God, a threat to America's public ethos. But the sexual freedoms and individual choices afforded by modernity are not perceived by all Americans as a threat to the well-being of individuals, their families, or their larger community. When we add to the literal reading of the Bible, a good amount of religious cultural captivity to the 1950s middle-class standards of morality, we create the perfect conditions for an all-out cultural war; one where there seems to be no room for compromise, or middle ground with other segments of society. Under the guise of sanitizing America's public square, religious conservatives seek to wipe out decades of cultural change, denying us some of the most basic freedoms a tolerant, modern society should protect.

PUSHING FOR A CHRISTIAN PUBLIC SQUARE

The First Session of the 109th U.S. Congress was coming to an end and weighty matters remained unresolved. There was the additional military funding for the Iraq and Afghanistan wars, the money needed for the Katrina victims, the tax cuts to be made permanent for the well-to-do, some $40 billion worth of social welfare to be shed from the budget, and the important (if not controversial) provisions of the Patriot Act to renew. But on a mid-December evening in 2005, more pressing matters kept the House of Representatives working late. The Honorable Jo Ann Davis of Virginia submitted the following resolution (H. RES. 579) on her own behalf, and on that of Mr. Bartlett of Maryland, and Mr. Goode and Mr. Jones of North Carolina:

> Expressing the sense of the House of Representatives that the symbols and traditions of Christmas should be protected.
> Whereas Christmas is a national holiday celebrated on December 25; and
> Whereas the Framers intended that the First Amendment to the Constitution of the United States would prohibit the establishment of religion, not prohibit any mention of religion or reference to God in civic dialog: Now, therefore, be it
> *Resolved*, That the House of Representatives—
> (1) recognizes the importance of the symbols and traditions of Christmas;
> (2) strongly disapproves of attempts to ban references to Christmas; and
> (3) expresses support for the use of these symbols and traditions.

Described by a home district newspaper as the "outspoken Christian conservative from Gloucester,"[32] Rep. Davis was quite surprised by opposition to her resolution. Rep. Gary Ackerman, a Jewish Democrat from New York, tried to educate her on its lack of inclusion: "You've drawn me out. Why not protect my symbols?" When Rep. Anthony Weiner (D-NY) suggested that Davis amend the resolution to include other holiday symbols, she made it clear she did not see other faiths being threatened: "The attack has not been on the menorah or any symbols of the other religions...I will leave it as the resolution stands." Her resolve drew praise from conservative quarters, but left fellow lawmakers perplexed or bemused. Rep. Lynn Woolsey (D-CA), a Presbyterian, remarked, "You can always tell when the right wing is in trouble. They invariably cook up some kind of culture war." Sadly, the resolution passed, with 401 Representatives voting in favor and 22 opposing it.

Indefatigable in her defense of the faith, Rep. Davis had a previous resolution (H. RES. 302), in support of America's national motto—"In God We Trust." She felt the motto was under attack from "secular, liberal forces," and hoped for a swift response from the House. After all, she reasoned, "In God We Trust is as old as the Republic itself, and has always been an integral part of the First Amendment."[33] She did not seem to know that the motto had been established in 1956, during the Second Session of the 84th Congress (July 30 to be precise);[34] or that her interpretation of the First Amendment seemed quite unique among constitutional experts. The point being made here is that the conservative Church sees Christianity under attack in the public square. Rep. Davis saw the defense of Christianity as part of her *public mandate*. In the case of the national motto, she equated her resolution with the defense of "America's religious heritage," a well-known Christian conservative terminology.

For Christian conservatives, the way to restore America is to press for its official acknowledgment of Christian symbols, themes, and motifs all over the public square. Conservative religious leaders seek constant official recognition for Christian holidays, for their faith to be recognized as the country's very foundation. To them, there is only one "American religious heritage," and it is sectarian Christianity; which is why that faith should inform our most fundamental laws, system of representative government, economy, and national mores. Suburban megachurches, like the 10,000-member Coral Ridge Presbyterian Church in Florida, are quite eager to provide the structure and resources needed to see the fight to the end. One of Coral Ridge's most visible ministries is a national annual conference—"Reclaiming America for Christ"—staged as training ground for Christian political activists.

The church also sponsors two politically oriented centers: the *Center for Christian Statesmanship* (CCS) and the *Center for Reclaiming America* (CRA). The CCS, in Washington, DC, was created "to evangelize members of Congress and their staffs, and to counsel conservative Christian officeholders."[35] The CRA was created to build a national grassroots alliance that would pressure Congress to adopt the conservative agenda. The CRA hopes to double its current 500,000 membership, while developing twelve regional offices. The goal is to plant a grassroots chapter in all 435 U.S. House districts. Its DC lobbying arm is also dedicated to push for the "right" judicial nominations.

The fascinating thing here is that twenty-five years ago none of these activities would be considered as a real, authentic church ministry by working-class conservative Christians. Gone is the sense that mission meant only the salvation of individual souls, or the preaching of God's redemptive love. A reporter covering the last "Reclaiming America for Christ" conference described the participants' motivation this way:

> Their mission is not simply to save souls. The goal is to mobilize evangelical Christians for political action to return society to what they call "the biblical worldview of the Founding Fathers." Some speak of "restoring a Christian nation." Others shy from the phrase, but agree that the Bible calls them not only to evangelize, but also to transform the culture.[36]

Last year's conference showcased Alabama's Ten Commandments monument. Conservative pressure to display the Ten Commandments in Texas and Kentucky incited suits that went all the way to the Supreme Court. The court handed a mixed decision: the Texas display was not an unconstitutional governmental promotion of religion, but Kentucky's was. Right after the verdict, religious groups announced a nationwide campaign to install Texas-like displays in a hundred cities and towns within a year.[37]

Perhaps no event in 2005 symbolized the Christian conservative-Republican partnership better than "Justice Sunday." A nationwide telecast event, the program was sponsored by conservative Christians to denounce Democrats as enemies of "people of faith."[38] Since Democrats were threatening to filibuster the President's nomination of conservative judges, religious groups sought to paint them as obstructionist, antifaith politicians. Counting with the participation of then Senate Majority Leader Bill Frist, "Justice Sunday" was a national event pitching the forces of Christianity against the "secular, liberal forces" in our society; people who were actively moving our nation away from its Christian heritage. Speaker after speaker raged against the "liberal minority" in the Senate who kept President George W. Bush's conservative judicial nominees hostage. To explain the event, the *Family Research Council* issued a rallying communiqué (see The Family Research Council Communiqué):

The Family Research Council Communique

Dear Friend:

A day of decision is upon us. Whether it was the legalization of abortion, the banning of school prayer, the expulsion of the 10 Commandments from public spaces, or the starvation of Terri Schiavo, decisions by the courts have not only changed our nation's course, but even led to the taking of human lives. As the liberal, anti-Christian dogma of the left has been repudiated in almost every recent election, the courts have become the last great bastion for liberalism.

For years activist courts, aided by liberal interest groups like the ACLU, have been quietly working under the veil of the judiciary, like thieves in the night, to rob us of our Christian heritage and our religious freedoms. Federal judges have systematically grabbed power, usurping the constitutional authority that resides in the other two branches of government and, ultimately, in the American people.

We now have a President who is committed to nominate judicial candidates who are not activists, but strict constructionists—judges who will simply interpret the Constitution as it was written. We now have a majority in the U.S. Senate that will confirm these nominees. However, there is a radical minority that has launched an unprecedented filibuster against these outstanding men and women.

Many of these nominees to the all-important appellate court level are being blocked, not because they haven't paid their taxes or because they have used drugs or because they have criminal records or for any other reason that would disqualify them from public service; rather, they are being blocked because they are people of faith and moral conviction. These are people whose only offense is to say that abortion is wrong or that marriage should be between one man and one woman.

Only 51 votes are needed to approve these nominees and most of these candidates, if not all, would receive more than 51 votes if a vote were held on the Senate floor. But a radical minority in the Senate is using the filibuster to block an up or down vote on the Senate floor. They are requiring a super majority, 60 votes, to proceed on these nominees. This liberal minority does not respect the will of the people: they want judge-made law because our elected officials will not give them the social anarchy they demand.

The Senate Majority Leader, Bill Frist of Tennessee, is committed to returning Constitutional order to the Senate by requiring an up-or-down vote on these nominees. To do this, he urgently needs the help of every "values voter." Without doubt, this will be the most important vote cast in the United States Senate in this term. If this effort fails, the best we can hope for are likely to be mediocre judges who meet the approval of Ted Kennedy, Charles Schumer and Hillary Rodham Clinton.

We must stop this unprecedented filibuster of people of faith. Join us on Sunday, April 24, as we observe Justice Sunday. On that date, just around the corner, FRC will host a nationwide, live simulcast to engage value voters in this all-important issue of reining in our out-of-control courts.

The simulcast will originate from Highview Baptist Church in Louisville, KY. Participants joining me include Dr. James Dobson, Dr. Al Mohler, and Chuck Colson.

For more information on how your church can participate or how you can find a venue to participate in this critically important simulcast, click the links below. This is an event you won't want to miss, an historic debate we can't afford to lose!

Sincerely, Tony Perkins
President, FRC Action

Source: http://www.frc.org/get.cfm?i=EVO5DO2&f=LHO5DO2.

The communiqué makes a straightforward case for producing "Justice Sunday." Its politically astute approach shows the level of sophistication reached by conservative religious groups in the United States. It also reveals the level of marginality and bifurcation that continues to inform their efforts. While Perkins rallies every "value voter" to battle, the *Alliance Defense Fund* (ADF), a religious legal aid organization, assures pastors and church members that they are legally clear to participate in the event, and to pressure their senators to end the filibuster. Should there be any legal threats "by government officials or activist groups," warned the ADF memorandum, ADF staff would "promptly review your situation and make every effort to defend your constitutional rights. ADF is here to protect the precious constitutional rights of churches and Christians. Do not be silenced by fear or intimidation!"

The combative tone behind "Justice Sunday" shows both the "under siege" mentality of current religious groups *and* their militant disposition. That disposition finds a home in some of our political leaders too. Former U.S. Representative Bill Dannemeyer (R-CA), addressing another conservative gathering, argued that:

> The principal problem facing America is not the battle in Iraq, as important as that is, or federal spending that's out of control. The issue we are dealing with my friends, and let's face it, the current leadership of this nation, led by Congress, has to make a basic decision sooner or later: Will we as a people acknowledge that God exists? The Christian heritage on which this nation was founded has been stolen from us by decisions of the U.S. Supreme Court and the federal courts over the last half-century.[39]

The irony in this eager defense of "America's religious heritage" is precisely that it comes at a time when the conservative faith has reached its apex in the public square. Rather than showing any real evidence of a threat against Christianity, the boisterous organizing only proves how strong the movement has become. "Justice Sunday" was broadcast, without a hitch, to more than 1,000 churches by the *Christian Television Network*. Nationally known politicians and religious leaders attended the event and addressed a large audience of middle-class followers. All major American secular print and broadcast media reported on the event. Suffice it to say, no ADF attorney spent a single minute defending any church that participated in the event. No suits were filed against religious intrusion on political matters by "by government officials or activist groups." No churches were harassed by the Internal Revenue Service for their full-fledged participation. *In other words, there was NO threat.* How could this be construed as a faith under siege?

An equal level of visibility was obtained by a two-day gathering that preceded "Justice Sunday." "Confronting the Judicial War on Faith," sponsored by the *Judeo-Christian Council for Constitutional Restoration* in Washington, DC, brought together conservative speakers who railed against the judicial activism of liberal judges. Participants included two House members, aides to two Senators, representatives from the *Family Research Council*, and *Concerned Women for America*, conservative activists Alan Keyes and Morton C. Blackwell, the lawyer for Terri Schiavo's parents, and Alabama's judge Roy Moore. House Leader Tom DeLay had to cancel his appearance to attend Pope John Paul II's funeral.[40]

In a perceptive *Washington Post* editorial, Paul Gaston presented a different take on "Justice Sunday." He argued that conservative Christians were not defending Christianity, but waging a culture war against *other American Christians*:

"To simplify: Right-wing and fundamentalist Christians are really at war with left-wing and mainstream Christians. It is a battle over both the meaning and practice of Christianity as well as over the definition and destiny of the republic. Secular humanism is a bogeyman, a smoke screen obscuring the right-wing Christians' struggle for supremacy."[41] In the same vein, former U.S. Senator John C. Danforth, a long-term Republican and an Episcopal priest, rebuked his own party for acquiescing with the hegemonic ambitions of the Christian Right:

> When government becomes the means of carrying out a religious program, it raises obvious questions under the First Amendment. But even in the absence of constitutional issues, a political party should resist identification with a religious movement. While religions are free to advocate for their own sectarian causes, the work of government and those who engage in it is to hold together as one people a very diverse country. At its best, religion can be a uniting influence, but in practice, nothing is more divisive. For politicians to advance the cause of one religious group is often to oppose the cause of another.[42]

Both authors see the conservative push for Christian preeminence as a power grab—the desire of religious conservatives to rule and impose their worldview upon the rest of society. They find no evidence of a besieged faith. Many forms of Christianity are flourishing in America today. No Christian church has had to close its doors due to secular persecution. Some 45 percent of Americans polled by *Newsweek* in September 2005 said they attend worship services weekly, a figure virtually identical to the Gallup poll used by *Time* in 1966.[43] Surely, those critics argue, no external godless threats have prevented conservative Christians from practicing their faith, within the sanctity of their own sanctuaries, within their church-sponsored schools and parachurch organizations. This is not about lack of Christian visibility, or a faith under siege. No part of Western culture is as influenced by Christianity as the United States.

Rather, the religious cultural war is a sign of the affluence and strength of the conservative Church. As a resource-rich community, rich in numbers and human capital, the new conservative Church can afford to mount nationwide campaigns to push for Christian preeminence in the public arena. Never has the Church had so many well-educated leaders; nor have its groups and organizations been so professionally trained or so well funded; nor have its members been so deeply embedded in America's middle class. Ironically, the more Christian conservatives stage a cultural war, the more they reveal the real strength of their community, and how far they have succeeded in becoming a part of the body politic.

Take the issue of liberal judges, for instance. The judges who disappointed conservatives the most are all but devout Christians and they were appointed by conservative Republicans, no less. It was a Supreme Court Christian majority who ruled against Creationism in 1987. A Lutheran judge and Republican appointee of President Bush, Judge John E. Jones III, rendered the decision on the Dover, PA, court case, ruling that Intelligent Design is "an extension of religious fundamentalism."[44] Judge George Greer, who presided over the Schiavo case, is a lifelong Southern Baptist and a conservative Republican. Most of the judges who upheld his ruling in the 11th Circuit are devout churchgoing Christians as well.[45]

To make matters worse, the conservative cry against liberal activist judges in the Supreme Court is countered by a review by Gewirtz and Golder of Yale Law School, which shows that the most activist Supreme Court Justices since 1994 have been precisely the politically conservative appointees, not their liberal counterparts.[46] So the point of staging "Justice Sunday" events is not simply to gain court appointments, but to keep the conservative Church's agenda as publicly visible as possible.

As the White House pondered a replacement for Justice Sandra Day O'Connor, and pressed its religious allies to tone down their rhetoric, they responded by ratcheting it up. Gary Bauer, president of *American Values*, suggested that "a lot of people feel that the administration shouldn't be reluctant to talk about the values we hope the nominee will embrace. If all my side does is talk about process—'we want a fair hearing, etc.'—while Ted Kennedy is talking about 'we are not going to let somebody on the court who is going to take away the rights of individuals...' it will affect the way people think about the battle."[47] Tom Minnery, public policy director of *Focus on the Family* claimed that his group intended to "continue to address mainly social and cultural issues 'to get our constituents to understand how important this battle is.'" Once again, it is about keeping strong middle-class organizations and their issues on the cultural forefront.

Organizations like the *Family Research Council*, the *Judeo-Christian Council for Constitutional Restoration*, *Vision America*, the *American Christian Liberty Society*, the *Christian Defense Coalition*, the *Christian Policy Network*, the *Movement for Christian Democracy*, the *National Alliance against Christian Discrimination*, or the *American Center for Law and Justice*, are large, well-funded, public relations programs, existing to push the conservative agenda. They have but one mission—the public promotion of a particular worldview, *the formation of a public, conservative Christian ethos*. To accomplish it, they must find as many divisive issues as possible and use them to drive a wedge against those who do not share that worldview. Any cultural battle that pushes the conservative agenda is quite welcome. The tone is always strident and urgent; the time is always at hand: the nation's welfare always lying in the balance:

> The United States of America has come to a critical moment in its history. The challenge which confronts us today, is neither economic nor military. It is moral. Our nation is abandoning the bedrock moral values, which are our heritage from God, and the very foundation of our liberty. There are those in America, whose goal is nothing less than the transformation of our country in their own image, who openly ridicule and belittle people of faith. They seek to silence our witness and to banish Christianity from the public square. We cannot allow this to happen!

Christian involvement in civil government is not optional. It is an essential part of our calling from God to be salt and light in a dying culture. God's people in Christ must address the great moral issues now before the nation. The church has been entrusted by Almighty God with the tools necessary to reverse America's moral decline and effect lasting change if only she will engage in this momentous struggle before it is too late![48]

For religious conservatives we are always at a critical moment in U.S. history; the Christian message always under threat. Secular forces are always conspiring to "banish Christianity from the public square." Left to their own devices, these godless, immoral people would destroy any decency left in American society. That approach, incidentally, is not restricted to marginal believers. Americans in every generation have waxed nostalgically about a more decent past, imagining it better politically, economically, or spiritually. Marcus Cunliffe sees that tendency as a need for a "golden age"; a longing for old ways that have disappeared, or whose ideals no longer provide a "useful guide to a newer generation."[49] Remarkably, his research finds solid continuity in U.S. history. Our country's ethos has been one of the most stable among industrialized nations.

So, our nostalgia may be more a function of ignorance of the past, than of a golden age truly lost. To any student of American history, the claim that "the United States has come to a critical moment in its history" is completely befuddling. Two hundred plus years of American independence, and Christian influence is widespread in our literature, music, the arts, and politics. Christianity is part and parcel of our history, customs, and mores. The country is run by an overwhelming majority of Christians, in every branch of government. How is the faith in any danger? Were every threat that we face these days as dangerous as this one, we would have nothing to fear.

6

SHALL WE GATHER AT THE RIVER? RELIGIOUS ZEAL AND AMERICAN PLURALISM

"Today, the calls for diversity and multiculturalism are nothing more than thinly veiled attacks on anyone willing, desirous, or compelled to proclaim Christian truths."[1]
—Frank Wright, President of the National Religious Broadcasters

Christian conservatism has undergone an important change in the last twenty-five years. Conservative believers have gone from avoiding modernity at the beginning of the twentieth century to *Christianizing* it at the century's end. Conservative congregations have shed their rural and storefront origins, sporting these days suburban campuses filled with plenty of modern activities. The level of affluence reached by the conservative Church has transformed its agenda, but more importantly, the very nature of the faith. From its Arminian beginnings to its current Dominionist leanings, the Church has become triumphant in structure and suburban in worldview. Its public agenda is simply a consequence of that change.

For the first time in its history, Christian conservatism boasts an expanded network of megachurches with enormous auditoriums, radio and TV broadcast capabilities, multiple-use buildings, and exercise programs. Christian companies now promote born-again clubs and services that closely follow the secular trends of the American consumer market. And Christian organizations have become a permanent part of the American political landscape. In fact, the alliance between religious conservatives and the Republican Party provide this suburban and rising religious community with the opportunity to push for key issues in the public square. Multiple single-issue organizations enabled the Church to set up the most daring conservative religious agenda in American history. That the conservative

Church is playing such a prominent role in the public square is the most unusual development in its history.

In truth, the changes experienced by Christian conservatism are part of a larger realignment in American Christianity. The marginal faith, once home to working-class religious communities, greatly benefited from the migration of wealthier and better-educated conservative Christians from mainline denominations. As its numbers rose, and its membership changed, conservative Christianity became more vocal, combative, and politically savvy. This surge in resources and cultural capital emboldened Christian conservatism to challenge the separation of Church and State. Through a series of strategically placed issues, the Church has continuously assaulted that wall of separation. Efforts to bring prayer to public schools, to introduce Intelligent Design and Christian values in public school curricula, to develop a "pro-family" agenda, to ban abortion and gay marriage, and to multiply Protestant symbols in public spaces have grown exponentially in the last two and a half decades, the same time period in which the Church grew in prosperity.

The final goal, of course, is the creation of a biblically based society, whose laws are set to a conservative, suburban, middle-class reading of Scriptures, and whose public mores are similar to those found in the new conservative Christian communities. Success in any small scale only encourages the Church to keep pushing for the final *Christianization* of the country.

DOMINION AS A DEFENSE MECHANISM

To better understand the Christian conservative agenda it is necessary to frame it as a defensive reaction against modernity. Religious conservatives are still keen to protect their communities from certain secular aspects of reality. They wish to preserve religious autonomy in matters of family life and schooling. Self-defense also requires Christian conservatives to go out into society to further sanitize the public square. As long as America maintains "lax" sexual mores and fails to honor its Christian roots the situation will continue to deteriorate. In their eyes, a Christian public square guarantees the integrity of the conservative Christian community life.

But *the push to "restore" a Christian America raises questions for the larger society*. Is it possible for a modern, postindustrial nation to become a theocratic State? Would *Christianization* drastically alter our national character? Can the country respond in measured ways to an all-out threat to religious liberty? If so, which segments of the nation will stand for our constitutional freedoms? Past American mass movements have used the courts to push for greater freedom and inclusiveness. Labor unions, the Suffragists, Civil Rights leaders, the women's movement, and the gay movement have all placed their trust in the inclusiveness of the American compact. Will a suburban form of Christian conservatism be able to stem that tide, and curtail those freedoms? Will the courts reverse the trend toward greater individual protection and roll back the freedoms already gained? These are weighty matters.

The push to restore a Christian America raises questions for conservative Christianity as well. Will the conservative Church's numbers, resources, and political connections suffice to produce its desired revolution? Can a particularistic, dogmatic religious movement find a broader base of support among the larger American population? Moreover, can Christian conservatives immerse themselves in partisan politics without losing their integrity? Will a suburban lifestyle continue to refashion the conservative faith? Will political action and social mobility ultimately radically transform the nature of conservative Christianity?

What would happen to an Arminian-based, working-class faith if it is employed as the ideological tool of a middle-class combative and militant political movement? Will the tradition lose its *free will* bearings? Is it possible for the conservative faith to hold on to its original vision, while adapting to the needs of its new middle-class congregants? How will the many conservative clubs and services transform that vision? These are some of the questions that will continue to redefine Church and State relations for the next few decades of our century. Those relations have changed so much already that public officials who served under Presidents Roosevelt, Truman, Eisenhower, or Kennedy would hardly recognize our public square. There is far greater tolerance for religious language in the halls of power, and a greater number of presidential and congressional initiatives backing a particular sectarian religious worldview with large sums of taxpayer dollars.

In January 2006, when the White House director of faith-based initiatives addressed a Catholic conference celebrating the fortieth anniversary of "Dignitas Humanae," he claimed that "enforcing a strict separation between church and state curtails religious freedom and deprives state-funded social programs of a 'spiritual dimension.'"[2] One cannot imagine a mid-century U.S. official, one who served under the four presidents named above, making a similar statement.

THE NATURE OF THE AMERICAN COMPACT

Our country was founded upon religious tolerance. Respect for religious diversity is an intrinsic component of our Republic. The lack of religious language in our Constitution, the preventive dispositions in Article VI and the First Amendment, all point to the secular nature of our nation. As we survey the Founders' debates on the matter, we find again and again their resolve to make ample room in their brand new country for the practice of multiple faiths. Despite the desire in some Federalist quarters to establish an official faith for the United States, and the good intentions of some Founders who saw religion as a practical means to curb social vices, the Continental Congress affirmed our freedom of conscience and our religious liberty as it set the Constitution. This first new nation would be known for its welcoming of multiple confessions, and preservation of a secular public square.

No candidate for public office in the United States would have to swear a religious oath in order to serve. No faith could claim government favor for its practice or propagation. And despite all the *Dominionist* arguments to the contrary, that original constitutional welcome extended well beyond Christianity. In defense of his *Virginia Act*, Thomas Jefferson argued that tolerance should be afforded even to those who were not Christian or religiously affiliated:

> The bill for establishing religious freedom, the principles of which had, to a certain degree, been enacted before, I had drawn in all the latitude of reason & right. It still met with opposition; but with some mutilations in the preamble, it was finally passed; and a singular proposition proved that its protection of opinion was meant to be universal. Where the preamble declares, that coercion is a departure from the plan of the holy author of our religion, an amendment was proposed by inserting "Jesus Christ," so that it would read "A departure from the plan of Jesus Christ, the holy author of our religion;" the insertion was rejected by the great majority, in proof that *they meant to comprehend, within the mantle of its protection, the Jew and the Gentile, the Christian and Mohametan, the Hindoo and Infidel of every denomination.*[3]

The secular public square has held us in good stead for more than two centuries, even at our nation's most trying moments. It has protected America's religious minorities throughout our history. Contrary to the belief of many, our country never shared a single religious heritage, or cultural or ethnic background. From the native American traditions that preceded the Pilgrims, to the California Catholic missions that predated Jamestown's religious services, to the Muslim or animistic faiths of American slaves in colonial Virginia, to the mid-1600s Jewish Sabbath prayers in New Amsterdam, to the philosophical Deism of our Founders, to the eighteenth-century Santéria of French Louisiana, to the nineteenth-century West Coast Buddhists who bridged our continent by rail, we have been a country of many faiths, and we remain so today:

> The assertion that there exists a set of shared and fundamental beliefs about personal and social morality in the United States is, at a minimum, quite controversial, and is, in all likelihood, false. As an empirical matter, it is difficult to specify the content of a religio-moral consensus in a society in which issues such as abortion, homosexuality, stem cell research, and gender equality are contested among and within American faith traditions. While it is not clear whether such a consensus ever existed, it seems likely that the diversity of American religion makes the cognitive basis of communal or covenantal characterizations of religious politics in the United States rather implausible. Stephen Carter has argued that "Christian America" is not, and never was, a live possibility.[4]

Will our legal and political institutions withstand the current drive for America's *Christianization*? So far, despite the Religious Right ingenious attacks, our freedoms seem to hold intact. But crucial battles will continue to be fought, especially as our country becomes more, not less, diverse in faith and ethnicity.

Witness, for instance, the 2005 Guilford County, North Carolina case, where a judge prevented a Muslim woman from swearing upon the Koran before testifying in court. All experts agreed that the First Amendment supported her petition.[5] Judge Albright's refusal unleashed a wave of requests by other religious groups to have their holy texts allowable under law. This is precisely why we need a secular public square.

A crucial battle line in this war is the issue of *public* proselytism. To the conservative faithful, proselytism is intrinsic to Christianity. Jesus commissioned them to make disciples. So they must be public in their efforts to gather converts. But what happens if that argument were made by other faiths? If all go public, where will it end? How will we find a common language or a common identity as Americans, save as a secular community? Christian conservatives have a long history of proselytism in our country, but one that was performed in the privacy of their sanctuaries, revival tents, camp meetings, and city crusades; places *where the choice of other Americans to participate* was preserved. That practice never threatened the health of the Republic. Using public resources for proselytism, however, would cross that line, jeopardizing toleration in a multicultural, multifaith society.

Nevertheless, that push is on right now, as Christian broadcasters are battling the FCC's *Fairness Doctrine*, and conservative military chaplains are suing the Armed Forces to offer public sectarian prayers in official ceremonies. They also want permission to convert American soldiers of other religious orientations.[6] Even if Christian conservatives were allowed to proselytize publicly, would a Christian America be truly feasible? At a third or a quarter of the American electorate, Christian conservatives may have reached their apex. These days, their largest denomination—the *Southern Baptist Convention*—cannot find enough converts to keep its membership base from shrinking.[7]

It is hard to imagine how the conservative Church's overall numbers can continue to rise to encompass the whole nation. In fact, some social scientists argue that conservative Christian membership has remained steady for quite a while. The faithful may circulate from mainline churches to more conservative ones; from evangelical to charismatic circles. But the larger American public remains untouched by such religious recycling. In the end, the same people end up following the conservative religious broadcasting, attending born-again revivals, and seeking refuge in Christian suburbia. Unless there is a mandatory, forceful conversion ordered by a theocratic State, the conservative kingdom might not be at hand.

No one doubts the sincerity of the Church's foot soldiers; nor the drive, ambition, and intensity of their leaders; nor the conviction of every Christian political operative about the justness of the cause. But it seems rather unlikely that America will ever be the theocratic nation these folks pray, hope, and work for. We are too diverse in too many ways to all gather under the same religious canopy. At some point, even the most ardent true believer has to face that reality. At some point the conservative community will have to realize two important things: that our constitutional framework will not allow the *public Christianization* of America; and that even the conservative Church might not have the resources or the power to convert *every single American*. When that happens, how will the Church respond? More importantly, will Christian conservatives ever learn to live with other Americans in a diversely religious country?

STEERING THE CONSERVATIVE JUGGERNAUT

The problem is that this generation of Christian conservatives has consumed a quarter of a century and untold amounts of money, time, and energy pushing for America's restoration, for the *Christianization* of their beloved country. Would such earnest faith workers ever imagine a time when turning America into a Christian paradise is no longer the utmost goal? How does one reverse the faith from its current Dominionist approach? More importantly, what will Christian conservatives do when the public square remains solidly secular and tolerant? How will they react when they realize they must share a nation with the same religious and social minorities they have so fiercely battled? *How will they manage to remain equally loyal to a triumphant faith and a tolerant country?* Will secular resistance cause a religious retreat similar to the one that took place after the Scopes monkey trial in the 1920s? How will religious conservatives recover from the failed dream of national restoration? And if they do, where will they spend their energies next? What goal will drive their earnest practices? At this point, it is too early to tell. But we can foresee some of the issues they will be dealing with in the future.

The Problem of Affluence

There is a limit to a religious renewal fueled by social mobility. How will Christian conservative affluence affect its quest for America's restoration? On one hand conservative affluence provides the Church with greater resources to push for a public agenda; on the other hand, it creates a comfortable, middle class exclusive world for its members. The two trends are not necessarily complementary nor mutually sustaining. Will Christian suburbia continue to staff a combative restoration movement, or will it choose to revel in the joys of its "born-again only" clubs and services? Affluence could tone down the conservative Church's religious intransigence or it might enable it to undertake even more quixotic charges. If the suburban lifestyle of current religious conservatives clashes with the constant waging of cultural wars, will the faithful retreat into their Christian clubs or will they remain in the battlefront?

Putting it differently, how many "Justice Sundays" will it take before the rank and file decides that there should be more to faith than charging at political windmills? How many political rallies will suburban believers have to staff before they realize that energy, dedication, and organization alone will not change the character of a country as democratic and diverse as the United States? Unlike the camp meetings of yore, modern religious spectacles are harder to stage and control. Outcomes are more uncertain, both in the short and long term. Nineteenth-century handbooks gave detailed explanations on how to stage a camp meeting so as to obtain the greatest spiritual yield possible.[8] There were practical tricks that could be used to "aid" the Holy Spirit in convincing sinners of their need for redemption. An era of instant communication, round-the-clock news coverage, and political spinning makes it harder to create equal results. Nowadays, a political rally is no guarantee that the unchurched will be greatly impressed, or that symbolic rallies alone will sustain the resolve of the faithful.

For all the political smoke and mirrors of "Justice Sunday," all the organizing the *Family Research Council* did on its behalf, all the work the 1,000 congregations did to link up to the broadcast, and all the media hype generated by other conservative Church groups, the event was completely preempted by a Senate agreement between fourteen moderate Democrats and Republicans. With quiet competence, those members dispatched the "nuclear option" fiercely promised by the Senate Majority Leader. Fourteen sensible politicians, willing to find common ground, sufficed to take away the wedge created by the entire conservative movement on this issue. In the end it all fizzled away. The symbolism of "Justice Sunday" remained an empty effort.

The Problem of Mass Conversion

To be sure, religious energies can be harnessed for long-term projects. But in order to last, they require more than a short string of small symbolic successes. They depend upon *feasible* long-term goals. And how feasible is the *Christianization of America*? How do Christian conservatives propose to convert every individual in every family, in every town, in every county, in every state, and in every region of the country? The drastic strategies needed to create such a large-scale, top-down transformation of our society are gigantic. And the quest is made more absurd by the willful independence of American citizens. No nation in the world treasures autonomy and individualism more highly than we do. Fiercely proud of our freedom, we "regard [our] selves as autonomous possessors of individual rights, which are generally conceived as non-negotiable prerogatives, and which lie beyond the reach of any authority."[9]

How do you convert an entire country made up of individuals who enjoy their independence and their freedom to choose too much? As if that was not enough, our country is becoming *more*, not less, diverse. Never have we been as ethnically, socially, or religiously diverse as we are today. Since the 1965 changes in immigration laws, America has witnessed a surge in Asian, African, and Latino immigrants. These new groups are not as easily absorbed into a uniform Anglo, conservative, and religious worldview.[10] In fact, during the last forty years immigrants have brought to America an array of non-European religious practices that are quite distinct from the Judeo-Christian panoply.

This greater variety of faith is literally rearranging the religious landscape: There are more American Muslims today than Presbyterians.[11] As the new immigrants cope with the demands of a new culture, they also negotiate a valid space for their faiths.[12] Mosques, and Hindu and Buddhist temples, have become a part of large American cities like Houston, Dallas, Atlanta, Los Angeles, and Boston. One can find Buddhist retreats as far as upstate New York, in Colorado, or in California.

American rituals are now as diverse as the multiple faiths that create our vast religious landscape. New Year celebrations brought Afro-Brazilian religious practices to the shores of Lake Michigan. Afro-Caribbean religions have expanded in the United States beyond their traditional Atlantic/Gulf Coast basin. Afro-Catholic devotion to the Virgin of Guadalupe, along with its array of votive candles, icons, and medals has spread from Texas to Minnesota, and from Chicago to Seattle. Ancient Mayan rituals have followed Central American communities as they migrated north. Mexican Huichol traditions have crossed the Southwest borders. Taoism, Sufism, Shiite and Sufi versions of Islam, and a varied array of tribal ethnic devotions have spread throughout the country from coast to coast. The thought that somehow this more diverse society could join a golden-age WASP Puritan village hailing a single religious heritage is hard to fathom.

Furthermore, we are also *more* not less secular. While some 60 percent of us today find religion very important, that figure was 75 percent in 1952. If "religious traditionalists" make up 58 percent of all Republicans, they represent only 29 percent of the American population.[13] Americans are by nature a pragmatic people, and our version of modernity reflects that cause and effect practical orientation to everyday life:

> "The religious right's organisational prowess is impressive. But it still leaves a movement that represents a minority point of view on many issues and is just as capable of over-reaching as liberal judges are. 'Some leaders of the religious right think they are far more powerful than they actually are,' argues one Republican veteran. 'As religious as this country and this president are, neither wants a theocracy.'"[14]

The Problem of Secular Modernity

Late modernity presents a constant challenge to those who rely on a literal interpretation of the Bible. Seeing conservative Christians battle evolution time and again, only to have science stand its ground, leads one to wonder whether there will ever be hope of relief. Will the conservative mind ever make its peace with a scientifically grounded world? The more we learn about our origins, the greater effort it takes to hide from the evidence. Bishop Spong, discussing how science exiled the Christian faith, asks whether,

> Many citizens of our century have given up believing and have assumed citizenship in the secular city. They no longer call themselves Christian or religious people or even believers. Others, reeling in the face of these pressures, have tried to dismiss all the data derived from the explosion of knowledge in the last few centuries as if it were false or evil or even as if it did not exist. These people maintain their pre-modern convictions with hostile vigor while asserting that everyone must be wrong but them. With great vehemence, they deny the realities that have produced the exile. They refuse to engage in the debate. They even produce bumper stickers, designed to defend their biblical source of authority, which say, "God wrote it! I believe it! That does it!"[15]

Similarly, modernity erodes the symbolic power of religious display. How many monuments to the Ten Commandments will have to be erected before conservative Christians realize that public blocks of marble do not automatically change the hearts or the behavior of average Americans? How many public defenses of Christmas will it take before they see that the rest of the country continues to celebrates "the holidays"? How many bans on gay marriage will they pass, before it becomes clear that gays and lesbians will continue to share a lifetime of committed relationships? Outlawing people's lives do not prevent them from being lived. How many Christian clubs will be formed in public schools before they realize that praying and reading the Bible will not curb adolescent behavior?

The Problem of Biblical Scholarship

More importantly, can religious conservatives hold on to a rigid interpretation of the Scriptures as new evidence from biblical scholarship mounts to challenge the literal truth of their faith? Current archaeological and historical data have cast doubts on the existence of important biblical figures, on the possibility of a large-scale exodus, and on the importance of King David's realm. Literary evidence questions whether Yeshua of Nazareth could ever have been the Hellenistic Messiah created by later Christianity.[16] Can conservative Christians ignore all the evidence amassed by professional organizations like the American Academy of Religion or the Society of Biblical Literature? Will they ever find a better way to approach the sacred text? These are questions that are yet to be answered as we continue to observe the development of the conservative Church.

As conservative seminaries flourish, will their scholars avoid probing certain aspects of the faith? How do you leave out the evidence? What happens when conservative scholarship catches up to secular scholarship? Will seminary professors train new generations of conservative pastors who are still shackled by the dogmatic constraints of a premodern tradition, or will they foster a quiet revolution in the faith's theological development?

The Problem of Political Partisanship

Finally, how will the effort to reclaim America affect *the integrity* of the conservative faith? Engaging in politically expedient action rather than theologically authentic behavior, dealing in half-truths and double-speaks, making pacts with shady politicians, or staging bad-faith political theatrics may yield immediate success, but at what long-term costs? When does victory trump faithfulness?

President Bush received unanimous support in religious conservative quarters for the Iraq war. In a 2004 essay Jerry Falwell boasted that "God is pro-war."[17] Charles Stanley, pastor of Atlanta's First Baptist Church, urged Christians to support the President's war policy. Not surprisingly, 87 percent of all white evangelical Christians were in favor of the war in April 2003.[18] As the war effort unraveled, the evangelical support dropped to 68 percent and continued in a downward spiral. Eventually, disillusion with the war contributed to the Republican Party's loss of both houses of Congress in the 2006 election. At that point, how did the pastors explain to disillusioned congregants that they might have been mistaken about God's will on the matter?

Another case involving religion and politics shows how easy it is for a religious leader to lose his balance in the pursuit of political partisanship. During the 2004 presidential election, Pastor Chan Chandler of the East Waynesville Baptist Church in North Carolina declared his unquestioned support for George W. Bush, and asked all his congregants to similarly support the president's bid. When nine long-term church members refused to vote Republican, he quickly kicked them out of the church membership. One, a congregational leader, was shocked: "We're there to learn and worship, not worship Bush. I just couldn't believe what I was hearing coming from the Lord's podium." The pastor was sued. His actions were reported in the national media. He eventually resigned, but not before splintering the congregation.[19]

Religious dishonesty for the sake of political expediency takes its toll. Already the nation has found that Christian conservatives are willing to spread medical misinformation in their push for abstinence. The White House had to cut funding for some abstinence organizations until those issues were addressed. We have also found out that Christian conservatives cannot be trusted when it comes to political expediency in school boards. Religious conservative members of the Dover, Pennsylvania, Board of Education were caught skirting the truth *under oath*, in their futile effort to promote Intelligent Design. By the time the judge rebuked them, they had already lost their public offices. The deception brought shame to their cause and turned Intelligent Design into a legal dead end.[20]

Examples of bad-faith multiply. The national religious leaders, who rallied in their unqualified support to Tom DeLay, must have watched with dismay as the Speaker of the House was indicted for breaking Texas electoral laws, and then resigned his post due to his connections with lobbyist Jack Abramoff and the K Street Project. The Christian leadership of the House of Representatives was similarly caught red-handed in their response to Representative Foley's sexual advances to underage congressional pages.

When NBC decided to feature Pastor Ted Haggard's *New Life Church* on *Dateline*, the president of the *National Association of Evangelicals* e-mailed instructions to all his congregants about being on TV: "If a camera is on you during a worship service, worship; don't dance, jump," he warned, "secular people watching TV are touched by authentic worship, but jumping and dancing in church looks too bizarre for most to relate to." When approached by reporters, he instructed, "Don't talk about the devil, demons, voices speaking to you, God giving you supernatural revelations." "If Barbara Walters talks to you, don't be spooky or weird. Don't switch into a glassy-eyed heavenly mode, just answer, 'Heaven is real. It's the place where God will be fully present with his people.'"[21] Apparently spontaneous Christian conservatism makes for bad press coverage.

This is the same Ted Haggard who in 2006 had to resign from the presidency of the NAE and from his pastorate after revelations of a three-year relationship with a male prostitute and their regular use of methamphetamine surfaced. Haggard's resignation came on the heels of his high profile, statewide, crusade against same-sex marriage in Colorado. In fact, it was the media coverage that alerted the male prostitute to Haggard's real identity. Sometimes, suburbia makes Christian conservatism far more public than it can stand to be.

Caught in its rush to reclaim the nation, the conservative leadership may be inadvertently trading in its hard-won credibility. When Jerry Falwell blamed 9/11 on America's tolerance for feminism, homosexuality, and abortion rights, he horrified the nation, including a Christian-friendly White House.[22] When Pat Robertson explained Prime Minister Sharon's stroke as divine retribution for territory he conceded to the Palestinians, he was quickly and unequivocally rebuked by the White House, and lost the opportunity to build a Christian theme park in Israel.[23] When Ralph Reed, once paraded on the cover of *Time* magazine as "The Right Hand of God," took $4.2 million of Indian gambling money from Jack Abramoff to organize opposition to gambling interests in Texas and Louisiana, he lost the moral high ground.[24] When religious leaders callously attributed Hurricane Katrina to God's punishment for gambling and homosexuality in New Orleans, they were rebuked publicly for adding to the pain of innocent, homeless citizens.[25]

WHERE NEXT?

All forms of McCarthyism, even religious ones, eventually run their course. At some point, American tolerance for self-righteous fire and brimstone preaching wanes, especially as religious conservatism is tested and found wanting. Decades long of the unwavering imposition of a rigid Christian worldview upon the nation will end up galvanizing an equally strong opposition or simply wearing out its welcome. Christian conservatives represent only a fraction of the U.S. population.

As they pursue one divisive issue after another, their moderate supporters will falter. Some middle-of-the-road American may be galvanized about abortion, but not be as indignant about evolution, or stem cell research, or gay marriage, or gender equity. The single-issue approach may hide the overall agenda, but it certainly fragments the united front needed to sustain the war:

> It is in the nature of these groups, however, to focus on single issues, such as abortion or gay rights, and thus be limited in the extent to which they can be regarded as harbingers of an all-out cultural cleavage. The conservative Christian Coalition, for example, purports to be concerned with a wide range of fundamental values but in reality is seldom able to elicit agreement from its constituents on issues other than abortion and homosexuality.[26]

At some point the country will engage in a course correction. After all, that is the nature of a democratic nation. Nixon's "law and order" supposedly corrected Lyndon Johnson's race riots. Carter's moral high ground was seen as a reaction to Watergate. The Reagan era represented a course correction to the cultural excesses of the 1960s and 1970s. The Clinton presidency curbed the yuppie excesses of the 1980s. Similarly, the religious conservative movement will win some and lose some in the political arena. What happens to their combative, religious ethos when there is no final, supreme victory? How does the Church regroup? What vision drives its reorganization? To what ends will its energies be applied? Some leaders may have benefited from political theatrics to build comfortable personal careers. But as some fall, what will happen to the earnest foot soldiers?

The problem with large-scale movements is that they eventually reach a momentum of their own, escaping the control of their creators. It happened to other mass movements in the twentieth century. The construction of a large, nationwide subculture of combative religious conservatism has clear long-term consequences. It will continue to affect American society long after its creators are gone from the public scene. So, predisposing dedicated people to wage wars that cannot be ultimately won carries serious social consequences. One cannot go on for decades teaching people to hate the secular world, and then expect them at some point to come to terms with its necessity and simply make their peace with it. One cannot teach the faithful to bifurcate the world, and then expect them to show kindness toward those who are not their spiritual kin.

So what will be the long-term impact of religious conservatism for our society? Political theorists who studied American democracy in the mid-twentieth century argued that a stable political system cannot be built upon institutions that promote divisiveness.[27] Unlike European class-based socialist or communist parties, American political parties have to constantly elicit crossover loyalties, holding members of multiple political ideologies, religions, classes, races, genders, ages, incomes, and education within their rolls. At mid-century, no party spoke for a single faith, a single gender, or a single social class. There were extremists and moderates in both parties, minimizing the amount of polarization in our country.[28] By comparison, our current cultural wars are a constant tear at the political fabric. The rise of Christian activism clearly paralleled the rise of harsh political partisanship.

Our nation's political loyalties have never been so clearly aligned. When most churchgoers vote for Bush, and the unchurched lean toward Kerry, one can be sure that the crossover loyalties are no longer operative in terms of religion. Such divisiveness preempts us from much needed common ground, as it generates arbitrary political divisions. As our country grows and becomes more diverse, as our social infrastructure creaks under the weight of its age, whether we are talking about social welfare, health care, or public education, divisiveness will makes us less able to meet the needs of all Americans, especially those who are uncomfortable with taking permanent sides on a polarized political scene.

The focus on Blue and Red states diverts us from what we have in common—our lifestyle, vocations, dreams, and even the loftier matters of ideals and values. Tragically, cultural commentators find us more akin than dissimilar:

> When it comes to fundamental questions about human nature, the formation of character, qualities of good and evil, and the sources of moral authority, our respondents have roughly the same views. There is a common American moral philosophy, and it is broad and inclusive enough to incorporate people whose views of the actual issues of the day are at loggerheads.[29]

If our past is any indication, our nation will continue to move toward greater freedom and inclusiveness. Despite cultural wars, we will continue to embrace diversity, faith included. In his book, *Moral Freedom*, Alan Wolfe argues that America is an experiment in human freedom: nineteenth-century America delivered economic freedom to us; twentieth-century America, political freedom. Wolfe predicts that twenty-first-century America will bring us moral freedom. He sees Americans increasingly developing more independent moral views, rather than taking dogma at its face value.[30]

Nevertheless, if America will not turn into a Christian theocracy, the conservative Church will not go away either. It is critical to acknowledge that Christian conservatives have created an important space for themselves in America's late modernity. They are now a public presence in American politics, culture, and society. American politics will continue to be marked by the conservative religious influence. Without Christian conservatives the stark electoral divisions between Blue and Red states might not have escalated into the current level of scorched earth politics, but their presence have brought to the fore the valid political concerns of a unique kind of suburbia.

Conservative believers have also affected the larger Christian culture. At a time when mainline denominations are waning, and spirituality has become more privatized, Christian conservatives are reinventing congregational life, updating worship and missionary work, and developing new and creative ways to weave together large intentional religious communities within the vast wasteland of American cities. The push to reclaim the nation drove suburban Christian conservatives into building the largest religious infrastructure in the country. Its loose coalition of denominations, independent megachurches, schools and colleges, professional associations, music enterprise, and single-issue political coalitions has transformed the face of Christian conservatism, and turned Christian conservatism into a dominant force in American Christianity.

Culturally, Christian modernity will continue to extend the influence of religious conservatives into American suburbia. Today's marginal believers are knowledge workers, developing cultural products for broader audiences, reaching into segments of the American consumer market that are not necessarily part of their congregations. Their media skills give them the chance to develop sophisticated Christian programming. Their music festivals, pod casting, Web services, and Christian clubs allow them to find new ways to package an ancient, simpler message. As a megachurch pastor put it:

> Growing churches and congregations, like growing businesses, have a reflexive thirst for market share. They tend to equate rising numbers with self-worth and bricks and mortar with godliness. But growth is also an expression of the evangelical mission. When I marveled to Bill Hybels, of Willow Creek, about his church's phenomenal growth and size—more than 15,000 attend a worship service every weekend—he frowned. "There are two million people within a one-hour drive of this place," he said. "In business parlance, we've got two percent of market share. We've got a long way to go."[31]

So, if the conservative Church is not going away, what happens when Christian restoration fails to materialize? Right now the *Christianization* of the United States provides a lot of impetus for the conservative presence in the public arena. The dream of a Christian America funds single-issue church groups, policy centers, and religious lobbying efforts. If that goal does not materialize, what will the Church do next? It will not stop growing, but it will have to find another reason to exist.

THE DREAM OF A CHRISTIAN NATION

The effort to *Christianize* America is not new. It was there at the creation of the Republic. The Federalist Party supported established religion. The clergy then considered Jefferson's deism a threat to the social order. As early as 1802, Hamilton was proposing the creation of a Christian Constitutional Society to promote Christianity *and* the Constitution.[32] The truth is that religion is a quick sell. It offers politicians a convenient, populist appeal and serves as a proxy for tradition in a country that is still relatively young. The Federalist religious expediency irritated Thomas Jefferson:

> In every country and in every age, the priest has been hostile to liberty. He is always in alliance with the despot, abetting his abuses in return for protection of his own. It

is easier to acquire wealth and power by this combination than by deserving them, and to effect this, they have perverted the purest religion ever preached to man into mystery and jargon, unintelligible to all mankind, and therefore the safer engine for their purpose.[33]

Every generation of Americans has seen its fair share of religious efforts to *Christianize* our society. Fortunately, other factors in the American character keep those efforts in check: America's open religious market and social mobility curbs the religious impetus to push for a "winner-takes-all" approach.[34] Another consequence of American "voluntarism" is the constant diffusion of doctrinal intransigence. In pre-Westphalia Europe, being Lutheran was as irrevocable as living in Saxony, being Catholic as definite as being Spaniard. Under those circumstances, doctrines can be used to divide. In the United States, the ability to move from faith to faith, as one moves from one region to another or from a social class to the next, helps Americans develop an appreciation for the relative truth of all faiths. Father Giovanni Grassi, an Italian Jesuit who served as president of Georgetown College between 1812 and 1817, was astonished by this mobility:

> Every sect there is held as good, every road as correct, and every error as the insignificant weakness of poor mortals.... Those who describe themselves as members of one or another of the sects do not thereby profess an abiding adherence to the doctrines of the founders of the sect.... And many, when asked, do not answer "I believe," but simply, "I was brought up in such a persuasion."[35]

We should be relieved that our Founders knew better than to wish for earthly Christian perfection. They were never inclined to create a divinely sanctioned nation, nor a divinely instructed political order. Products of the Enlightenment, they saw their task as creating a government established *by the people, for the people*. The people alone were its source of legitimacy. Similarly, they did not speak of THE perfect Union, but "a more perfect Union." Bound by the practical limits of their age and the political compromises required to create the Republic, they knew their endeavor was a "work in progress." The Bill of Rights is proof enough of the evolving nature of the American compact.

The vision that drives contemporary Christian conservatives comes dangerously close to idolatry: loyalty to country that runs as deep as loyalty to the Kingdom of God. There is, of course, no biblical basis for this version of American Exceptionalism. A sympathetic observer such as Charles Marsh, professor of religion at the University of Virginia, takes stock of conservative Christianity these days by lamenting:

> What will it take for evangelicals in the United States to recognize our mistaken loyalty? We have increasingly isolated ourselves from the shared faith of the global Church, and there is no denying that our Faustian bargain for access and power has

undermined the credibility of our moral and evangelistic witness in the world. The Hebrew prophets might call us to repentance, but repentance is a tough demand for a people utterly convinced of their righteousness.[36]

The dream of legitimating America as God's perfect country may inspire zealous Christian patriots; but is bad religion and bad politics. It is bad religion because no temporal nation can be on equal footing with God's realm. It is bad politics because the American project *is still being perfected*. A Christian America might tarnish the faith in the way the Crusades and the religious wars did back in Europe. It might also end the ongoing evolution of the first new nation.

The Founders hoped to create a framework that was flexible enough to hold us all together while we evolved into "the people of these United States." But the project was unfinished, open-ended. It took far too long, for instance, to rid ourselves of slavery, and only at the cost of a bloody civil war. American women waited nearly 150 years to win the franchise in a land where "all [were supposedly] created equal." The Civil Rights movement, the women's movement, and the gay movement in the second half of the twentieth century certainly remind us that the Founders' dream for an inclusive nation is yet to be fully achieved. The wave of new immigrants at the end of the century indicates there are still exciting new chapters to be written. As an ideal, national religious perfection might inspire some. But as a concrete reality it would be a heavy burden—freeing the chosen, and imprisoning the rest of us.

Each age contributes to America's long-term goal of a more perfect Union. Ours will be no different. There is yet much work to be done. In their efforts to "restore" a Christian nation, conservative Christians are trying to make their own contribution to this process. Unfortunately, they are double-yoked to a simplistic faith (Dominionism) and an imaginary country (a sectarian Republic). Thus, they end up bestowing upon their earthly citizenship a status that ought to be reserved for their heavenly home. And they transform a beautiful Arminian faith into a Constantinean political juggernaut. One can only hope that mistaken loyalties and misplaced righteousness do not last for long, and that eventually they will run their due course.

NOTES

CHAPTER 1

1. For the purposes of this work, Church with a capital C is used in a theological sense. It represents the universal community of Christian believers. It includes the myriad denominations that fall under the Christian banner. It does not mean established religion as described by Troeltsch (1960).

2. Several students of American religion have outlined these three strategies for dealing with modernity. For a theological treatment see H. Richard Niebuhr, *Christ and Culture* (1951). For a sociological one see Peter L. Berger, *The Heretical Imperative* (1979).

3. Alan Cooperman, "Coming Soon to a Church Near You: Hollywood Skips Movie Theaters with 3,200-Screen Opening" (2005), A1.

4. Stephen Warner's work (1993, 1997) details the larger societal processes that affected American denominations during the period in question. So does Robert Wuthnow's. Wuthnow argues that "in religion, the so-called seeker phenomenon is the most visible example of loose connections.... While attendance at religious services has held fairly steady over the past half-century, membership in religious organizations has declined significantly since the 1950s, and interest in nontraditional forms of spirituality, ranging from self-help groups to books about angels and near-death experiences, has increased. Fewer people belong to the same denomination or congregation as their parents did or expect to remain in the same religious organization as long as they once did. In the process, spirituality has not so much become privatized as personalized, meaning that individuals connect themselves loosely with a large number of traditions, groups, and spiritual networks." (Robert Wuthnow, "Democratic Liberalism and the Challenge of Diversity in Late-Twentieth-Century America" [1999], 29.)

5. For more on the shift see Robert Wuthnow's *The Restructuring of American Religion* (1988).

6. For a description of America's civil religion, see Robert Bellah's "Civil Religion in America" (1967). See also James Reichley's, *Religion in American Public Life* (1985). For a

review of how religion influenced our moral vision see Rhys H. Williams, "Visions of the Good Society and the Religious Roots of American Political Culture" (1999).

7. I am grateful to N. J. Demerath III for his framing of civil religion and the U.S. denominational autonomy in the article, "Civil Society and Civil Religion as Mutually Dependent" (2003).

8. "The emphasis upon equality, between religions as among men, which intensified after the American revolution, gave the subsequent development of religious institutions in America its special character. Democratic and religious values have grown together. The results have been that, on the one hand, Americans see religion as essential to the support of the democratic institutions they cherish, and therefore feel that all Americans should profess some sort of religious faith; on the other hand, American denominations stress the ethical side of religion, which they all have in common (and which is closely associated with other democratic values) rather than stressing transcendental beliefs wherein they differ. At the same time, democracy, by giving religious institutions a specific role in American society, has allowed them to proliferate, to adjust to peculiar needs, and to have a limited influence on their members' lives," Seymour Lipset, *The First New Nation* (1963), 169.

9. "Just as the three great religions are the basic subdivisions of the American people, so are the three great communions felt to be recognized expressions of the spiritual aspect of the American Way of Life. This underlying unity not only supplies limits within which their conflicts and tensions may operate and beyond which they cannot go—it also supplies the common content of the three communities," Will Herberg, *Protestant, Catholic, Jew* (1955), 247.

10. See Andrew Greeley, *The Denominational Society* (1972).

11. "I believe in an America where the separation of church and state is absolute—where no Catholic prelate would tell the President (should he be Catholic) how to act, and no Protestant minister would tell his parishioners for whom to vote—where no church or church school is granted any public funds or political preference—and where no man is denied public office merely because his religion differs from the President, who might appoint him, or the people who might elect him.

> —I believe in an America that is officially neither Catholic, Protestant, nor Jewish—where no public official either requests or accepts instructions on public policy from the Pope, the National Council of Churches, or any other ecclesiastical source—where no religious body seeks to impose its will directly or indirectly upon the general populace or the public acts of its officials—and where religious liberty is so indivisible that an act against one church is treated as an act against all.
>
> —For while this year it may be a Catholic against whom the finger of suspicion is pointed, in other years it has been, and may someday be again, a Jew—or a Quaker—or a Unitarian—or a Baptist. It was Virginia's harassment of Baptist preachers, for example, that helped lead to Jefferson's statute of religious freedom. Today I may be the victim—but tomorrow it may be you—until the whole fabric of our harmonious society is ripped at a time of great national peril.
>
> —Finally, I believe in an America where religious intolerance will someday end—where all men and all churches are treated as equal—where every man has the same right to attend or not attend the church of his choice—where there is no Catholic vote, no anti-Catholic vote, no bloc voting of any kind—and where Catholics, Protestants, and Jews, at both the lay and pastoral level, will refrain from those attitudes of disdain and division, which have so often marred their works in the past, and promote instead the American ideal of brotherhood.

—That is the kind of America in which I believe. And it represents the kind of Presidency in which I believe—a great office that must neither be humbled by making it the instrument of any one religious group nor tarnished by arbitrarily withholding its occupancy from the members of any one religious group. I believe in a President whose religious views are his own private affair, neither imposed by him upon the nation or imposed by the nation upon him as a condition to holding that office.

—I would not look with favor upon a President working to subvert the first amendment's guarantees of religious liberty. Nor would our system of checks and balances permit him to do so—and neither do I look with favor upon those who would work to subvert Article VI of the Constitution by requiring a religious test—even by indirection—for it. If they disagree with that safeguard they should be out openly working to repeal it.

—I want a Chief Executive whose public acts are responsible to all groups and obligated to none—who can attend any ceremony, service, or dinner his office may appropriately require of him—and whose fulfillment of his Presidential oath is not limited or conditioned by any religious oath, ritual, or obligation.

—This is the kind of America I believe in—and this is the kind I fought for in the South Pacific, and the kind my brother died for in Europe. No one suggested then that we may have a "divided loyalty," and that we did "not believe in liberty," or that we belonged to a disloyal group that threatened the "freedoms for which our forefathers died."

—And in fact this is the kind of America for which our forefathers died—when they fled here to escape religious test oaths that denied office to members of less favored churches—when they fought for the Constitution, the Bill of Rights, and the Virginia Statute of Religious Freedom—and when they fought at the shrine I visited today, the Alamo. For side by side with Bowie and Crockett died McCafferty, and Bailey, and Carey—but no one knows whether they were Catholic or not. For there was no religious test at the Alamo." President John F. Kennedy, "Address of Senator John F. Kennedy to the Greater Houston Ministerial Association" (1960), http://www.jfklibrary.org/j091260.htm.

12. "'The government of the United States is not in any sense founded on the Christian Religion.' Those words, penned in Article 11 of the 1797 Treaty of Tripoli, are as succinct a statement as we have from the Founding Fathers on the role of religion in our government. Their authorship is ascribed variously to George Washington, under whom the treaty was negotiated, or to John Adams, under who it took effect, or sometimes to Joel Barlow, U.S. Consul to Algiers, friend of Thomas Jefferson and Thomas Paine, and himself no stranger to the religious ferment of the era, having served as a chaplain in the Revolutionary Army. But the validity of the document transcends its authorship for a simple reason: it was ratified. It was debated in the U.S. Senate and signed into law by President Adams without a breath of controversy or complaint concerning its secular language, and so stands today as an official description of the founders' intent." Editorial, "The Great Debate of Our Season," *Mother Jones* (2005), 26.

13. Finkel, "It's a Victory for People Like Us" (2004), A03.

14. Zernike and Broder, "The Mood of the Electorate: War? Jobs? No, Character Counted Most to Voters" (2004), 1.

15. CNN Presents, *The Fight over Faith*, November 20, 2004.

16. Here I include groups whose faith sets them at odds with secular America. While I am aware that there are important differences among these (see, for instance, Nancy

Ammerman, *Bible Believers: Fundamentalists in the Modern World* [1987], 3–6, for a careful description of the differences between Evangelicals and Fundamentalists), they are similar in their experience of marginality. Gallup and Castelli put their numbers at 31 percent of Americans in *The People's Religion* (1989), 93.

17. Cooperman and Edsall, "Evangelicals Say They Led Charge for GOP" (2004), A1.
18. Ibid.
19. Lampman, "A 'Moral Voter' Majority? The Cultural Wars Are Back" (2004), 4.
20. Seelye, "Moral Values Cited as a Defining Issue of the Election" (2004), 4.
21. Incidentally, the high-level of church attendance in America is not a recent phenomenon. Alexis de Tocqueville remarked after his tour of the United States in 1930 that "there is no country in the world where the Christian religion retains a greater influence over the souls of men than in America," *Democracy in America* (1954) 1, 314. A summary of reports from other nineteenth-century travelers finds in America "religious assemblages (that) were being held at one place or another practically all the time.... Church services were always crowded on Sundays.... Church going... was all the rage in New York... the high percentage of males in the audience was in sharp contrast to their paucity in English services," Max Berger, *The British Traveller in America, 1836–1860* (1943), 133–134.
22. See James Davison Hunter's book, *American Evangelicalism* (1983), for a full analysis of how the 1920s battles are related to the return of Fundamentalism in the 1970s and the 1980s.
23. Luke, chapter 6, verses 20–23.
24. World with a capital W is used here in a theological sense as well. It means all that is not divine, not sacred; and therefore all that is perishable, sinful, and depraved in everyday reality.
25. Darren Sherkat argues that supernatural "compensators" add value to the religious practices of believers. In describing religious preferences, dynamics, and choices, Sherkat claims that "religious choices are often driven by adaptive preferences. People are comforted by familiar religious explanations, and they find value and solace in the supernatural rewards and compensators of familiar religious goods." "Religious Socialization: Sources of Influence and Influences of Agency" (2003), 153. Rodney Stark and William Sims Bainbridge proposed an earlier version of this form of *exchange theory* in their work *The Future of Religion* (1985).
26. For a comparison of similarities and dissimilarities between Fundamentalist movements in Christianity, Judaism, and Islam, see the edited works of Martin Marty and Scott Appleby (1993a, 1993b, 1994, and 1995).
27. For an analysis of the early Christian community, see Blasi, Turcotte, and Duhaime, *Handbook of Early Christianity* (2002); Gillian Clark, *Christianity and Roman Society* (2004); Kyu Sam Han, *Jerusalem and the Early Jesus Movement* (2002); and Charles Horton, *The Earliest Gospels* (2004).
28. On the emergence of Christendom—the merging of the Christian faith with temporal political power in Europe, see Karl Baus, *The Imperial Church from Constantine to the Early Middle Ages* (1980); Karl Baus and Hubert Jedin, *From the Apostolic Community to Constantine* (1980); and Jean Danielou and Henri Marrou, *The Christian Centuries* (1964).
29. Stanley Chodorow et al., *The Mainstream of Civilization* (1989), 281.
30. Andrew Greeley, *The Catholic Imagination* (2000), 11–12.
31. For a theological analysis of Christian marginality, see chapter 2 ("Christ against Culture") of H. Richard Niebuhr's *Christ and Culture* (1951).
32. For more on that research see Roger Finke and Rodney Stark's *The Churching of America, 1776–1990* (1992). See also Roger Finke and Rodney Stark's "The Dynamics

of Religious Economies" (2003). Laurence Iannaccone's "Religious Markets and the Economics of Religion" (1992), and "Why Strict Churches are Strong" (1994) provide similar data.

33. Finke and Stark, op. cit., 254. The authors' italics are retained.

34. See Max Weber, *Economy and Society* (1978); Ernst Troeltsch, *The Social Teaching of the Christian Churches* (1960); and H. Richard Niebuhr, *The Social Sources of Denominationalism* (1957).

35. David Tracy offers the best theological description of an "analogical" faith in *The Analogical Imagination* (1981). For a sociological treatment I recommend Andrew Greeley's *The Catholic Imagination* (2000).

36. This is not to say that Roman Catholicism in America does not have its own tensions with the secular world. Witness the issues of lay empowerment, ordination of women, clerical celibacy, and church governance faced by the American Church.

37. Needless to say, not all conservative or Evangelical groups would fall into the category of *marginal Christianity*. Research shows that even among those groups there is a divide between *traditionalists*, *centrists*, and *modernists*: "Every four years since 1992 a group of political scientists sponsored by the Pew Forum on Religion and Public Life has attempted to track these shifting loyalties; with each survey," says John C. Green, a professor of political science at the University of Akron and a member of the group, "the argument for the culture war in religion gets more convincing." "The survey subdivides the three largest religious groups—evangelicals, mainstream Protestants, and Catholics—into 'traditionalists,' 'centrists,' and 'modernists.' Traditionalists are defined as having a 'high view of the authority of the Bible' and worshipping regularly; they say they want to preserve 'traditional beliefs and practices in a changing world.' Centrists are defined as wanting to adapt beliefs to new times, while modernists have unabashedly heterodox beliefs, worship infrequently, and support upending traditional doctrines to reflect a modern view. The three categories are similar in size (centrists are a little larger and modernists a little smaller) and have remained the same size over the dozen-year of the survey. On a wide range of issues, traditionalists agree with one another across denominations, while strongly disagreeing with modernists in their own religion. For example, 32 percent of traditionalist evangelicals and 26 percent of traditionalist Catholics say abortion should always be illegal, compared with only 7 percent of modernist evangelicals and 3 percent of modernist Catholics. Perhaps the survey's most surprising finding is the degree to which evangelicals are splintering along the same lines as all other denominations. About half of the evangelicals surveyed in 2004 defined themselves as centrist or modernist. This reflects a new movement of what are sometimes called 'freestyle evangelicals.' They are often married women with children who attend one of those suburban megachurches where the doctrine is traditional but the style is modern. Their morals are conservative but their politics are more heterodox, featuring considerable support for education and the environment. In time they may erode the stereotype of evangelicals as overwhelmingly conservative," Hanna Rosin, "Beyond Belief" (2005), 118.

38. *Dispensationalism* is the theological system of Biblical interpretation that describes different periods of human history as "dispensations." God works out distinct covenants for each period as part of the process of redeeming his chosen among humankind. For detailed explanation of the system see Hal Harless, *How Firm a Foundation* (2004). Other works of relevance include Michael D. Williams, *This World Is Not My Home* (2003); and Ronald M. Henzel, *Darby, Dualism, and the Decline of Dispensationalism* (2003).

39. Philippians chapter 2, verses 10–11.

40. There is a whole series of popular novels by Tim LaHaye and Jerry B. Jenkins solely dedicated to the issue of history's endpoint: *Left Behind* (1995), *Tribulation Force* (1996), *Soul Harvest* (1998), *Apollyon* (1999), *Assassins* (1999), *The Mark* (2000), and *The Indwelling* (2000). These books can be found in supermarkets and popular bookstores all over the United States. They describe the last days of humanity and Jesus Christ's return to rule over his followers and all creation. The whole series has sold more than 70 million copies so far. Three of the novels have been made into movies.

41. Its rationality runs along the lines described by Max Weber in *The Protestant Ethic and the Spirit of Capitalism* (2002).

42. A common practice among mainline Protestant churches in America is the sharing of resources in areas where their presence is scarce. In those areas, churches affiliated with two different denominations may share a sanctuary; or a local congregation with an equally divided membership may affiliate with one particular denomination for a limited term (say three years or so) before switching to cooperative work with the other denomination.

43. This paragraph is based on a number of theological, sociological, and historical works. For a theological treatment of the marginal worldview I recommend Timothy George and Alister E McGrath, *For All the Saints* (2003); R. C. Sproul, *Getting the Gospel Right* (2003); James Boyce and Benjamin Sasse, *Here We Stand* (2004); and Anthony Campolo, *Speaking My Mind* (2004). For a sociological analysis of that world, see Nancy T. Ammerman, *Bible Believers* (1987); and James D. Hunter, *American Evangelicalism* (1983) and *Evangelicalism* (1987). Among historical reviews I would suggest Winthrop Hudson and John Corrigan, *Religion in America* (1999); and Darryl Hart, *That Old-Time Religion in Modern America* (2002). To understand how the faith relates to public affairs, see Michael Cromartie, *A Public Faith: Evangelicals and Civic Engagement* (2003); and Esther Kaplan, *With God on Their Side* (2004).

44. Meredith McGuire, *Religion: The Social Context* (2002), 303.

45. Wade Clark Roof, *A Generation of Seekers* (1993), 154, 177, and 179.

46. Megachurches have become an increasing topic of interest for graduate theological theses and dissertations. Those studies range from profiling the churches, to discussing their leadership, or just documenting how megachurches come into being. Among graduate research on the topic I found Wilson Beardsley, *The Pastor As Change Agent in the Growth of a Southern Baptist Megachurch Model* (1991); Charles Hughes, *Developing An Effective Ministry with Mid Life Single Adults in a Mega Church* (2000); Louis Attles, *Leadership That Facilitates Church Numerical Growth: An Epistemology of Mega Church Leadership* (2001); and Eugene Voss, *Surviving and Thriving in the Shadows of the Mega-Church* (2001).

47. Jane Lampman, "For Evangelicals, a Bid to 'Reclaim America'" (2004), 16.

48. On the matter of the transformation of American conservative politics, see Sara Diamond, *Roads to Dominion* (1995); and Godfrey Hodgson, *The World Turned Right Side Up* (1996). For a treatment of the current religious mix in American conservatism see Kenneth Heineman, *God Is a Conservative* (1998), and an edited volume by Kenneth Wald, *Religion and Politics in the United States* (1997).

CHAPTER 2

1. Lois Romano, "For Wednesday Church Services, a Youth Revival" (2005), A3.
2. Ibid.
3. "Jesus, himself an astonishing master of irony, emulates Yahweh in the hyperbolical demands of his teaching, with insistence upon perfections that mere humans scarcely can achieve. Rhetorical excess in Jesus seeks to persuade us to yield up easier moralities for more

difficult ethical choices, for what might be called the Sublime awareness of others at the expense of our all-too-natural selfishness. Since Jesus, unlike Christianity, never asserted he was the Messiah, his hyperbolical ethics are all the more unnerving. Can Yahweh and Jesus be one in this regard, since the Law, despite St. Paul's misreading of it, does not ask us for perfection? The Pharisees made that clear, and if Jesus sometimes argued with and against them, essentially the disagreement turned upon his fierce yearnings for perfection. That may be why he asserted that he came to fulfill the Law, and not to abolish it," Harold Bloom, *Jesus and Yahweh: The Names Divine* (2005), 133–134.

4. Max Weber was perhaps the first sociologist to point out the inevitable clash between religion's lofty ideals and the imperfect conditions of social reality, especially in his discussion of the different types of religious leadership (prophetic versus priestly) and religious salvation in *Economy and Society* 1 (1978): 439–451, 529–601.

5. For more on the Shakers see Stephen J. Stein, *The Shaker Experience in America* (1992); or Edward Andrews, *The People Called Shakers* (1963).

6. For a thoughtful reflection on the conditions of late modernity, see Anthony Giddens' *Modernity and Self-Identity* (1991) and *Runaway World* (2000).

7. http://www.gospelcom.net/nehemiah/ (Spring 2005).

8. Tamara Eaton, "How to Know God's Will?" http://www.chfweb.com/articles/week45.htm.

9. The information for the *Lakewood Church* and the Osteen ministry comes from an article by Lois Romano, "'The Smiling Preacher' Builds on Large Following" (2005), A1, A10.

10. Ibid., A10.

11. On the social conditions of biblical times, see for instance, the work of Norman K. Gottwald, particularly *The Tribes of Yahweh* (1979), *The Hebrew Bible* (1985), and *The Politics of Ancient Israel* (2001).

12. Alan Cooperman, "Coming Soon to a Church Near You: Hollywood Skips Movie Theaters with 3,200-Screen Opening" (2005), A9.

13. Ibid.

14. Ibid.

15. Information on Gwen Shamblin's enterprises comes from R. Marie Griffith's "The Gospel of Born-Again Bodies" (2005), B6–B8.

16. http://www.loc.gov/catdir/description/random0413/2003055707.html.

17. R. Marie Griffith, op. cit., B8.

18. http://www.christiansoulmates.com.

19. http://www.adammeeteve.com/.

20. http://www.adammeeteve.com/pages/home.html.

21. http://www.kingsingles.com/Soul_Mate.htm.

22. http://www.christiansingleseniors.com/.

23. http://christianparadise.com/singles05.html.

24. http://www.AmericanSingles.com.

25. For a tour of the constellation of CCM styles, visit the *Christian Music* Web site, http://www.christianmusic.com/genres/rock.htm. Musicians for each style are listed in separate pages. One can download the most popular songs, sample the CDs, and read music reviews on each band and each style.

26. For more on the debate see Samuele Bacchiocchi, *The Christian and Rock Music* (2000); Jeff Godwin, *What's Wrong with Christian Rock?* (1990); Jay R. Howard and John M. Steck, *Apostles of Rock* (2004); Mark Joseph, *Faith, God & Rock 'n' Roll* (2003); Dana Key and Steve Rabey, *Don't Stop the Music* (1989); John J. Thompson, *Raised by Wolves:*

The Story of Christian Rock & Roll (2000); and Jack Wheaton, *The Crisis in Christian Music* (2000).

27. Bacchiocchi, op. cit., vi.
28. http://www.av1611.org/crock/crockids.html.
29. http://www.delafont.com/gospel.htm.
30. http://www.roarbush.com/ccmplus/crcnseur.htm.
31. For CCM *Magazine* go to http://www.ccmcom.com. For *Christian Rock Net* go to http://www.christianrock.net. For *Christian Music* go to http://www.christianmusic.com/genres/rock.htm. For *CC Music* go to http://www.ccmusic.org.
32. For *Jesus Freak Hideout* go to http://www.jesusfreakhideout.com. For *Worship Circus* go to http://www.worshipcircus.com.
33. http://powerlight.org/fest/fest.html.
34. For more on the process of splintering modern life into the public and the private see Robert Bellah et al., *Habits of the Heart* (1985), especially the last sections of chapter 2 ("The Manager," and "The Therapist").
35. For a more in-depth treatment of Christianity's view of work, see James Cochrane and Gerald West (eds.), *The Three-Fold Cord: Theology, Work and Labour* (1991); Arthur Geoghegan, *The Attitude toward Labor in Early Christianity and Ancient Culture* (1945); John Houck and Oliver Williams (eds.), *Co-Creation and Capitalism: John Paul II's "Laborem Exercens"* (1983); Peter Johnson and Chris Sugden (eds.), *Markets, Fair Trade and the Kingdom of God* (2001); Paul Marshall, Edward Vanderkloet, and Peter Nijkamp, *Labour of Love* (1980); Thomas Nitsch, Joseph Philips Jr., and Edward Fitzsimmons (eds.), *On the Condition of Labor and the Social Question One Hundred Years Later* (1994); and Gregory F. Pierce (ed.), *Of Human Hands: A Reader in the Spirituality of Work* (1991).
36. For a discussion of the Lutheran approach to work see Heinrich Bornkamm, *Luther's Doctrine of the Two Kingdoms* (1966); and F. E. Cranz, *An Essay on the Development of Luther's Thought on Justice, Law and Society* (1969).
37. See Max Weber, *The Protestant Ethic and the Spirit Of Capitalism* (2002).
38. For more on the Church's relation to middle-age and premodern economies see Jacques Le Goff, *Your Money or Your Life* (1988); Nigel Saul, *The Oxford Illustrated History of Medieval England* (1997); Virginia Bainbridge, *Gilds in the Medieval Countryside* (1996); Martin Heale, *The Dependent Priorities of Medieval English Monasteries* (2004); Angus MacKay, *Society, Economy, and Religion in Late Medieval Castile* (1987); James Stayer, *The German Peasant's War and Anabaptist Community of Goods* (1991); and Clifford Backman, *The Decline and Fall of Medieval Sicily* (1995).
39. For a general treatment of the American churches role in the industrial era see Sydney Ahlstrom, *A Religious History of the American People* (1972); Hudson and Corrigan, *Religion in America* (1999); and James Reichley, *Religion in American Public Life* (1985). For a more specific treatment of American religion in the industrial age see Susan Curtis, *A Consuming Faith* (1991); Gary Dorrien, *The Making of American Liberal Theology* (2001); Donald Gorrell, *The Age of Social Responsibility* (1988); Paul Phillips, *A Kingdom on Earth* (1996); and Robert Wauzzinski, *Between God and Gold* (1993).
40. http://www.cmdahome.org.
41. http://www.clsnet.com.
42. http://www.clsnet.com/clsPages/vision.php.
43. For nurses see http://www.intervarsity.org/ncf/ncfindex.html; for pharmacists see http://www.cpfi.org/cp3/; for entrepreneurs see http://www.christianjobs.com/cen_home.asp; for accountants see http://finance.groups.yahoo.com/group/christianaccountants/;

for managers see http://www.christianity.com/partner/0,,7419,00.html; for engineers see http://engr.calvin.edu/ces/; for sociologists see http://www.christiansociology.com/; for economists see http://www.gordon.edu/ace/; for biologists see http://home.messiah.edu/~ghess/acbhome.htm; for geologists see http://www.wheaton.edu/ACG/; for writers see http://www.christianwritersguild.com); for periodical publishers see http://www.epassoc.org/about_epa.html; for booksellers see http://www.cbaonline.org/; for broadcasters see http://www.icbinternational.com/about/; for real estate agents see http://www.hismove.com/; for farmers see http://www.fcfi.org/; for firefighters see http://fellowshipofchristianfirefighters.com/; for police officers see http://www.fcpo.org/; for military officers see http://www.gospelcom.net/ocf/index.php; for pilots see http://www.christianpilots.org/Mission/mission.html; and for airline personnel see http://www.fcap.org/aboutfcap.htm.

44. For *Christian Jobs* see http://www.christianjobs.com. The *Salem Web Network* can be found at http://www.salemwebnetwork.com/.

45. The *Christian Career Center* is located at http://www.christiancareercenter.com/, while the *Gospel Com Net*'s URL is http://www.gospelcom.net/. *Christian Employments* is found at http://www.christianemployments.com, and its parent company is found at http://www.enterglobe.com/.

46. *Christian Employment*'s URL is http://www.christianemployment.com. *Christia Net* is found at http://www.christianet.com/christianjobs/. *Christian Find It* is located at http://www.christian-findit.com/. *Praize Jobs* is at http://www.praize.com/Jobs/. *Jobs 4 Jesus* is at http://landing.domainsponsor.com/ds. *America's Christian Job Source*'s URL is http://ministryemployment.com/.

47. *InterCristo*'s URL is http://intercristo.searchease.com. For *CRISTA Ministries* go to http://www.crista.org/.

48. *Christian Placements* is located at http://www.churchstaffing.com/cp/index2.htm. The first part of the URL also serves as the address for *Church Staffing*.

49. Sandra G. Boodman, "Seeking Divine Protection" (2005), F5.

50. Information for this section comes from the plans' Web sites (Medi-Share's is at http://www.medi-share.org; Samaritan Ministries International is at http://www.samaritanministries.org/; *Christian Brotherhood Newsletter* is found at http://christianbrotherhood.org/index2.html) and Sandra Boodman, op. cit., F1.

51. http://christianbrotherhood.org/h/welcome.html.

52. http://www.medi-share.org/.

53. http://www.medi-share.org/.

54. http://www.tccm.org/.

55. Sandra G. Boodman, op. cit., F5.

56. .Ibid.

57. For more on confraternities in general see Christopher Black, *Italian Confraternities in the Sixteenth Century* (1989); John Donnelly and Michael Maher, *Confraternities & Catholic Reform in Italy, France, and Spain* (1999); Donald Durnbaugh, *Every Need Supplied* (1974); Maureen Flynn, *Sacred Charity* (1989); and John Henderson, *Piety and Charity in Late Medieval Florence* (1994). For the role of Church gilds in Europe see Virginia Bainbridge, *Gilds in the Medieval Countryside* (1996); Judith Bennett, *Sisters and Workers in the Middle Ages* (1989); David Crouch, *Piety, Fraternity, and Power* (2000); and Sylvia Thrupp, *Society and History* (1977). The civic role of confraternities is discussed by Nicholas Terpstra, *Lay Confraternities and Civic Religion in Renaissance Bologna* (1995); Susan Webster, *Art and Ritual in Golden-Age Spain* (1988); and Barbara Wisch and Diane Ahl, *Confraternities and the Visual Arts in Renaissance Italy* (2000). For the role of confraternities in the New

World, see David Beito, *From Mutual Aid to the Welfare State* (2000); and Albert Meyers and Diane Hopkins, *Manipulating the Saints* (1988).

58. Meredith McGuire, *Religion: The Social Context* (2002), 42.

59. Christopher Ellison, "Religious Involvement and Self-Perceptions among Black Americans" (1993), 1028.

60. That sense of optimism was present at the founding of our country and remains strong throughout American history. Crèvecoeur's words describe the general feeling about our new nation at the early days of the Republic: "What then is the American, this new man? He is an American, who leaving behind him all his ancient prejudices and manners, receives new ones from the new mode of life he has embraced.... He becomes an American by being received in the broad lap of our great *Alma Mater*. The American is a new man, who acts upon new principles; he must therefore entertain new ideas and form new opinions," *Letters from an American farmer* (n.d.), 49–50.

61. This desire to create a theocratic social order dates back to the early days of our nation, and even then came mixed with politics. In his efforts to reenergize the political fortunes of the Federalist Party, Alexander Hamilton tried to create a Christian Constitutionalist Society, whose explicit goal was to promote Christianity and the Constitution, but more importantly to take the religious vote from the Democratic-Republican Party (see Clifford S. Griffin, *Their Brothers' Keepers* [1960]). Lyman Beecher, a Congregationalist leader and founder of the *Connecticut Moral Society*, successively involved in Federalist, Whig, and Republican politics (in that order), pushed for a "clerically dominated social order by means of voluntary social and moral reform societies that would give the clergy an influential role in forming public opinion and molding public legislation," William G. McLoughlin, introduction to Charles G. Finney, *Lectures on the Revivals of Religion* (1960), xviii.

Some of our Founders saw the need for an established religion for the more practical purpose of controlling the mobs, and instilling in them some sense of morality: "After the revolution, conservatives among the Virginia leadership, including George Washington, John Marshall, and the volatile Patrick Henry became convinced that restoration of direct state support for religion was needed to strengthen social stability. In 1784 Henry introduced a bill that would authorize 'a moderate tax or contribution annually for the support of the Christian religion, or of some Christian church, denomination or communion of Christians, or for some form of Christian worship.' Henry argued that state support for Christianity was justified on purely secular grounds. 'The general diffusion of Christian knowledge [has] a natural tendency to correct the morals of men, restrain their vices, and preserve the peace of society,'" James Reichley, *Religion in American Public Life* (1985), 87. Those feelings were echoed by Benjamin Franklin as well: "The great mass of men and women have need of the motives of religion to restrain them from vice, to support their virtue, and retain them in the practice of it till it becomes habitual," James Reichley, op. cit., 101. In response James Madison in his *Memorial and Remonstrance against Religious Assessments*, argued that "The Religion ... of every man must be left to the conviction and conscience of every man; and it is the right of every man to exercise it as these may dictate ... [Public taxation for the support of religion necessarily] violates equality by subjecting some to peculiar burdens ... [To claim that Christianity needs the support of government] is a contradiction to the Christian religion itself; for every page of it disavows a dependence on the powers of this world: it is a contradiction to fact: for it is known that this Religion both existed and flourished, not only without the support of human laws, but in spite of every opposition from them," James Reichley, op. cit., 88.

CHAPTER 3

1. Jane Lampman, "For Evangelicals, a Bid to 'Reclaim America'" (2004), 17.
2. Ralph Blumenthal, "Texas Governor Draws Criticism for a Bill-Signing Event at an Evangelical School" (2005), A12.
3. Information for this paragraph comes from Peter Slevin's article, "Judge Upholds Prayer Limits in Indiana State House" (2006), A3.
4. All one has to do to document the bipartisan nature of the times is to read about President Lyndon Johnson's dealings with Republican Congressional leaders. See for instance, Robert Dallek, *Flawed Giant: Lyndon Johnson and His Times, 1961–1973* (1998); or Tom Wicker, *JFK and LBJ* (1968). Or read the transcription of the president's tapes in two volumes: Johnson and Beschloss, *Taking Charge: The Johnson White House Tapes, 1963–1964* (1997); and *Reaching for Glory: Lyndon Johnson's Secret White House's Tapes, 1964-1965* (2001).
5. Information regarding the study comes from Ceci Connolly, "Teen Pledges Barely Cut STD Rates, Study Says" (2005), A3; and Ronald J. Sider, "The Scandal of the Evangelical Conscience" (2005), http://www.christianitytoday.com/bc/2005/001/3.8.html.
6. See Frederick Clarkson, "Theocratic Dominionism Gains Influence" (1994), http://www.publiceye.org/magazine/v08n1/chrisrel.html.
7. Ibid.
8. "You Ain't Seen Nothing Yet," *The Economist* (2005), http://www.economist.com/world/na/printerfriendly.cfm?storyID=4102212.
9. http://www.yuricareport.com/Dominionism/TheDespoilingOfAmerica.htm.
10. For more information on the *Dominionist* ideology see Bruce Barron, *Heaven on Earth? The Social and Political Agendas of Dominion Theology* (1992); Frederick Clarkson, *Eternal Hostility: The Struggle between Theocracy and Democracy* (1997); and Sara Diamond's *Roads to Dominion* (1995). Chris Hedges provide a short and chilling description of the ideology: "What the disparate sects of this movement, known as Dominionism, share is an obsession with political power. A decades-long refusal to engage in politics at all following the Scopes trial has been replaced by a call for Christian 'dominion' over the nation and, eventually, over the earth itself. Dominionists preach that Jesus has called them to build the kingdom of God in the here and now, whereas previously it was thought that we would have to wait for it. America becomes, in this militant Biblicism, an agent of God, and all political and intellectual opponents of America's Christian leaders are viewed, quite simply, as agents of Satan. Under Christian dominion, America will no longer be a sinful and fallen nation but one in which the Ten Commandments form the basis of our legal system, Creationism and 'Christian values' form the basis of our educational system, and the media and the government proclaim the Good News to one and all. Aside from its proselytizing mandate, the federal government will be reduced to the protection of property rights and 'homeland security.' Some Dominionists (not all of whom accept the label, at least not publicly) would further require all citizens to pay 'tithes' to church organizations empowered by the government to run our social-welfare agencies, and a number of influential figures advocate the death penalty for a host of 'moral crimes,' including apostasy, blasphemy, sodomy, and witchcraft. The only legitimate voices in this state will be Christian. All others will be silenced." In "Feeling the Hate with the National Religious Broadcasters" (2005), 58.
11. http://zena.secureforum.com/Znet/smag/articles/feb95diamond.htm.
12. Pat Robertson, *700 Club*, January 5, 1986 program as quoted in http://www.yuricareport.com/Dominionism/TheDespoilingOfAmerica.htm.

13. The preferred modus operandi of the Christian Right these days is to work through a decentralized set of loose coalitions. These groups enjoy a great deal of autonomy but there is constant networking between leaders, so the reverberations of their work are felt as a united front. For instance, when Roy Moore, the Chief Justice of the Alabama Supreme Court was removed from office in 2004 for refusing to remove a Ten Commandments monument from the Alabama Judiciary Building, over sixty heads of major ministries flew to Dallas at the invitation of *Vision America* to discuss "the threat of activist judges." There are plenty of similar examples of this sort of coordination taking place.

14. More information on the Baptist battles can be found in the work of Nancy Ammerman, *Baptist Battles* (1990) and her edited work, *Southern Baptists Observed* (1993); Grady Cothen, *What Happened to the Southern Baptist Convention* (1993); Bill Leonard, *God's Last and Only Hope* (1990); David Morgan, *The New Crusades, the New Holy Land: Conflict in the Southern Baptist Convention, 1969–1991* (1996); Ellen Rosenberg, *The Southern Baptists: A Subculture in Transition* (1989); and Oran Smith, *The Rise of Baptist Republicanism* (1997).

15. My discussion of the rise of conservative Christianity in American politics is influenced by several works. See, for instance, Sharon Georgianna, *The Moral Majority and Fundamentalism* (1989); or James D. Hunter, *American Evangelicalism* (1983) and *Evangelicalism* (1987). I also use a series of edited works that examined in depth the initial impact of the rise. Among those works I would list David Bromley and Anson Shupe, *New Christian Politics* (1984); Ted Jelen, *Religion and Political Behavior in the United States* (1989); Robert Liebman et al., *The New Christian Right* (1983); and Rhys H. Williams, *Cultural Wars in American Politics: Critical Reviews of a Popular Myth* (1997).

16. Francis Schaeffer, *700 Club*, originally broadcast in 1982; rebroadcast in the week of July 7, 1986, http://www.yuricareport.com/Dominionism/TheDespoilingOfAmerica.htm.

17. All one has to do is to measure the level of education of conservative Christians is to look at the credentials of their leaders: James Dobson has a Ph.D. in child development from the University of Southern California; Pat Robertson has a Doctor of Law degree from Yale University; John Whitehead has a Doctor of Law degree from the University of Arkansas; James Kennedy has two masters' degrees from different universities and a Ph.D. from New York University; Gary North has a Ph.D. in History; Tim Lahaye has a Doctor of Ministry; Jay Grimstead has a Doctor of Ministry, and the list goes on with leaders who hold Doctors of Theology, Education, and Law as well. These are also people who have job experience to be highly effective organizers. Prior to his work with the Christian Right, for instance, Gary Bauer served as President Reagan's Chief Domestic Policy Advisor during the last two years of his administration. Before that he was Under Secretary of Education (beginning in July 1985). Paul Weyrich was the founding president of the Heritage Foundation, and prior to that served as a reporter and radio news director, contributing editorials to the *New York Times*, the *Washington Post*, and the *Wall Street Journal*. Jerry Regier, who preceded Tony Perkins at the Family Research Council was a Reagan Administration official at the Department of Health and Human Services. Tony Perkins, the current president of Family Research Council, served as a two-term state representative in Louisiana, where he authored and passed the nation's first covenant marriage law. These are not the usual storefront ministers who sustained the work of the conservative Church prior to the late 1970s.

18. For more on the class-based rise of marginal Christianity see Martin Riesebrodt, *Pious Passion* (1993); Trollinger, *God's Empire* (1990); and Wagner, *The New Temperance* (1997). Thaddeus Coreno, in an insightful article, summarizes the argument well

(see Coreno, "Fundamentalism as a Class Culture" [2002], 335–360). For more on the theory that marginal Christianity attracted more educated members of mainline denominations see Roof and McKinney, *American Mainline Religion* (1987); and Wuthnow, *The Restructuring of American Religion* (1988).

19. John Sugg, "A Nation under God" (2005), 78.

20. See Margaret Ann Latus, "Ideological PACs and Political Action" (1983), 75–99.

21. See James D. Hunter, *Culture Wars: The Struggle to Define America* (1991), 299.

22. Chris Hedges, op. cit., 55.

23. Jeff Sharlet, "Soldiers of Christ" (2005), 47.

24. In his 2004 address to the National Association of Evangelicals President Bush outlined the common agenda between his government and evangelical causes: a constitutional amendment banning same-sex marriage, support for various antiabortion measures, and opposition to human cloning (David B. Kirkpatrick, "Bush Assures Evangelicals of His Commitment to Amendment on Marriage" [2004], A14). There seems to be no grand plan for large-scale public initiatives in the current American political landscape.

25. See Alan Wolfe, *Return to Greatness: How America Lost Its Sense of Purpose and What It Needs to Do to Recover It* (2005).

26. Howard Kurtz, "Faint Praise from the Left" (2005), http://www.washingtonpost.com/wp-dyn/content/blog/2005/03/03/BL2005040701166.html.

27. Mike Allen, "GOP House Member Calls Democrats Anti-Christian" (2005), A4.

28. For reactions to the Pentagon's inquiry into the Air Force Academy problems, see the *New York Times* Editorial, "Obfuscating Intolerance," June 23, 2005.

29. http://www.renewamerica.us/columns/weyrich/041203.

30. Gary DeMar and Colonel Doner (eds.), *The Christian Worldview of Government* (1989), 4.

31. "COR's vision is to see Christians everywhere doing all they can in the power of the Holy Spirit *to take every thought captive to the obedience of Christ (2 Cor. 10:5), in every aspect of life*. Toward that end, we have developed a series of worldview documents that set forth what we believe are the fundamental and essential points of the total Christian world and life view. The COR worldview documents state what we believe are the biblical principles for all spheres of human life including theology, evangelism, discipleship, law, civil governments, economics, education, family, medicine, psychology and counseling, arts and media, business and professions, and science and technology. We believe that the COR worldview documents state where the entire Church must stand and what action it must take to accomplish its task in this new millennium," http://www.reformation.net/cor/about_us.htm.

32. The author's dissertation reviewed Christian participation in U.S. presidential elections from Kennedy's to Reagan's second election. In every single presidential election during the period, no matter who ran or what issues dominated the campaigns, conservative Protestants had the lowest rates of voting in comparison to liberal and moderate Protestants as well as Catholics, *including* the two Reagan elections. For more details see H. B. Cavalcanti, *Opiate of the People?* (1990).

33. DeMar and Doner, op. cit., 5.

34. Lester Kurtz, *Gods in the Global Village* (1995), 173.

35. DeMar and Doner, op. cit., 6. All further comments in this section stem from the document as well.

36. DeMar and Doner, op. cit., 9.

37. Ibid.

38. Ibid.

39. Jerry Falwell makes that case when he warns Americans not to grow complacent about God's blessings: "Psalm 9:17 admonishes 'The Wicked shall be turned into Hell, and all the nations that forget God.' America will be no exception: If she forgets God, she too will face His Wrath and judgment like every other nation in the history of humanity. But we have the promise in Psalm 33:12, which declares 'Blessed is the nation whose God is the LORD.' When nations' ways please the Lord, the nation is blessed with supernatural help" *Listen, America!* (1980), 24. But the vision of America as God's blessed model of society for the world, his beacon of light on earth, has been part of American conservative doctrine from colonial times. James Reichley argues that Jonathan Edwards links America's chosen status to Christ's return: "From the time of the first settlements in the New World, many had believed that God selected America for some great work. Now it was clear to the evangelicals what this work must be: development of a model for the 'unspeakably happy and glorious' human society that was to precede the last judgment.... Belief in progress toward a better society became for eighteenth century evangelicals not simply a secular passion but a conclusion drawn from religious prophecy." *Religion in American Public Life* (1985), 72.

40. Robert Green Ingersoll, "God in the Constitution" (1912–1929), microform.

41. All quotes from the manifesto come from its PDF form, which can be downloaded at http://www.nae.net/images/civic_responsibility2.pdf.

42. http://www.nae.net/index.cfm?FUSEACTION=nae.mission.

43. Jeff Sharlet, op. cit., 43.

44. This lack of concern with the social consequences of a postindustrial economy is not surprising. The theme of self-sufficiency for the poor has a long history in the conservative/evangelical frame of mind. Gordon Bigelow, describing the evangelical approach to the free market during the early Industrial Revolution, had this to say: "The group that bridled most against these pessimistic elements of Smith and Ricardo was the evangelicals. These were middle-class reformers who wanted to reshape Protestant doctrine. For them it was unthinkable that capitalism led to class conflict, for that would mean that God had created a world at war with itself. The evangelicals believed in a providential God, one who built a logical and orderly universe, and they saw the new industrial economy as a fulfillment of God's plan. The free market, they believed, was a perfectly designed instrument to reward good Christian behavior and to punish and humiliate the unrepentant. At the center of this early evangelical doctrine was the idea of original sin: we were all born stained by corruption and fleshly desire, and the true purpose of earthly life was to redeem this. The trials of economic life—the sweat of hard labor, the fear of poverty, the self-denial involved in saving—were earthly tests of sinfulness and virtue. While evangelicals believed salvation was ultimately possible only through conversion and faith, they saw the pain of earthly life as means of atonement for original sin. These were the people that writers like Dickens detested. The extreme among them urged mortification of the flesh and would scold anyone who took pleasure in food, drink, or good company. Moreover, they regarded poverty as part of a divine program. Evangelicals interpreted the mental anguish of poverty and debt, and the physical agony of hunger or cold, as natural spurs to prick the conscience of sinners. They believed that the suffering of the poor would provoke remorse, reflection, and ultimately the conversion that would change their fate. In other words, the poor were poor for a reason, and helping them out of poverty would endanger their mortal souls." In "Let There Be Markets" (2005), 35. Judging by the COR document and the NAE manifesto those attitudes still prevail today.

45. Gernot Sydow, "1648—Peace of Westphalia: Turning Point in German History" (1998), http://www.germanembassy-india.org/news/GN98Okt/gn08.htm.

46. Immanuel Wallerstein, commenting on the process of nation-state formation and its relation to religion, argues: "Once, however, the religious uniformity had created the basic cement for nationalism, the uniformity began to seem less useful, even harmful to the creation and maintenance of national identity. For successful nation-states, which became loci of capital accumulation within the world-economy, found that religious monolithism conflicted with two other tendencies. On the one hand, there was a steady trend to secularism among the more educated, wealthier portions of the population who chafed at the constraints of religious dogma and practice. And on the other hand, successful nation-states found it useful to encourage immigration for multiple reasons, but in particular to fill the whole range of occupational niches they were developing. And with immigration came inevitably minority religions." In "Render unto Caesar? The Dilemmas of a Multicultural World" (2005), 125. I'm also indebted to Wallerstein for the Latin phrase that I quote in parentheses on the text.

47. For those interested in exploring the Peace of Westphalia in greater depth I recommend Derek Croxton, *Peacemaking in Early Modern Europe* (1999); William Guthrie, *Battles of the Thirty Years War* (2002); and Randall Lesaffer, *Peace Treaties and International Law in European History* (2004).

48. Thomas Jefferson, *Virginia Act for Establishing Religious Freedom* (1786), http://religiousfreedom.lib.virginia.edu/sacred/vaact.html.

49. Ibid.

50. Constitution of the United States of America, Applewood Books edition, 17.

51. I'm indebted to Frederick Clarkson for his perceptive analysis of the *Dominionist* failure to address Article VI. For more on the subject see Clarkson's "Theocratic Dominionism Gains Influence" (1994), http://www.publiceye.org/magazine/v08n1/ chrisrel.html.

52. *Constitution of the United States of America*, Applewood Books edition, 18.

53. Bernard Bailyn, *The Federalist Papers* (1998), 23–24.

54. My presentation of the *nonpreferential* interpretation of the First Amendment is based on works such as Walter Berns' *The First Amendment and the Future of American Democracy* (1976); Robert Cord, *Separation of Church and State* (1982); Max Farrand, *The Records of the Federal Convention of 1878* (1911); and Gordon Wood, *The Creation of the American Republic 1776–1787* (1969). Notice also that in the Annals of the Congress of the United States, under the Debates and Proceedings, vol. 1, 731, James Madison argues that "the people feared one sect might obtain a preeminence, or two combine together, and establish a religion to which they would compel others to conform."

55. Seymour Lipset, *The First New Nation* (1963), 81, 164–165.

CHAPTER 4

1. http://www.crpc.org/2000/About%20CRPC/index.html.
2. http://christianexodus.org/index.php?module=PostWrap&page=home.
3. http://christianexodus.org/index.php?module=PostWrap&page=plan.
4. Ibid.
5. The group's leaders have law and management degrees.
6. http://christianexodus.org/index.php?module=PostWrap&page=home.
7. "On the conservative side of the religious spectrum, orthodox Congregationalists gave strong support to the Federalists, the party of order in the early years of the Republic. About nine out of ten Congregationalist ministers were 'staunchly Federalist,' and many

of them were 'energetic politicians.' Congregationalists were drawn to Federalism not only because they regarded the Federalist party as the special guardian of their establishment status in three New England states but also because emphasis on the social fitted naturally with their dour view of human nature.... Episcopalians, though deprived of the establishment status they had held in several colonies before the Revolution, also generally enlisted on the side of the party of order ... in New England most Episcopalians were probably Federalists, 'reflecting their generally high status, Anglican tastes, and elitism.' In the Middle Atlantic States, Episcopalians were almost all Federalists ... Presbyterians, in contrast, usually lined up with the party of equality, partly as a continuation of long-standing struggles against Congregationalist establishments in New England and against socially dominant Anglicans in New York and Pennsylvania," James Reichley, *Religion in American Public Life* (1985), 178–180.

8. For more on the lasting presence of the Protestant Establishment in the circles of power, see Prof. James D. Davidson, "Religion among America's Elite" (1994) and "Persistence and Change in the Protestant Establishment" (1995).

9. Lipset, *The First New Nation* (1963), 167–168.

10. William James, *The Varieties of Religious Experience* (1958), 191.

11. Hymn by Albert E. Brumley, "This World is Not My Home" (1965).

12. Peter Applebome, "Jerry Falwell, Leading Religious Conservative, Dies at 73" (2007), http://www.nytimes.com/2007/05/15/obituaries/15cnd-falwell.html?pagewanted=2&hp.

13. The temperance movement is a good example of the past conservative dislike for large-scale redemption. Sydney Ahlstrom argues that the movement unfolded in three waves. The first wave, led by Lyman Beecher and fellow Congregationalists, focused on changing state law, but attracted little religious conservative attention. The second wave, led by Frances Willard, president of the Women's Christian Temperance Union, also failed to attract conservative support because of its desire to link drinking with a number of other social causes. The third wave, starting with the Anti-Saloon League in 1893, gathered widespread support from the Christian conservative community because it concentrated exclusively on Prohibition, using the same single-issue approach that modern religious conservatives employ. For more on the effort see Ahlstrom, *A Religious History of the American People* (1972).

14. For more on the religious worldview of working-class Christians see Gordon A. Cotton, *Of Primitive Faith and Order* (1974); Bill Leonard, *Christianity in Appalachia* (1999); Larry G. Morgan, *Old Time Religion in the Southern Appalachians* (2005); and Herman Albert Norton, *Religion in Tennessee, 1777–1945* (1981).

15. Speaking about unique characteristics of American religion Seymour Lipset notes that "new sects have developed more readily here than anywhere else in the world. For the most part, these are drawn from economically and socially depressed strata, and their theology reflects this fact, such as in the belief that wealth or ostentation is sinful and corrupting," *The First New Nation* (1963), 157.

16. See Max Weber, "Elective Affinities" (1946), 62–63, and 284–285.

17. Timothy Smith, reviewing the connections between revivalism and social reform in nineteenth-century America, sees in Arminianism the more egalitarian means for social redemption, whereby working-class religious groups benefited from "doctrines of free will, free grace, and unlimited hope for the conversion of all men," *Revivalism and Social Reform in Mid-Nineteenth Century America* (1957), 88–89.

18. On the rich man's story see Mark, chapter 10, verses 17–25; for Zaccheus' story see Luke, chapter 19, verses 1–10.

19. Matthew, chapter 5, verse 45.

20. Alan Cooperman, "Coming Soon to a Church Near You: Hollywood Skips Movie Theaters with 3,200-Screen Opening" (2005), A9.

21. Richard Niebuhr, *The Social Sources of Denominationalism* (1957).

22. My claim here is based on research done by Alan Wolfe and others on the mores of the American middle class.

23. On the matter of denominational coexistence see, for instance, the work of Andrew Greeley, *The Denominational Society* (1972).

24. Wolfe, *One Nation After All: What Middle-Class Americans Really Think about: God, Country, Family, Racism, Welfare, Immigration, Homosexuality, Work, the Right, the Left, and Each Other* (1998), 51.

25. Ibid., 55.

26. Ibid., 126.

27. To follow the marginal logic, the complementary natures of men and women are physically and psychologically self-evident. These differences are created and natural, not primarily socially constructed. Sexuality is ordered for the procreation of children and the expression of love between husband and wife in the covenant of marriage. Marriage between a man and a woman forms the sole moral context for natural sexual union. Whether through pornography, promiscuity, incest, or homosexuality, deviations from these created sexual norms cannot truly satisfy the human spirit. They lead to obsession, remorse, alienation, and disease. Child molesters harm children and no valid legal, psychological, or moral justification can be offered for the odious crime of pedophilia. Culture and society should encourage standards of sexual morality that support and enhance family life. See http://www.profam.org/THC/xthc_principles.htm.

28. http://www.profam.org/THC/xthc_principles.htm.

29. Ibid.

30. http://www.geocities.com/Heartland/Plains/8218/family.html.

31. Error! Main Document Only http://www.geocities.com/Heartland/Plains/8218/family.html. The focus on the husband and father as a provider and a spiritual leader has been renewed by the born-again male movement of the *Promise Keepers*. This concern with male leadership in the family ties in nicely with the conservative Christian view of the nuclear family. For a sociological analysis of the *Promise Keepers* see Rhys H. Williams, *Promise Keepers and the New Masculinity: Private Lives and Public Morality* (2001).

32. The discussion on the benefits of marriage follows the outline provided by Bridget Maher in her article, "The Benefits of Marriage," published in the *Family Research Council* Web site, http://www.frc.org/get.cfm?i=IS05B01.

33. "The reality is that our government is permanently in the business of dealing with the social fallout of marital and family decline whether we acknowledge the fact or not. This is because decades of social science studies have proven that most of our nation's most daunting social problems are driven more by family breakdown than any other social variable including race and economics," Matt Daniels, "Healthy Marriages Are Good Social Policy" (2004), http://www.allianceformarriage.org/site/PageServer?pagename=HealthyMarriages).

34. Bridget Maher, op. cit.

35. http://www.thefamily.com/teaching_values.asp.

36. "Government should protect and support the family, and not usurp the vital roles it plays in society. When the state or its agent attempts to exercise a right or responsibility that belongs to the family, albeit with good intentions to address a vexing social problem, its effect is to undermine and displace the family and make matters worse. Government

policies should not create pressure for mothers to enter the workplace when they would prefer to care for their families' full-time. Government should secure an orderly, lawful, and just society that allows families freely and responsibly to: form in the covenant of marriage and bear children, pursue meaningful work, provide for their material and health needs, direct the education and upbringing of their children, participate in charitable, civic and recreational activities, care for elderly family members, build estates for their present and future generations, and practice their religion," http://www.profam.org/THC/xthc_principles.htm.

37. http://www.allianceformarriage.org/site/PageServer?pagename=mic_mission.
38. Bridget Maher, op. cit.
39. http://www.allianceformarriage.org/site/PageServer?pagename=mic_mission.
40. Ibid.
41. For more on the social forces that have impacted the American family see the work of Stephanie Coontz, especially *The Way We Never Were: American Families and the Nostalgia Trap* (1992), and *The Way We Really Are: Coming to Terms with America's Changing Families* (1998).
42. Alan Wolfe, *Moral Freedom: The Search for Virtue in a World of Choice* (2001), 49.
43. For more on the topic see Juliet B. Schor, *The Overworked American: The Unexpected Decline of Leisure* (1992).
44. Ronald Sider, "The Scandal of the Evangelical Conscience" (2005), http://www.christianitytoday.com/bc/2005/001/3.8.html.
45. Ibid.
46. Ibid.
47. http://www.frc.org/file.cfm?f=RESEARCH&iss=MF.
48. The three "R's," http://honestedu.org/.
49. http://www.profam.org/THC/xthc_principles.htm.
50. http://honestedu.org/.
51. http://www.homeschoolchristian.com/Beginner.html.
52. http://www.aacs.org/.
53. http://www.aacs.org/about/welcome.aspx.
54. http://www.accsedu.org/.
55. http://www.acsi.org/web2003/default.aspx?ID=1606.
56. http://community.gospelcom.net/Brix?pageID=2831.
57. http://www.ag.org/acts/.
58. http://www.christiancollegementor.org/AboutMentor/cccu.asp.
59. http://www.ceai.org/about.htm.
60. http://www.ceai.org/about.htm.
61. http://www.bibleinschools.net/.
62. http://www.bibleinschools.net/sdm.asp?pg=implemented.
63. Ralph Blumenthal and Barbara Novovitch, "Bible Course Becomes A Test For Public Schools in Texas" (2005), A9.
64. http://www.iam4schools.com/.
65. http://www.religioustolerance.org/equ_acce.htm.
66. http://www.itvs.org/schoolprayer/issue3.html.
67. http://www.ffrf.org/nontracts/schoolprayer.php.
68. As cited in Lipset, op. cit., 165.
69. For more on the elimination of sectarianism in public schools, and the public support of American institutions for a sectarian-free public education in the country

see Joel Spring's work, especially *The American School, 1642–2000* (2000) and *American Education* (2002).

70. By comparison the Roman Catholic Church, whose foundations were shaken by Galileo's research, has no problem conciliating faith with evolution's scientific views. After the Dover, PA, court decision was handed down, deeming Intelligent Design an extension of the Fundamentalist faith, the reaction from the Vatican was one of support for the teaching of evolution: "The official Vatican newspaper published an article this week labeling as 'correct' the recent decision by a judge in Pennsylvania that intelligent design should not be taught as a scientific alternative to evolution. 'If the model proposed by Darwin is not considered sufficient, one should search for another,' Fiorenzo Facchini, a professor of evolutionary biology at the University of Bologna, wrote in the January 16–17 edition of the paper, *L'Osservatore Romano*. 'But it is not correct from a methodological point of view to stray from the field of science while pretending to do science,' he wrote, calling intelligent design unscientific. 'It only creates confusion between the scientific plane and those that are philosophical or religious,'" Fisher and Dean, "In 'Design' vs. Darwinism, Darwin Wins a Point in Rome" (2006), http://www.nytimes.com/2006/01/19/science/sciencespecial2/19evolution.html?th&emc=th.

71. Lisa Anderson, "A Museum of Supernatural History: Dinos Share Earth with Adam & Eve in Creationist Dioramas" (2005), C2. All the information on creationist museums comes from Lisa Anderson's article.

72. Ted G. Jelen, "Political Esperanto: Rhetorical Resources and Limitation of the Christian Right in the United States" (2005), 315.

73. Some of the documentaries, *Volcanoes of the Deep Sea* for instance, had been vetted by scientific panels as presenting the most accurate scientific information on earth's origins. It was sponsored in part by the National Science Foundation. See the *New York Times* editorial, "Censorship in the Sciences Museum" (March 28, 2005), A16.

74. As Verlyn Klinkenborg so eloquently states in his article in the *New York Times*: "Last month a team of paleontologists announced that it had found several fossilized dinosaur embryos that were 190 million years old—some 90 million years older than any dinosaur embryos found so far.... The universe is perhaps 14 billion years old. Earth is some 4.5 billion years old. The oldest hominid fossils are between 6 million and 7 million years old. The oldest distinctly modern human fossils are about 160,000 years old.... It's been approximately 3.5 billion years since primeval life first originated on this planet.... Evolution is a robust theory, in the scientific sense, that has been tested and confirmed again and again. Intelligent design is not a theory at all, as scientists understand the word, but a well-financed political and religious campaign to muddy science. Its basic proposition—the intervention of a designer, a.k.a. God—cannot be tested. It has no evidence to offer, and its assumptions that humans were divinely created are the same as its conclusions. Its objections to evolution are based on syllogistic reasoning and a highly selective treatment of the physical evidence. Accepting the fact of evolution does not necessarily mean discarding a personal faith in God. But accepting intelligent design means discarding science. Much has been made of a 2004 poll showing that some 45 percent of Americans believe that the Earth—and humans with it—was created as described in the book of Genesis, and within the past 10,000 years. This isn't a triumph of faith. It's a failure of education. The purpose of the campaign for intelligent design is to deepen that failure. To present the arguments of intelligent design as part of a debate over evolution is nonsense. From the scientific perspective, there is no debate. But even the illusion of a debate is a sorry victory for antievolutionists, a public relations victory based, as so

many have been in recent years, on ignorance and obfuscation. The essential, but often well-disguised, purpose of intelligent design, is to preserve the myth of a separate, divine creation for humans in the belief that only that can explain who we are. But there is a destructive hubris, a fearful arrogance, in that myth. It sets us apart from nature, except to dominate it. It misses both the grace and the moral depth of knowing that humans have only the same stake, the same right, in the Earth as every other creature that has ever lived here. There is a righteousness—a responsibility—in the deep, ancestral origins we share with all of life. Grasping the depth of time is a first step in understanding evolution," *New York Times* (August 23, 2005), A16.

75. Elisabeth Bumiller, "Bush Remarks Roil Debate over Teaching of Evolution" (2005), A14.

76. Cornelia Dean, "Scientists Speak Up on Mix of God and Science" *The New York Times* (August 23, 2005), A1.

CHAPTER 5

1. *AdvanceUSA*, http://www.advanceusa.org/pro4.asp.
2. Ralph Reed, *Politically Incorrect: The Emerging Faith Factor in American Politics* (1994), 18, 41; as quoted in Jelen, "Political Esperanto: Rhetorical Resources and Limitation of the Christian Right in the United States" (2005), 310.
3. http://www.advanceusa.org/pro4.asp.
4. http://www.nrb.org/.
5. Mariah Blake, "Stations of the Cross" (2005), http://www.cjr.org/issues/2005/3/blake-evangelist.asp.
6. The NRB information used in this chapter comes from the association's Web site and Chris Hedges' "Feeling the Hate with the National Religious Broadcasters" (2005), 56. Other sources on the topic are footnoted as well.
7. Mariah Blake, "Stations of the Cross" (2005).
8. Meredith McGuire, *Religion: The Social Context* (2002), 215–216.
9. Chris Hedges, op. cit., 56.
10. Ibid., 57.
11. John Sugg, "A Nation under God" (2005), 35.
12. Several organizations list numerous articles against those activities in their Web sites. The most thorough is the *Family Research Council* (http://www.frc.org/get.cfm?c=RESEARCH). Other groups would include the *American Coalition for Traditional Values*, the *American Family Association*, the *Child and Family Protection Institute*, the *Christian Family Coalition*, *Concerned Women for America*, the *Culture and Family Institute*, *Families Across America*, the *Family.Com* group, and the *Family Policy Network*. Some Internet ministries offered to Christians also provide in-depth coverage on sexual issues. Among them, the most popular are *Christian Answers* (http://www.christiananswers.net), *Love Fruit* (http://www.geocities.com/SouthBeach/Suite/6839), *The Marriage Bed* (http://www.themarriagebed.com), and *This* (http://hometown.aol.com/mytlv4b/websample4/index.html). Some organizations, like *Focus on Family* offer short booklets that can be easily purchased through its bookstore.
13. "We are not tolerant of behaviors that destroy individuals, families, and our culture. Individuals may be free to pursue such behaviors as sodomy, but we will not and cannot tolerate these behaviors. They frequently lead to death. We do not believe it is loving to permit someone to kill themselves by engaging in a self-destructive behavior. We believe

in 'discrimination' in the good sense: choosing between good and evil, right and wrong, the better and the best. We believe in discrimination in the sense of being discerning between good and bad choices. Popular culture maintains that all forms of discrimination are wrong. This is incorrect. A person with 'discriminating taste' is one who uses wisdom in making choices. In short, we believe in intolerance to those things that are evil; and we believe that we should discriminate against those behaviors which are dangerous to individuals and to society," *Traditional Values Coalition*, http://www.traditionalvalues.org/defined.php.

14. For the sake of parsimony I am using here a list provided by *The Marriage Bed* (http://www.themarriagebed.com/pages/sexuality/splay/whatisokay.shtml). But that list is supported by citations from other organizations, and books on Christian sexual counseling such as Bob Davies' *Coming out of Homosexuality* (1994); Linda Dilllow, *Intimate Issues* (1999); Joshua Harris, *I Kissed Dating Goodbye* (2003); Earl Johnson, *Single Life* (1999); Tim and Beverly LaHaye, *The Act of Marriage* (1998); Lewis Smedes, *Sex for Christians* (1994); and Ed and Gay Wheat, *Intended for Pleasure* (1997).

15. Ceci Connolly, "Some Abstinence Programs Mislead Teens, Report Says" (2004), A1.

16. Amanda Paulson, "Culture War Hits Local Pharmacy" (2005), 11.

17. Brad Knickerbocker, "Ripples Spread As States Vote on Same-Sex Marriages" (2005), 2.

18. Connolly, op. cit.

19. Ibid.

20. http://www.cmdahome.org/index.cgi?BISKIT=2302340612&CONTEXT=art&art=2553.

21. Ibid.

22. For a thorough treatment of the Church's traditional listing of moral sins, see Pope Gregory I, *Moralia in Job* (1979). For a summary of the work, see Joseph Gildea's *Source Book of Self-Discipline: A Synthesis of Moralia in Job by Gregory the Great* (1991).

23. "We now make a great distinction between 'inner' and 'outer,' and those of us who are Protestants, or heirs to the Protestant tradition, distrust external forms. It should be remembered that, to ancient Jews, 'love thy neighbor' and 'love the stranger' were not vague commandments about the feelings in one's heart, but were quite specific. 'Love' meant, 'Use just weights and measures;' 'Do not reap your field to the border, but leave some for the poor;' 'Neither steal, deal falsely nor lie;' 'Do not withhold wages that you owe;' 'Do not take advantage of the blind or deaf;' 'Do not be biased in judgment;' 'Do not slander,'—and so on through the verses of Leviticus 10 and many others," E. P. Sanders, *Jewish Law from Jesus to the Mishnah* (1990), 271. For more on the prophetic tradition see Harry Meyer Orlinsky (ed.), *Interpreting the Prophetic Tradition* (1969).

24. Ronald J. Sider, "The Scandal of the Evangelical Conscience" (2005), http://www.christianitytoday.com/bc/2005/001/3.8.html.

25. Jane Lampman, "Churches Confront an 'Elephant in the Pews'" (2005), 14.

26. Sider, op. cit.

27. Jane Lampman, op. cit.

28. For more on that dominant heterosexual pattern see John D'Emilio, *Sexual Politics, Sexual Communities* (1983); Steven Seidman, *Embattled Eros* (1992); and Jeffrey Weeks, *Invented Moralities* (1995).

29. CNN Presents: *The Fight over Faith*, November 20, 2004.

30. See for instance Peter Allen, *The Wages of Sin* (2000); James Brundage, *Law, Sex, and Christian Society in Medieval Europe* (1987); Vern Bullough and James Brundage, *Sexual*

Practices and the Medieval Church (1982); and Pierre Payer, *Sex and the Penitentials: The Development of a Sexual Code, 550–1150* (1984). For a more sociological treatment see Michel Foucault, *The History of Sexuality* (1988).

31. "I have suggested that a key site of sexual conflict pivots around the moral logics that justify social norms, rules, and therefore a system of sexual hierarchy, and I have proposed that in contemporary America there is an opposition between a morality of the sex act and a communicative sex ethic. The former appeals to some notion of a fixed or transcendent social and moral order that gives to sexual desires and practices an inherent meaning and social role. The latter asserts that sexual-intimate practices have no intrinsic social and moral meaning: their meaning is derived by agents in a social context, and the moral status of particular sexual practices hinges on the presence or absence of certain formal qualities of the social interaction, for example, consent, respect, and reciprocity. In the communicative sexual ethic, transcendent moral imperatives or norms are replaced by broad ethical guidelines that leave a lot of room for individual discretion, judgment, and ambiguity.... A chief feature of the morality of the sex act is that it makes assumptions about what sex is and, on that basis, proscribes sexual norms. For example, if we assume that the meaning and purpose of sex is to express and consolidate 'love,' only those sex acts and social interactions are legitimate that exhibit the qualities of love. Although such an ethical position provides strong normative and regulatory guidance, it also devalues and sometimes pollutes or stigmatizes a wide range of very different kinds of behaviors that deviate from such social norms. In other words, a morality of the sex act inevitably suppresses, devalues, pathologizes, and renders immoral a heterogeneous cluster of practices, many of which seem freely chosen, involves only adults, are meaningful to the agents, and lack any obvious 'harm' to the individual or to others. This hostility to difference, especially in a sexual culture characterized by a plurality of sexual values, patterns, identities, and communities has made it less credible," Steven Seidman, "Contesting the Moral Boundaries of Eros" (1999), 184, 185.

32. David Lerman, "Representative Davis Wants to Protect Symbols of Christmas" (2005), http://www.dailypress.com/news/local/dp-39306sy0dec15,0,1382931.story?coll=dp-news-local-final. The other quotes used in the paragraph come from this reporting.

33. http://joanndavis.house.gov/HoR/VA01/News/Press+Releases/2005/Davis+Introduces +Congressional+Resolution+Supporting+In+God+We+Trust.htm.

34. http://www.dar.org/natsociety/Citizenship.cfm?TP=Show&ID=67.

35. Jane Lampman, "For Evangelicals, a Bid to 'Reclaim America'" (2004), 16. The rest of the paragraph is based on her reporting as well.

36. Ibid., 16.

37. Alan Cooperman, "Christian Groups Plan More Monuments: Many Expect Confusion and Litigation on Ten Commandments to Continue" (2005), A6.

38. Editorial, "The Disappearing Wall" (2005), 18.

39. Rob Garver, "Justice Sunday: The Family Research Council Says Anticlerical Judges Pose a Greater Danger than Al-Qaeda" (2005)., http://www.prospect.org/web/.

40. Dana Milbank, "And the Verdict on Justice Kennedy Is: Guilty" (2005), A3.

41. Paul Gaston, "Smearing Christian Judges" (2005), A19.

42. John C. Danforth, "In the Name of Politics" (2005), http://www.nytimes.com/2005/03/30/opinion/30danforth.html?ex=1135918800&en=64ef0af5b6a20f85&ei=5070.

43. Jerry Adler, "In Search of the Spiritual" (2005), 49.

44. Michael Powell, "Judge Rules against 'Intelligent Design': Dover, PA, District Can't Teach Evolution Alternative" (2005), A1.

45. Gaston, op. cit., A19.

46. "Declaring an act of Congress unconstitutional is the boldest thing a judge can do. That's because Congress, as an elected legislative body representing the entire nation, makes decisions that can be presumed to possess a high degree of democratic legitimacy.... Since the Supreme Court assumed its current composition in 1994, by our count it has upheld or struck down 64 Congressional provisions. That legislation has concerned Social Security, church and state, and campaign finance, among many other issues. We examined the court's decisions in these cases and looked at how each justice voted, regardless of whether he or she concurred with the majority or dissented. We found that justices vary widely in their inclination to strike down Congressional laws. Justice Clarence Thomas, appointed by President George H. W. Bush, was the most inclined, voting to invalidate 65.63 percent of those laws; Justice Stephen Breyer, appointed by President Bill Clinton, was the least, voting to invalidate 28.13 percent.... One conclusion our data suggests is that those justices often considered more "liberal"—Justices Breyer, Ruth Bader Ginsburg, David Souter and John Paul Stevens—vote least frequently to overturn Congressional statutes, while those often labeled 'conservative' vote more frequently to do so. At least by this measure (others are possible, of course), the latter group is the most activist," Paul Gewirtz and Chad Golder, "So Who Are the Activists?" (2005), 19.

47. David D. Kirkpatrick and Carl Hulse, "G.O.P. Asks Conservative Allies to Cool Rhetoric over the Court" (2005), 1. Tom Minnery's quote comes from the same article.

48. http://www.visionamerica.us/.

49. Marcus Cunliffe, "American Watershed" (1961), 479.

CHAPTER 6

1. Chris Hedges, "Feeling the Hate with the National Religious Broadcasters" (2005), 57.

2. "Bush Aid Denounces Strict Church-State Line," *The Washington Post* (2006), B9.

3. Thomas Jefferson, *Autobiography*, "In Reference to the Virginia Act for Religious Freedom." In George Seldes (ed.), *The Great Quotations* (1983), 363.

4. Ted Jelen, "Political Esperanto: Rhetorical Resources and Limitation of the Christian Right in the United States" (2005), 305–306.

5. Patrik Jonsson, "A Carolina Fight over Swearing on the Koran in Court" (2005), 2.

6. See Alan Cooperman, "Fasting Chaplain Declares Victory: Navy Denies That He Couldn't Pray in Jesus' Name" (2006), A13; Julia Duin, "Military Chaplain Told to Shy from Jesus" (2005), http://www.washtimes.com/national/20051221-121224-6972r.htm; Laurie Goodstein, "Evangelicals Are Growing Force in the Military Chaplain Corps" (2005), 1; and Leo Shane III, "Christian Lawmakers Want to Protect Chaplains' Speech" (2005), http://www.freerepublic.com/focus/f-news/ 1507039/ posts.

7. "Far from being a provincial denomination of rural churches, the Southern Baptist Convention has evolved into an organization that asserts its political clout and claims its prominence as the largest Protestant denomination, with 15.7 million members. Now convention leaders admit that figure is inflated by as much as a third. And since more reliable figures show that membership has remained flat throughout the '90s, they are searching for ways to start the church growing again ... 'We've known for a long time the

boasting numbers were inflated,' said Convention President Paige Patterson. 'Some of us were having a hard time with our consciences about it. Churches have been cleaning up their rolls, so I do not view the drop as unfortunate. We needed to get more honest about the numbers.' Patterson, who is 56 and who is expected to be reelected without opposition this week, attributes some of the membership drop to an attempt to make the reporting more honest. Referring to the 15.7 million total members, Patterson said, 'As far as I'm concerned, it's accurate only to the degree it represents people who have affiliated with Southern Baptist churches. We probably couldn't find 3 million of them because they're non-resident Baptists.' It's more like 5 million that couldn't be found. According to Cliff Tharp, coordinator for constituent information for the Southern Baptist Convention, the number of resident members in 1998 is 10.7 million, or 32 percent less than total membership. That is also fewer resident members than the convention had in 1991. While total membership figures did not drop until 1998, resident members have fallen since 1995." Cary McMullen, "Any Way You Count It, Fewer Southern Baptists" (1999), http://www.palatkadailynews.com/pages/0615/count.html.

8. For the general details of the camp meeting staging see Roger Finke and Rodney Stark's *The Churching of America, 1776–1990* (1992); for specific research on the staging itself, see John Corrigan, *Business of the Heart* (2002); or Donald Pitzer, *Professional Revivalism in Nineteenth-Century Ohio* (1966).

9. Ted Jelen, op. cit., 304. On the independence and individualism of Americans, see also Michael Alzer, "The Communitarian Critique of Liberalism" (1990).

10. See for instance Russell A. Kazal, "Revisiting Assimilation" (1995); and Rubén G. Rumbaut's "Ties That Bind" (1997) for thorough appraisals of how diverse America has become.

11. For more on the faith variety of new Americans, see Helen Ebaugh and Janet Chafez, *Religion and the New Immigrants* (2000); Diana Eck, *A New Religious America* (2001); Peter Kivisto, "Religion and the New Immigrants" (1992); Bruce L. Lawrence, *New Faiths, Old Fears* (2002); and R. Stephen Warner, "Approaching Religious Diversity" (1998).

12. See for instance Steven Gregory, *Santeria in New York City* (1999); Yvonne Haddad and Adair Lummis, *Islamic Values in the United States* (1987); Prema Kurien, "Becoming American by Becoming Hindu" (1998); Irene Lin, "Journey to the Far West: Chinese Buddhism in America" (1996); or Joseph M. Murphy, *Working the Spirit* (1994).

13. "You Ain't Seen Nothing Yet," *The Economist* (2005), http://www.economist.com/world/na/printerfriendly.cfm?story_ID=4102212.

14. Ibid.

15. John Spong, *Why Christianity Must Change or Die* (1998), 40–41.

16. Daniel Lazare, "False Testament: Archaeology Refutes the Bible's Claim to History" (2002), 39–47. See also Donald Akerson, *Surpassing Wonder: The Invention of the Bible and the Talmuds* (2001); Charlotte Allen, *The Human Christ* (1998); and Richard Rubenstein, *When Jesus Became God* (2000).

17. Charles Marsh, "Wayward Christian Soldiers" (2006), http://www.nytimes.com/2006/01/20/opinion/20marsh.html?th&em=th.

18. Ibid.

19. Patrik Jonsson, "Limits of Pulpit Politics Tested in N.C." (2005), 3.

20. "On December 20, 2005, Judge Jones ruled that the defendants' intelligent design policy violated the Establishment Clause of the First Amendment. In a withering 139-page opinion, he found that the goal of the intelligent design movement is religious in nature, that intelligent design is not science and cannot be taught in Dover schools,

and that the board's claimed reason for including intelligent design in the curriculum—solely because it was good science—was a 'sham.' In referring to board members, he used such words as 'striking ignorance' and 'breathtaking inanity.' Additionally, he wrote that Buckingham and Bonsell 'had either testified inconsistently, or lied outright under oath on several occasions,' and that 'It is ironic that several of these individuals who so staunchly and proudly touted their religious convictions in public, would time and again lie to cover their tracks and disguise the real purpose behind the ID policy,'" Matthew Chapman, "God or Gorilla: A Darwin Descendant at the Dover Monkey Trial" (2006), 63.

21. "Judgment Day," *Harper's Magazine* (2005), 23.

22. "Falwell Apologizes to Gays, Feminists and Lesbians," *CNN.com* (2001), http://archives.cnn.com/2001/US/09/14/Falwell.apology/.

23. "White House Blasts Robertson's Sharon Remark," *MSNBC News Services* (2006), http://www.msnbc.msn.com/id/10728347/.

24. Thomas Edsall, "In Georgia, Abramoff Scandal Threatens a Political Ascendancy" (2006), A1.

25. David Krowe, "Katrina: God's Judgment on America" (2006), http://beliefnet.org/story/174/story_17439_1.html.

26. Robert Wuthnow, "Democratic Liberalism and the Challenge of Diversity in Late-Twentieth-Century America" (1999), 27.

27. See Gabriel Almond and Sidney Verba, *The Civic Culture* (1963); Robert Dahl, *A Preface to Democratic Theory* (1956), or his *Pluralist Democracy in the United States* (1967); Seymour Lipset, *Political Man* (1960); and Sidney Verba and Norman Nie, *Participation in America* (1972).

28. "The secret of liberal democracy lies partly in giving individual citizens enough room to disagree so that they do not feel compelled to arrive at consensus on all levels. Moreover, individual freedom is a 'decoupling' mechanism that allows people to work together despite different interests and convictions." Robert Wuthnow, op cit., 25.

29. Alan Wolfe, *Moral Freedom: The Search* (2001), 168.

30. Ibid.

31. Charles Trueheart, "Welcome to the Next Church" (1996), 48.

32. Arthur Schlesinger, Jr., *The Age of Jackson* (1946), 16.

33. Thomas Jefferson, letter to Horatio Spofford, March 17, 1814, found in George Seldes, *The Great Quotations* (1983), 371.

34. "The norms of political tolerance and religious tolerance have been mutually reinforcing. The special pressure on churches to proselytize *and* to tolerate each other, brought about by 'voluntarism,' is reinforced by another particular trait of American society—its geographic, occupational, and class mobility. This means that people have to be won over and over again as they move geographically and as they change in their class orientations and find different aspirations for themselves." Seymour M. Lipset, *The First New Nation* (1963), 167.

35. Quoted in Oscar Handlin, *This Was America* (1949), 147–148. Gustave de Beaumont, traveling companion of de Tocqueville, puzzled over the American indifference to doctrinal distinctions: "As a matter of fact, nothing is commoner in the United States than this indifference toward the nature of religions, which doesn't however eliminate the religious fervour of each for the cult he has chosen. Actually, this extreme tolerance on the one hand towards religions in general—on the other this considerable zeal of each

individual for his own religion, is a phenomenon I can't yet explain to myself. I would gladly know how a lively and sincere faith can get on with such a perfect toleration; how one can have equal respect for religions whose dogmas differ." Quoted in George W. Pierson, *Tocqueville in America* (Garden City, NY: Doubleday/Anchor, 1959), 70.

36. Charles Marsh, op. cit.

REFERENCES

Adler, Jerry. "In Search of the Spiritual." *Newsweek* (August 29/September 5), 2005: 48–50.
Ahlstrom, Sydney E. *A Religious History of the American People*. New Haven, CT/London, UK: Yale University Press, 1972.
Akerson, Donald Harman. *Surpassing Wonder: The Invention of the Bible and the Talmuds*. Chicago, IL: University of Chicago Press, 2001.
Allen, Charlotte. *The Human Christ: The Search for the Historical Jesus*. New York: Free Press, 1998.
Allen, Mike. "GOP House Member Calls Democrats Anti-Christian." *The Washington Post* (June 21, 2005): A4.
Allen, Peter L. *The Wages of Sin: Sex and Disease Past and Present*. Chicago, IL: University of Chicago Press, 2000.
Almond, Gabriel A. and Sidney Verba. *The Civic Culture: Political Attitudes and Democracy in Five Nations*. Princeton, NJ: Princeton University Press, 1963.
Alzer, Michael. "The Communitarian Critique of Liberalism." *Political Theory* 18 (1990): 6–23.
Ammerman, Nancy Taton. *Bible Believers: Fundamentalists in the Modern World*. New Brunswick, NJ: Rutgers University Press, 1987.
———. *Baptist Battles: Social Change and Religious Conflict in the Southern Baptist Convention*. New Brunswick, NJ: Rutgers University Press, 1990.
——— (ed.). *Southern Baptists Observed: Multiple Perspectives on a Changing Denomination*. Knoxville, TN: University of Tennessee Press, 1993.
Anderson, Lisa. "A Museum of Supernatural History: Dinos Share Earth with Adam & Eve in Creationist Dioramas." *The Washington Post* (August 15, 2005): C2.
Andrews, Edward Deming. *The People Called Shakers: A Search for the Perfect Society*. New York: Dover Publications, 1963.
Annals of the Congress of the United States: *The Debates and Proceedings in the Congress of the United States*, Vol. 1. Washington, DC: Gales and Seaton, 1834.

Applebome, Peter. "Jerry Falwell, Leading Religious Conservative, Dies at 73." *The New York Times* (May 15, 2007), http://www.nytimes.com/2007/05/15/obituaries/15cnd-falwell.html?pagewanted=2&hp.

Aquinas, St. Thomas. *Summa Theologica* (edited by Timothy McDermott). Allen, TX: Christian Classics, 1980.

Attles, Louis Prince. Leadership that Facilitates Church Numerical Growth: An Epistemology of Mega Church Leadership. *D. Min. Dissertation*. Newton Center, MA: Andover Newton Theological School, 2001.

Bacchiocchi, Samuele. *The Christian and Rock Music: A Study of Biblical Principles of Music*. Berrien Springs, MI: Biblical Perspectives, 2000.

Backman, Clifford R. *The Decline and Fall of Medieval Sicily: Politics, Religion, and Economy in the Reign of Frederick III, 1296–1337*. Cambridge, UK: Cambridge University Press, 1995.

Bailyn, Bernard. *The Federalist Papers*. Washington, DC: Library of Congress, 1998.

Bainbridge, Virginia R. *Gilds in the Medieval Countryside: Social and Religious Change in Cambridgeshire, C. 1350–1558*. Rochester, NY: Boydell Press, 1996.

Barron, Bruce. *Heaven on Earth? The Social and Political Agendas of Dominion Theology*. Grand Rapids, MI: Zondervan, 1992.

Baus, Karl. *The Imperial Church from Constantine to the Early Middle Ages*. New York: Seabury Press, 1980.

Baus, Karl and Hubert Jedin. *From the Apostolic Community to Constantine*. London, UK: Burns & Oates, 1980.

Beardsley, Wilson Hull. The Pastor as Change Agent in the Growth of a Southern Baptist Mega Church Model. *D. Min. Dissertation*. Pasadena, CA: Fuller Theological Seminary, 1991.

Beito, David T. *From Mutual Aid to the Welfare State: Fraternal Societies and Social Services, 1890–1967*. Chapel Hill, NC: University of North Carolina Press, 2000.

Bellah, Robert N. "Civil Religion in America." *Daedalus* 96 (1967): 1–21.

Bellah, Robert N., Richard Madsen, William M. Sullivan, Ann Swidler, and Steven M. Tipton. *Habits of the Heart: Individualism and Commitment in American Life*. Berkeley, CA: University of California Press, 1985.

Bennett, Judith M. *Sisters and Workers in the Middle Ages*. Chicago, IL: University of Chicago Press, 1989.

Berger, Max. *The British Traveller in America, 1836–1860*. New York: Columbia University Press, 1943.

Berger, Peter L. *The Heretical Imperative: Contemporary Possibilities of Religious Affirmation*. New York: Anchor Books, 1979.

Berns, Walter. *The First Amendment and the Future of American Democracy*. New York: Basic Books, 1976.

Bigelow, Gordon. "Let There Be Markets." *Harper's Magazine* (May 2005): 33–38.

Black, Christopher F. *Italian Confraternities in the Sixteenth Century*. Cambridge, UK: Cambridge University Press, 1989.

Blake, Mariah. "Stations of the Cross." *Columbia Journalism Review* (May/June 2005), http://www.cjr.org/issues/2005/3/blake-evangelist.asp.

Blasi, Anthony J., Paul-André Turcotte, and Jean Duhaime. *Handbook of Early Christianity:Social Science Approaches*. Walnut Creek, CA: AltaMira Press, 2002.

Bloom, Harold. *Jesus and Yahweh: The Names Divine*. New York: Riverhead Books, 2005.

Blumenthal, Ralph. "Texas Governor Draws Criticism for a Bill-Signing Event at an Evangelical School." *The New York Times* (June 6, 2005): A12.

Blumenthal, Ralph, and Barbara Novovitch. "Bible Course Becomes a Test for Public Schools in Texas." *The New York Times* (August 1, 2005): A9.
Boodman, Sandra G. "Seeking Divine Protection." *The Washington Post* (October 25, 2005): F1, F5.
Bornkamm, Heinrich. *Luther's Doctrine of the Two Kingdoms*. Philadelphia, PA: Fortress Press, 1966.
Boyce, James Montgomery, and Benjamin E. Sasse. *Here We Stand: A Call from Confessing Evangelicals for a Modern Reformation*. Phillipsburg, NJ: P & R Publishing, 2004.
Bromley, David G., and Anson D. Shupe. *New Christian Politics*. Macon, GA: Mercer University Press, 1984.
Brundage, James A. *Law, Sex, and Christian Society in Medieval Europe*. Chicago, IL: University of Chicago Press, 1987.
Bullough, Vern L., and James A. Brundage. *Sexual Practices and the Medieval Church*. Buffalo, NY: Prometheus Books, 1982.
Bumiller, Elisabeth. "Bush Remarks Roil Debate over Teaching of Evolution." *The New York Times* (August 3, 2005): A14.
"Bush Aid Denounces Strict Church-State Line." *The Washington Post* (January 21, 2006): B9.
Calvin, John. *Institutes of the Christian Religion* (edited by John T. McNeill), 2 vols. Philadelphia, PA: The Westminster Press, 1960.
Campolo, Anthony. *Speaking My Mind*. Nashville, TN: W Pub. Group, 2004.
Cavalcanti, H. B. Opiate of the People? Lower-Class Christianity and Political Alienation in America. *Ph.D. Dissertation*. Nashville, TN: Vanderbilt University, 1990.
"Censorship in the Sciences Museum." Editorial. *The New York Times* (March 28): A16.
Chapman, Matthew. "God or Gorilla: A Darwin Descendant at the Dover Monkey Trial." *Harper's Magazine* (February 2006): 54–63.
Chodorow, Stanley, Knox MacGregor, Conrad Schirokauer, Joseph R. Strayer and Hans W. Gatzke. *The Mainstream of Civilization*. 5th ed. San Diego, CA/New York: Harcourt Brace Jovanovich, 1989.
Clark, Gillian. *Christianity and Roman Society*. Cambridge, UK: Cambridge University Press, 2004.
Clarkson, Frederick. "Theocratic Dominionism Gains Influence." *The Public Eye Magazine* (March/June 1994), http://www.publiceye.org/magazine/v08n1/chrisrel.html.
———. *Eternal Hostility: The Struggle between Theocracy and Democracy*. Monroe, MA: Common Courage, 1997.
CNN presents: *The Fight over Faith* (Broadcast on November 20, 2004).
Cochrane, James R., and Gerald O. West (eds.). *The Three-Fold Cord: Theology, Work and Labour*. Hilton, South Africa: Cluster Publications, 1991.
Connolly, Ceci. "Some Abstinence Programs Mislead Teens, Report Says." *Washington Post* (December 2, 2004): A1.
———. "Teen Pledges Barely Cut STD Rates, Study Says." *The Washington Post* (March 19, 2005): A3.
Coontz, Stephanie. *The Way We Never Were: American Families and the Nostalgia Trap*. New York: Basic Books, 1992.
———. *The Way We Really Are: Coming to Terms with America's Changing Families*. New York: Basic Books. 1998.
Cooperman, Alan. "Christian Groups Plan More Monuments: Many Expect Confusion and Litigation on Ten Commandments to Continue." *The Washington Post* (June 28, 2005): A6.

———. "Coming Soon to a Church Near You: Hollywood Skips Movie Theaters with 3,200-Screen Opening." *The Washington Post* (October 21, 2005): A1, A9.

———. "Fasting Chaplain Declares Victory: Navy Denies That He Couldn't Pray in Jesus' Name." *The Washington Post* (January 10, 2006): A13.

Cooperman, Alan, and Thomas B. Edsall. "Evangelicals Say They Led Charge for GOP." *The Washington Post* (November 8, 2004): A1.

Cord, Robert L. *Separation of Church and State: Historical Fact and Current Fiction.* New York: Lambeth Press, 1982.

Coreno, Thaddeus. "Fundamentalism as a Class Culture." *Sociology of Religion* 63 (2002): 335–360.

Corrigan, John. *Business of the Heart: Religion and Emotion in the Nineteenth Century.* Berkeley, CA: University of California Press, 2002.

Coser, Lewis A. *Masters of Sociological Thought: Ideas in Historical and Social Context.* 2nd ed. New York: Harcourt Brace Jovanovich, 1977.

Cosgrove, Mark P. *The Amazing Body Human: God's Design for Personhood.* Grand Rapids, MI: Baker Book House, 1987.

Cothen, Grady C. *What Happened to the Southern Baptist Convention: A Memoir of the Controversy.* Macon, GA: Smyth & Helwys Publishers, 1993.

Cotton, Gordon A. *Of Primitive Faith and Order: A History of the Mississippi Primitive Baptist Church, 1780–1974.* Raymond, MS: Keith Press, 1974.

Cranz, F. E. *An Essay on the Development of Luther's Thought on Justice, Law and Society.* Cambridge, MA: Harvard University Press, 1969.

Crèvecoeur, J., Hector St. John. *Letters from an American Farmer.* New York: Dolphin Books, n. d.

Cromartie, Michael. *A Public Faith: Evangelicals and Civic Engagement.* Lanham, MD: Rowman & Littlefield, 2003.

Crouch, David J. F. *Piety, Fraternity, and Power: Religious Gilds in Late Medieval Yorkshire, 1389–1547.* Suffolk, UK: York Medieval Press, 2000.

Croxton, Derek. *Peacemaking in Early Modern Europe: Cardinal Mazarin and the Congress of Westphalia, 1643–1648.* Selinsgrove, NJ: Susquehanna University Press/London, UK: Associated University Presses, 1999.

Cunliffe, Marcus. "American Watershed." *American Quarterly* 13 (1961): 479–494.

Curtis, Susan. *A Consuming Faith: The Social Gospel and Modern American Culture.* Baltimore, MD: Johns Hopkins University Press, 1991.

D'Emilio, John. *Sexual Politics, Sexual Communities.* Chicago, IL: University of Chicago Press, 1983.

Dahl, Robert Alan. *A Preface to Democratic Theory.* Chicago, IL: University of Chicago Press, 1956.

———. *Pluralist Democracy in the United States: Conflict and Consent.* Chicago, IL: Rand McNally, 1967.

Dallek, Robert. *Flawed Giant: Lyndon Johnson and His Times, 1961–1973.* New York: Oxford University Press, 1998.

Danforth, John C. "In the Name of Politics." Editorial. *The New York Times* (March 30, 2005), http://www.nytimes.com/2005/03/30/opinion/30danforth.html?ex=1135918800&en=64ef0af5b6a20f85&ei=5070.

Daniélou, Jean, and Henri Irénée Marrou. *The Christian Centuries: A New History of the Catholic Church.* London, UK: Darton, Longman and Todd, 1964.

Daniels, Matt. "Healthy Marriages Are Good Social Policy." *Washington Times* (April 15, 2004), http://www.allianceformarriage.org/site/PageServer?pagename=HealthyMarriages.

Davidson, James D. "Religion among America's Elite." *Sociology of Religion* 55 (1994): 419–440.

———. "Persistence and Change in the Protestant Establishment." *Social Forces* 74 (1995): 157–175.

Davies, Bob. *Coming out of Homosexuality: New freedom for Men & Women*. Downer's Grove, IL: Inter Varsity Press, 1994.

Dean, Cornelia. "Scientists Speak Up on Mix of God and Science." *The New York Times* (August 23, 2005): A1.

DeMar, Gary. *America's Christian History: The Untold Story*. Atlanta, GA: American Vision Publishers, 1993.

———. *Liberty at Risk*. Atlanta, GA: American Vision Publishers, 1993.

DeMar, Gary and Colonel Doner (eds.). *The Christian Worldview of Government*. Murphys, CA: The Coalition on Revival, 1989.

Demerath III, N. J. "Civil Society and Civil Religion as Mutually Dependent." In Michele Dillon (ed.), *Handbook of the Sociology of Religion*, 348–358. New York: Cambridge University Press. 2003.

Demetre, Danna. *Scale Down: A Realistic Guide to Balancing Body, Soul, and Spirit*. Grand Rapids, MI: Fleming H. Revell, 2003.

Diamond, Sara. *Roads to Dominion: Right-Wing Movements and Political Power in the United States*. New York: Guilford Press, 1995.

Dillow, Linda. *Intimate Issues: 21 Questions Christian Women Ask about Sex*. Colorado Springs, CO: WaterBrook Press, 1999.

"The Disappearing Wall." Editorial. *The New York Times* (April 26, 2005): 18.

Donnelly, John Patrick, and Michael W. Maher. *Confraternities & Catholic Reform in Italy, France, & Spain*. Kirksville, MO: Thomas Jefferson University Press, 1999.

Dorrien, Gary J. *The Making of American Liberal Theology: Imagining Progressive Religion, 1805–1900*. Louisville, KY: Westminster/John Knox Press, 2001.

Duin, Julia. "Military Chaplain Told to Shy from Jesus." *The Washington Times* (December 21, 2005), http://www.washtimes.com/national/20051221-121224-6972r.htm.

Durnbaugh, Donald F. *Every Need Supplied: Mutual Aid and Christian Community in the Free Churches, 1525–1675*. Philadelphia, PA: Temple University Press, 1974.

Ebaugh, Helen R., and Janet S. Chafez. *Religion and the New Immigrants: Continuities and Adaptations in Immigrant Congregations*. Walnut Creek, CA: AltaMira, 2000.

Eck, Diana L. *A New Religious America*. New York: HarperSanFrancisco, 2001.

Edsall, Thomas B. "In Georgia, Abramoff Scandal Threatens a Political Ascendancy." *The Washington Post* (January 16, 2006): A1.

Ellison, Christopher G. "Religious Involvement and Self-Perceptions among Black Americans." *Social Forces* 71 (1993): 1027–1055.

Ethridge, Shannon, and Stephen Arterburn. *Every Young Woman's Battle: Guarding Your Mind, Heart, and Body in a Sex-Saturated World*. Colorado Springs, CO: WaterBrook Press, 2004.

"Falwell Apologizes to Gays, Feminists and Lesbians." CNN.com (January 14, 2001), http://archives.cnn.com/2001/US/09/14/Falwell.apology/.

Falwell, Jerry. *Listen, America!* Garden City, NY: Doubleday, 1980.

Farrand, Max. *The Records of the Federal Convention of 1787*. New Haven, CT: Yale University Press, 1911.

Finke, Roger, and Rodney Stark. *The Churching of America, 1776–1990: Winners and Losers in our Religious Economy*. New Brunswick, NJ: Rutgers University Press, 1992.

———. "The Dynamics of Religious Economies." In Michele Dillon (ed.), *Handbook of the Sociology of Religion*, 96–109. Cambridge, UK: Cambridge University Press, 2003.

Finkel, David. "It's a Victory for People Like Us." *The Washington Post* (November 5, 2004): A03.

Finney, Charles G. *Lectures on the Revivals of Religion*. Cambridge, MA: Belknap Press, 1960.

Fisher, Ian, and Cornelia Dean, "In 'Design' vs. Darwinism, Darwin Wins a Point in Rome." *The New York Times* (January 19, 2006), http://www.nytimes.com/2006/01/19/science/sciencespecial2/19evolution.html?th&emc=th.

Flynn, Maureen. *Sacred Charity: Confraternities and Social Welfare in Spain, 1400–1700*. Ithaca, NY: Cornell University Press, 1989.

For the Health of the Nations: An Evangelical Call to Civic Responsibility (September 2004), http://www.nae.net/images/civic_responsibility2.pdf.

Foucault, Michel. *The History of Sexuality*. London, UK: Allen Lane/Penguin Press, 1988.

Gallup, Jr., George, and Jim Castelli. *The People's Religion: American Faith in the '90s*. New York: Macmillan, 1989.

Garver, Rob. "Justice Sunday: The Family Research Council Says Anticlerical Judges Pose a Greater Danger than Al-Qaeda." *The American Prospect* (online edition) (April 13, 2005), http://www.prospect.org/web/.

Gaston, Paul. "Smearing Christian Judges." *The Washington Post* (April 23, 2005): A19.

Geoghegan, Arthur T. *The Attitude toward Labor in Early Christianity and Ancient Culture*. Washington, DC: The Catholic University of America Press, 1945.

George, Timothy, and Alister E McGrath. *For All the Saints: Evangelical Theology and Christian Spirituality*. Louisville, KY: Westminster/John Knox Press, 2003.

Georgianna, Sharon Linzey. *The Moral Majority and Fundamentalism: Plausibility and Dissonance*. New York: Mellen Press, 1989.

Gewirtz, Paul, and Chad Golder. "So Who Are the Activists?" *The New York Times* (July 6, 2005): 19.

Giddens, Anthony. *Modernity and Self-Identity: Self and Society in the Late Modern Age*. Stanford, CA: Stanford University Press, 1991.

———. *Runaway World*. New York: Routledge, 2000.

Gildea, Joseph. *Source Book of Self-Discipline: A Synthesis of Moralia in Job by Gregory the Great*. New York: Peter Lang Publishers, 1991.

Godwin, Jeff. *What's Wrong with Christian Rock?* Chino, CA: Chick Publications, 1990.

Goodstein, Laurie. "Evangelicals Are Growing Force in the Military Chaplain Corps." *The New York Times* (July 12, 2005): 1.

Gorrell, Donald K. *The Age of Social Responsibility: The Social Gospel in the Progressive Era, 1900–1920*. Macon, GA: Mercer University Press, 1988.

Gottwald, Norman K. *The Tribes of Yahweh: A Sociology of the Religion of Liberated Israel, 1250–1050 BCE*. Maryknoll, NY: Orbis Books, 1979.

———. *The Hebrew Bible: A Socio-Literary Introduction*. Philadelphia, PA: Fortress Press, 1985.

———. *The Politics of Ancient Israel*. Louisville, KY: Westminster/John Knox Press, 2001.

Greeley, Andrew. *The Denominational Society: A Sociological Approach to Religion in America*. Glenview, IL: Scott, Foresman, and Company, 1972.

———. *The Catholic Imagination*. Berkeley, CA: University of California Press, 2000.

Gregory I. *Moralia in Job: Cura et Studio*. Tournai, Belgium: Brepols, 1979.

Gregory, Steven. *Santeria in New York City: A Study in Cultural Resistance*. New York: Garland Publishers, 1999.

Griffin, Clifford S. *Their Brothers' Keepers*. New Brunswick, NJ: Rutgers University Press, 1960.

Griffith, R. Marie. "The Gospel of Born-Again Bodies." *The Chronicle of Higher Education* (January 21, 2005): B6–B8.

Guthrie, William P. *Battles of the Thirty Years War: From White Mountain to Nordlingen, 1618–1635*. Westport, CT: Greenwood Press, 2002.

Haddad, Yvonne Y., and Adair T. Lummis. *Islamic Values in the United States*. New York: Oxford University Press, 1987.

Han, Kyu Sam. *Jerusalem and the Early Jesus Movement: The Q Community's Attitude toward the Temple*. London, UK/New York: Sheffield Academic Press, 2002.

Handlin, Oscar. *This Was America*. Cambridge, MA: Harvard University Press, 1949.

Harless, Hal. *How Firm a Foundation: The Dispensations in the Light of the Divine Covenants*. New York: P. Lang, 2004.

Harris, Joshua. *I Kissed Dating Goodbye*. Sisters, OR: Multnomah, 2003.

Hart, Darryl G. *That Old-Time Religion in Modern America: Evangelical Protestantism in the Twentieth Century*. Chicago, IL: Ivan R. Dee, 2002.

Heale, Martin. *The Dependent Priorities of Medieval English Monasteries*. Woodbridge, UK: Boydell Press, 2004.

Hedges, Chris. "Feeling the Hate with the National Religious Broadcasters." *Harper's Magazine* (May 2005): 55–61.

Heineman, Kenneth J. *God Is a Conservative: Religion, Politics, and Morality in Contemporary America*. New York: New York University Press, 1998.

Henderson, John. *Piety and Charity in Late Medieval Florence*. Oxford, UK: Oxford University Press, 1994.

Henzel, Ronald M. *Darby, Dualism, and the Decline of Dispensationalism: Reassessing the Nineteenth-Century Roots of a Twentieth-Century Prophetic Movement for the Twenty-First Century*. Tucson, AZ: Fenestra Books, 2003.

Herberg, Will. *Protestant, Catholic, Jew: An Essay in American Religious Sociology*. Garden City, NY: Anchor Books, 1955.

Hodgson, Godfrey. *The World Turned Right Side Up: A History of the Conservative Ascendancy in America*. Boston, MA: Houghton Mifflin, 1996.

Holmes, Marjorie. *God and Vitamins: How Exercise, Diet, and Faith Can Change Your Life*. Garden City, NY: Doubleday, 1980.

Horton, Charles. *The Earliest Gospels: The Origins and Transmission of the Earliest Christian Gospels—The Contribution of the Chester Beatty Gospel Codex P45*. London, UK/New York: T & T Clark International, 2004.

Houck, John W., and Oliver F. Williams (eds.). *Co-creation and Capitalism: John Paul II's "Laborem Exercens."* Washington, DC: University Press of America, 1983.

House, Jean V. *Weight on the Lord: A Daily Devotional Book for Those Who Desire to Be Slim for Him*. Colorado Springs, CO: Hunter Publishing Company, 1983.

Howard, Jay R., and John M. Streck. *Apostles of Rock: The Splintered World of Contemporary Christian Music*. Lexington, KY: University Press of Kentucky, 2004.

Hudson, Winthrop S., and John Corrigan. *Religion in America*. 6th ed. Upper Saddle River, NJ: Prentice-Hall, 1999.

Hughes, Charles Richard. Developing an Effective Ministry with Midlife Single Adults in a Mega Church. *D. Min. Dissertation.* Lynchburg, VA: Liberty Baptist Theological Seminary, 2000.
Hunter, James Davison. *American Evangelicalism.* New Brunswick, NJ: Rutgers University Press, 1983.
———. *Evangelicalism: The Coming Generation.* Chicago, IL: University of Chicago Press, 1987.
———. *Culture Wars: The Struggle to Define America.* New York: Basic Books, 1991.
Iannaccone, Laurence R. "Religious Markets and the Economics of Religion." *Social Compass* 39 (1992): 123–132.
———. "Why Strict Churches Are Strong." *American Journal of Sociology* 99 (1994): 1180–1211.
Ingersoll, Robert Green. "God in the Constitution." [*The Arena* (Boston), 1890]. In *The Works of Robert G. Ingersoll* [microform]. New York: The Ingersoll League, 1912–1929.
James, Williams. *The Varieties of Religious Experience.* New York: New American Library, 1958.
Jantz, Gregory. *The Spiritual Path to Weight Loss: Praising God by Living a Healthy Life.* Lincolnwood, IL: Publications International, 1998.
Jaynes, Sharon. *The Ultimate Makeover: Becoming Spiritually Beautiful in Christ.* Chicago, IL: Moody, 2003.
Jefferson, Thomas. *Virginia Act for Establishing Religious Freedom.* 1786. Charlottesville, VA: University of Virginia, http://religiousfreedom.lib.virginia.edu/sacred/vaact.html.
Jelen, Ted. G. *Religion and Political Behavior in the United States.* New York: Praeger. 1989.
———. "Political Esperanto: Rhetorical Resources and Limitation of the Christian Right in the United States." *Sociology of Religion* 66 (2005): 303–321.
Johnson, Earl. *Single Life: Being Your Best for God as He Prepares His Best for You.* Lanham, MD: Pneuma Life Publishing, 1999.
Johnson, Lyndon B., and Michael R. Beschloss. *Taking Charge: The Johnson White House Tapes, 1963–1964.* New York: Simon & Schuster, 1997.
———. *Reaching for Glory: Lyndon Johnson's Secret White House's Tapes, 1964–1965.* New York: Simon & Schuster, 2001.
Johnson, Peter, and Chris Sugden (eds.). *Markets, Fair Trade and the Kingdom of God.* Oxford, UK: Regnum, 2001.
Jonsson, Patrik. "Limits of Pulpit Politics Tested in N.C." *The Christian Science Monitor* (May 12, 2005): 3.
———. "A Carolina Fight over Swearing on the Koran in Court." *The Christian Science Monitor* (July 20, 2005): 2–3.
Joseph, Mark. *Faith, God, & Rock 'n' Roll.* London, UK: Sanctuary Publishing, 2003.
"Judgment Day." *Harper's Magazine* (August 2005): 23.
Kaplan, Esther. *With God on Their Side: How Christian Fundamentalists Trampled Science, Policy, and Democracy in George W. Bush's White House.* New York: New Press. 2004.
Kazal, Russell A. "Revisiting Assimilation: The Rise, Fall, and Reappraisal of a Concept in American Ethnic History." *American Historical Review* 100 (1995): 437–471.
Kennedy, John F. "Address of Senator John F. Kennedy to the Greater Houston Ministerial Association" (September 12, 1960), http://www.jfklibrary.org/j091260.htm.
Key, Dana, and Steve Rabey. *Don't Stop the Music.* Grand Rapids, MI: Zondervan, 1989.

Kirkpatrick, David D. "Bush Assures Evangelicals of His Commitment to Amendment on Marriage." *The New York Times* (March 12, 2004): A14.

Kirkpatrick, David D., and Carl Hulse, "G.O.P. Asks Conservative Allies to Cool Rhetoric over the Court." *The New York Times* (July 6, 2005): 1.

Kivisto, Peter A. "Religion and the New Immigrants." In W. H. Swatos Jr. (ed.), *A Future for Religion? New Paradigms for Social Analysis*, 92–107. Newbury Park, CA: Sage, 1992.

Klinkenborg, Verlyn, "Grasping the Depth of Time as a First Step in Understanding Evolution." *The New York Times* (August 23, 2005): A16.

Knickerbocker, Brad. "Ripples Spread as States Vote on Same-Sex Marriages." *The Christian Science Monitor* (April 7, 2005): 2.

Kofahl, Robert E. *The Handy Dandy Evolution Refuter*. San Diego, CA: Beta Books, 1980.

Krowe, David. "Katrina: God's Judgment on America." *BeliefNet* (2006), http://beliefnet.org/story/174/story_17439_1.html.

Kurien, Prema. "Becoming American by Becoming Hindu." In R. S. Warner and J. Witnner (eds.), *Gatherings in Diaspora*, 37–70. Philadelphia, PA: Temple University Press, 1998.

Kurtz, Howard. "Faint Praise from the Left." *The Washington Post* (May 3, 2005), http://www.washingtonpost.com/wp-dyn/content/blog/2005/03/03/BL2005040701166.html.

Kurtz, Lester. *Gods in the Global Village*. Thousand Oaks, CA: Pine Forge Press, 1995.

LaHaye, Tim F., and Jerry B. Jenkins. *Left Behind: A Novel of the Earth's Last Days*. Wheaton, IL: Tyndale House, 1995.

———. *Tribulation Force: The Continuing Drama of Those Left Behind*. Wheaton, IL: Tyndale House, 1996.

———. *Soul Harvest: The World Takes Sides*. Wheaton, IL: Tyndale House, 1998.

———. *Apollyon: The Destroyer Is Unleashed*. Wheaton, IL: Tyndale House, 1999.

———. *Assassins*. Wheaton, IL: Tyndale House, 1999.

———. *The Mark: The Beast Rules the World*. Wheaton, IL: Tyndale House, 2000.

———. *The Indwelling: The Beast Takes Possession*. Wheaton, IL: Tyndale House, 2000.

LaHaye, Tim, and Beverly LaHaye. *The Act of Marriage: The Beauty of Sexual Love*. Grand Rapids, MI: Zondervan, 1998.

Lampman, Jane. "For Evangelicals, a Bid to 'Reclaim America.'" *The Christian Science Monitor* (March 16, 2004): 16–17.

———. "A 'Moral Voter' Majority? The Cultural Wars Are Back." *The Christian Science Monitor* (November 8, 2004): 4.

———. "Churches Confront an 'Elephant in the Pews.'" *The Christian Science Monitor* (August 25, 2005): 14.

Latus, Margaret Ann. "Ideological PACs and Political Action." In Robert C. Liebman and Robert Wuthnow (eds.), *The New Christian Right: Mobilization and Legitimation*, 75–99. New York: Aldine, 1983.

Lawrence, Bruce L. *New Faiths, Old Fears: Muslims and Other Asian Immigrants in American Religious Life*. New York: Columbia University Press, 2002.

Lazare, Daniel. "False Testament: Archaeology Refutes the Bible's Claim to History." *Harper's Magazine* (March 2002): 39–47.

Le Goff, Jacques. *Your Money or Your Life: Economy and Religion in the Middle Ages*. New York/Cambridge, MA: Zone Books (MIT Press), 1988.

Leonard, Bill. *God's Last and Only Hope: The Fragmentation of the Southern Baptist Convention*. Grand Rapids, MI: W. B. Eerdmans, 1990.

——— (ed.). *Christianity in Appalachia: Profiles in Regional Pluralism*. Knoxville, TN: University of Tennessee Press, 1999.

Lerman, David. "Representative Davis Wants to Protect Symbols of Christmas." *The Daily Press* (December 15, 2005), http://www.dailypress.com/news/local/dp-39306sy0dec15,0,1382931.story?coll=dp-news-local-final.

Lerner, Ben. *Body by God: The Owner's Manual for Maximized Living*. Nashville, TN: Thomas Nelson Publishers, 2003.

Lesaffer, Randall. *Peace Treaties and International Law in European History: From the late Middle Ages to World War One*. Cambridge, UK/New York: Cambridge University Press, 2004.

Ley, Beth M. *God Wants You Well*. Detroit Lakes, MN: BL Publications, 2001.

Liebman, Robert C., Robert Wuthnow, and James L. Guth. *The New Christian Right: Mobilization and Legitimation*. Hawthorne, NY: Aldine Publishing Company, 1983.

Lin, Irene. "Journey to the Far West: Chinese Buddhism in America." *Amerasia Journal* 22 (1996): 106–132.

Lipset, Seymour Martin. *Political Man: The Social Bases of Politics*. Garden City, NY: Doubleday, 1960.

———. *The First New Nation: The United States in Historical and Comparative Perspective*. New York: Basic Books, 1963.

MacKay, Angus. *Society, Economy, and Religion in Late Medieval Castile*. London, UK: Variorum Reprints, 1987.

Maher, Bridget. "The Benefits of Marriage." Washington, DC: Family Research Council, n. d., http://www.frc.org/get.cfm?i=IS05B01.

Marsh, Charles. "Wayward Christian soldiers." *The New York Times* (January 20, 2006), http://www.nytimes.com/2006/01/20/opinion/20marsh.html?th&em=th.

Marshall, Paul, Edward Vanderkloet, and Peter Nijkamp. *Labour of Love: Essays on Work*. Toronto, Canada: Wedge Publishing Foundation, 1980.

Marty, Martin E., and R. Scott Appleby. *Fundamentalisms and the State: Remaking Polities, Economies, and Militance*. Chicago, IL: University of Chicago Press, 1993a.

———. *Fundamentalisms and Society: Reclaiming the Sciences, the Family, and Education*. Chicago, IL: University of Chicago Press, 1993b.

———. *Accounting for Fundamentalisms: The Dynamic Character of Movements*. Chicago, IL: University of Chicago Press, 1994.

———. *Fundamentalisms Comprehended*. Chicago, IL: University of Chicago Press, 1995.

Maxwell, Randy. *"Weight" on the Lord*. Boise, ID: Pacific Press, 1985.

McMullen, Cary. "Any Way You Count It, Fewer Southern Baptists." *Paltka Daily News* (June 17, 1999), http://www.palatkadailynews.com/pages/0615/count.html.

McGuire, Meredith. *Religion: The Social Context*. Belmont, CA: Wadsworth, 2002.

Meyers, Albert, and Diane Elizabeth Hopkins. *Manipulating the Saints: Religious Brotherhoods and Social Integration in Postconquest Latin America*. Hamburg, Germany: Wabasha, 1988.

Milbank, Dana. "And the Verdict on Justice Kennedy is: Guilty." *The Washington Post* (April 9, 2005): A3.

Morgan, David T. *The New Crusades, the New Holy Land: Conflict in the Southern Baptist Convention, 1969–1991*. Tuscaloosa, AL: University of Alabama Press, 1996.

Morgan, Larry G. *Old Time Religion in the Southern Appalachians.* Boone, NC: Parkway Publishers, 2005.
Morris, Henry M. *The Bible and Modern Science.* Chicago, IL: Moody Press, 1968.
———. *Biblical Cosmology and Modern Science.* Nutley, NJ: Craig Press, 1982.
Morris, Julie. *Julie Morris Step Forward! Diet: Learn to Cast Your Cares on God—Not the Refrigerator.* Nashville, TN: Abingdon Press, 1999.
Murphy, Joseph M. *Working the Spirit: Ceremonies of the African Diaspora.* Boston, MA: Beacon Press, 1994.
Nelkin, Dorothy. *The Creation Controversy.* New York: W. W. Norton, 1982.
Neuhaus, Richard John, and Michael Cromartie. *Piety and Politics: Evangelicals and Fundamentalists Confront the World.* Washington, DC: Ethics and Public Policy Center/University Press of America, 1987.
Niebuhr, H. Richard. *Christ and Culture.* New York: Harper Torchbooks, 1951.
———. *The Social Sources of Denominationalism.* New York: Living Age Books, 1957.
Nitsch, Thomas O., Joseph M. Philips, Jr., and Edward L. Fitzsimmons (eds.). *On the Condition of Labor and the Social Question One Hundred Years Later: Commemorating the 100th Anniversary of Rerum Novarum, and the 50th Anniversary of the Association for Social Economics.* Lewiston, NY: Edwin Mellen, 1994.
Norton, Herman Albert. *Religion in Tennessee, 1777–1945.* Knoxville, TN: University of Tennessee Press, 1981.
Numbers, R. "Creationism in Twentieth Century America." *Science* 218 (1982): 538–544.
"Obfuscating Intolerance" (Editorial). *The New York Times* (June 23, 2005).
Orlinsky. Harry Meyer (ed.). *Interpreting the Prophetic Tradition.* Cincinnati, OH: Hebrew Union College Press, 1969.
Osteen, Joel. *Your Best Life Now: 7 Steps to Living at Your Full Potential.* New York: Warner Faith, 2004.
Paulson, Amanda. "Culture War Hits Local Pharmacy." *The Christian Science Monitor* (April 8, 2005): 11.
Payer, Pierre J. *Sex and the Penitentials: The Development of a Sexual Code, 550–1150.* Toronto/ Buffalo, NY: University of Toronto Press, 1984.
Pettit, Christie. *Starving: A Personal Journey through Anorexia.* Grand Rapids, MI: Fleming H. Revell, 2003.
Phillips, Paul T. *A Kingdom on Earth: Anglo-American Social Christianity, 1880–1940.* University Park, PA: Pennsylvania State University Press, 1996.
Pierce, Gregory F. (ed.). *Of Human Hands: A Reader in the Spirituality of Work.* Chicago, IL: ACTA, 1991.
Pierson, George W. *Tocqueville in America.* Garden City, NY: Doubleday/Anchor, 1959.
Pitzer, Donald Elden. *Professional Revivalism in Nineteenth-Century Ohio.* Ph.D. dissertation. Columbus, OH: Ohio State University, 1966.
Powell, Michael. "Judge Rules against 'Intelligent Design:' Dover, Pa., District Can't Teach Evolution Alternative." *The Washington Post* (December 21, 2005): A1.
Reed, Ralph. *Politically Incorrect: The Emerging Faith Factor in American Politics.* Dallas, TX: Word, 1994.
Reichley, A. James. *Religion in American Public Life.* Washington, DC: The Brookings Institution, 1985.
Riesebrodt, Martin. *Pious Passion: The Emergence of Modern Fundamentalism in the United States and Iran.* Berkeley, CA: University of California Press, 1993.

Roof, Wade Clark. *A Generation of Seekers: The Spiritual Journeys of the Baby Boom Generation.* San Francisco, CA: HarperSanFrancisco, 1993.

——— and William McKinney. *American Mainline Religion.* New Brunswick, NJ: Rutgers University Press, 1987.

Romano, Lois. "'The Smiling Preacher' Builds on Large Following." *The Washington Post* (January 30, 2005): A1, A10.

———. "For Wednesday Church Services, a Youth Revival." *The Washington Post* (April 27, 2005): A3.

Rosenberg, Ellen MacGilvra. *The Southern Baptists: A Subculture in Transition.* Knoxville, TN: University of Tennessee Press, 1989.

Rosin, Hanna. "Beyond Belief." *The Atlantic Monthly* (January/February 2005): 117–120.

Rubenstein, Richard E. *When Jesus Became God: The Struggle to Define Christianity during the Last Days of Rome.* New York: Harvest/HBJ Book, 2000.

Rubin, Jordan. *The Maker's Diet.* New York: Berkley Books, 2004.

Rumbaut, Rubén G. "Ties That Bind: Immigration and Immigrant Families in the United States." In A. Booth, A. C. Crouter, and N. S. Landale (eds.), *Immigration and the Family,* 3–46. Hillsdale, NJ: Lawrence Erlbaum, 1997.

Rushdoony, Rousas John. *The Nature of the American System.* Nutley, NJ: Craig Press, 1965.

Sanders, E. P. *Jewish Law from Jesus to the Mishnah.* Harrisburg, PA: Trinity Press International, 1990.

Saul, Nigel. *The Oxford Illustrated History of Medieval England.* Oxford, UK: Oxford University Press, 1997.

Schlesinger, Jr., Arthur. *The Age of Jackson.* Boston, MA: Little, Brown, 1946.

Schor, Juliet B. *The Overworked American: The Unexpected Decline of Leisure.* New York: Basic Books, 1992.

Seelye, P. "Moral Values Cited as a Defining Issue of the Election." *The New York Times* (November 4, 2004): 4.

Seidman, Steven. *Embattled Eros.* New York: Routledge, 1992.

———. "Contesting the Moral Boundaries of Eros: A Perspective on the Cultural Politics of Sexuality in the Late-Twentieth-Century United States." In Neil J. Smelser and Jeffrey C. Alexander (eds.), *Diversity and Its Discontents: Cultural Conflict and Common Ground in Contemporary American Society,* 167–189. Princeton, NJ: Princeton University Press, 1999.

Seldes, George (ed.). *The Great Quotations.* Secaucus, NJ: Citadel Press, 1983.

Setterfield, Barry. *The Velocity of Light and the Age of the Universe.* Australia: Creation Science Association, 1983.

Shamblin, Gwen. *Rise Above: God Can Set You Free from Your Weight Problems Forever.* Nashville, TN: Thomas Nelson, 2000.

Shane III, Leo. "Christian Lawmakers Want to Protect Chaplains' Speech." *Stars and Stripes* (European edition) (October 21, 2005), http://www.freerepublic.com/focus/f-news/1507039/posts.

Sharlet, Jeff. "Soldiers of Christ." *Harper's Magazine* (May 2005): 41–54.

Sherkat, Darren. "Religious Socialization: Sources of Influence and Influences of Agency." In Michele Dillon (ed.), *Handbook of the Sociology of Religion,* 151–163. New York: Cambridge University Press, 2003.

Sider, Ronald J. "The Scandal of the Evangelical Conscience." *Christianity Today* (2005), http://www.christianitytoday.com/bc/2005/001/3.8.html.

Slevin, Peter. "Judge Upholds Prayer Limits in Indiana State House." *The Washington Post* (January 1, 2006): A3.
Smedes, Lewis B. *Sex for Christians: The Limits and Liberties of Sexual Living.* Grand Rapids, MI: Willliam B. Eerdmans, 1994.
Smith, Oran P. *The Rise of Baptist Republicanism.* New York: New York University Press, 1997.
Smith, Timothy L. *Revivalism and Social Reform in Mid-Nineteenth Century America.* New York: Abingdon Press, 1957.
Snyder, Pamela E. *A Life Styled by God: A Women's Workshop on Spiritual Discipline for Weight Control.* Grand Rapids, MI: Zondervan, 1985.
Spong, John Shelby. *Why Christianity Must Change or Die: A Bishop Speaks to Believers in Exile.* New York: HarperCollins, 1998.
Spring, Joel. *The American School, 1642–2000.* New York: McGraw-Hill, 2000.
———. *American Education.* New York: McGraw-Hill, 2002.
Sproul, R. C. *Getting the Gospel Right: The Tie That Binds Evangelicals Together.* Grand Rapids, MI: Baker Books, 2003.
Stark, Rodney, and William Sims Bainbridge. *The Future of Religion: Secularization, Revival and Cult Formation.* Berkeley, CA: The University of California Press, 1985.
Stayer, James M. *The German Peasant's War and Anabaptist Community of Goods.* Buffalo, NY: McGill-Queen's University Press, 1991.
Stein, Stephen J. *The Shaker Experience in America: A History of the United Society of Believers.* New Haven, CT: Yale University Press, 1992.
Stephens, Andrea. *God Thinks You're Positively Awesome: Discover Your True Beauty—Inside and Out!* Ann Arbor, MI: Servant Publications, 1997.
Sugg, John. "A Nation under God." *Mother Jones* (December 2005): 33–34, 78.
Sydow, Gernot. "1648—Peace of Westphalia: Turning Point In German History." *German News* (October 1998), http://www.germanembassy-india.org/news/GN98Okt/gn08.htm.
Terpstra, Nicholas. *Lay Confraternities and Civic Religion in Renaissance Bologna.* Cambridge, UK: Cambridge University Press, 1995.
Tessler, Gordon S. *The Genesis Diet: The Biblical Foundation for Optimum Nutrition.* Raleigh, NC: Be Well Publications, 1996.
"The Great Debate of our Season." Editorial. *Mother Jones* (December 2005): 26.
Thompson, John J. *Raised by Wolves: The Story of Christian Rock and Roll.* Toronto, Canada: ECN Press, 2000.
Thrupp Sylvia L. *Society and History: Essays.* Ann Arbor, MI: University of Michigan Press, 1977.
Tocqueville, Alexis de. *Democracy in America.* New York: Vintage Books, 1954.
Tracy, David. *The Analogical Imagination: Christian Theology and the Culture of Pluralism.* New York: Crossroad, 1981.
Troeltsch, Ernst. *The Social Teachings of the Christian Churches.* 2 vols. London, UK/New York: George Allen & Unwin/The MacMillan Company, 1960.
Trollinger, William Vance. *God's Empire: William Bell Riley and Midwestern Fundamentalism.* Madison, WI: University of Wisconsin Press, 1991.
Trueheart, Charles. "Welcome to the Next Church." *The Atlantic Monthly* (August 1996): 37–58.
Verba, Sidney, and Norman H. Nie. *Participation in America: Political Democracy and Social Equality.* New York, Harper & Row, 1972.

Voss, Eugene H. Surviving and Thriving in the Shadows of the Mega-Church. D. Min. Dissertation. Deerfield, IL: Trinity International University, 2001.

Wagner, David. *The New Temperance: The American Obsession with Sin and Vice.* Boulder, CO: Westview Press, 1997.

Wald, Kenneth D. (ed.). *Religion and Politics in the United States.* 3rd ed. Washington, DC: CQ Press, 1997.

Wallerstein, Immanuel. "Render unto Caesar? The Dilemmas of a Multicultural World." *Sociology of Religion* 66 (2005): 121–134.

Warner, R. Stephen. "Work in Progress: Toward a New Paradigm for the Sociological Study of Religion in the United States." *American Journal of Sociology* 98 (1993): 1044–1093.

———. "Convergence toward the New Paradigm: A Case of Induction." In L. A Young (ed.), *Rational Choice Theory and Religion: Summary and Assessment,* 87–101. New York: Routledge. 1997.

———. "Approaching Religious Diversity: Barriers, Byways, and Beginnings." *Sociology of Religion* 59 (1998): 193–215.

Wauzzinski, Robert A. *Between God and Gold: Protestant Evangelicalism and the Industrial Revolution, 1820–1914.* Rutherford, NJ: Fairleigh Dickinson University Press, 1993.

Weaver, La Vita. *Fit for God: The 8 Weeks That Kicks the Devil out and Invites Health and Healing In.* New York: Doubleday, 2004.

Weber, Max. "Elective Affinities." In Hans Gerth and C.Wright Mills (eds.), *From Max Weber: Essays in Sociology,* 62–63, and 284–285, New York: Oxford University Press, 1946.

———. *Economy and Society.* Berkeley, CA: University of California Press, 1978.

———. *The Protestant Ethic and the Spirit of Capitalism.* 2nd ed. London, UK: Routledge Classics, 2002 [1930].

Webster, Susan Verdi. *Art and Ritual in Golden-Age Spain: Sevillian Confraternities and the Processional Sculpture of Holy Week.* Princeton, NJ: Princeton University Press, 1988.

Weeks, Jeffrey. *Invented Moralities.* New York: Columbia University Press, 1995.

Wheat, Ed, and Gay Wheat. *Intended for Pleasure: Sex Technique and Sexual Fulfillment in Christian Marriage.* New York: Revell, 1997.

Wheaton, Jack. *The Crisis in Christian Music.* Oklahoma City, OK: Hearthstone Publishing Company, 2000.

Whitcomb, John C. "Origin of the Planets." In K. L. Seagraves (ed.), *And God Created.* San Diego, CA: Creation Science Research Center, 1973.

"White House Blasts Robertson's Sharon Remark" MSNBC News Services (January 6, 2006), http://www.msnbc.msn.com/id/10728347/.

Wicker, Tom. *JFK and LBJ: The Influence of Personality upon Politics.* New York: Morrow, 1968.

Williams, Michael D. *This World Is Not My Home: The Origins and Development of Dispensationalism.* Fearn, Scotland: Mentor, 2003.

Williams Rhys H. *Cultural Wars in American Politics: Critical Reviews of a Popular Myth.* New York: Aldine de Gruyter, 1997.

———. "Visions of the Good Society and the Religious Roots of American Political Culture." *Sociology of Religion* 60 (1999): 1–34.

———. *Promise Keepers and the New Masculinity: Private Lives and Public Morality.* Lanham, MD: Lexington Books, 2001.

Wisch, Barbara, and Diane Cole Ahl. *Confraternities and the Visual Arts in Renaissance Italy: Ritual, Spectacle, Image.* Cambridge, UK: Cambridge University Press, 2000.

Wolfe, Alan. *One Nation After All: What Middle-Class Americans Really Think about: God, Country, Family, Racism, Welfare, Immigration, Homosexuality, Work, the Right, the Left, and Each Other.* New York: Penguin Books, 1998.

———. *Moral Freedom: The Search for Virtue in a World of Choice.* New York: W. W. Norton, 2001.

———. *Return to Greatness: How America Lost Its Sense of Purpose and What It Needs to Do to Recover It.* Princeton, NJ: Princeton University Press, 2005.

Wood, Gordon S. *The Creation of the American Republic 1776–1787.* New York: W. W. Norton, 1969.

Wuthnow, Robert. *The Restructuring of American Religion: Society and Faith since World War II.* Princeton, NJ: Princeton University Press, 1988.

———. "Democratic Liberalism and the Challenge of Diversity in Late-Twentieth-Century America." In Neil J. Smelser and Jeffrey C. Alexander (eds.), *Diversity and Its Discontents: Cultural Conflict and Common Ground in Contemporary American Society*, 19–35. Princeton, NJ: Princeton University Press, 1999.

"You Ain't Seen Nothing Yet." *The Economist* (June 23, 2005), http://www.economist.com/world/na/printerfriendly.cfm?story_ID=4102212.

Zeolla, Gary F. *Creationist Diet: Nutrition and God-Given Foods According to the Bible.* Bloomington, IN: 1st Books, 2000.

Zernike, Kate, and John Broder. "The Mood of the Electorate: War? Jobs? No, Character Counted Most to Voters." *The New York Times* (November 4, 2004): 1.

INDEX

Abortion, 5, 25–26, 39, 46, 48, 53, 60, 63, 72–73, 82, 84, 87, 103, 105, 110–11, 118, 120, 127–28
Abstinence, 47, 53, 74, 85, 87, 104, 126
Apostasy, 1, 11, 89, 98
Arlington Group, 49, 55
Arminianism/Arminian faith, 78–79, 117, 119, 132
Assemblies of God, 81, 90

Baptists, xi, 23, 48, 50–51, 68, 81, 114, 126
Bush, George, 6–7, 50, 53–54, 60, 72, 96, 100–104, 110, 113, 126, 129

Calvin, 20, 36
Calvinism, 65, 78–79
Catholic, 4, 6, 13, 21, 80, 119, 120, 124, 131
Catholic Church/Roman Catholicism, 36, 64–65, 94, 96, 106
Center for Christian Statesmanship, 49, 109
Center for Reclaiming America, 45, 49, 109
Charismatic circles, 38, 121
Christendom, 9, 65–66, 68

Christian conservatives, 2–4, 13–16, 25–26, 29, 32, 37, 42–43, 45, 50–51, 55, 73–74, 76, 78, 80, 89, 94–95, 97, 102, 108–10, 113, 118–19, 121–23, 126–27, 129–31
Christian dating, 30–32
Christian dieting/exercising, 32–34
Christian Exodus, 49, 72–74
Christian festivals, 32–35
Christian health insurance, 39–41
Christian Medical and Dental Associations, 37, 102
Christian modernity, 24, 32, 45, 74, 117, 130
Christian public square, x, 45–46, 48, 51, 54, 59, 64, 71, 74, 80, 92, 97–98, 102–3, 105, 106, 108–9, 112, 108–15, 118
Christian Right, 6, 48, 53, 71, 99, 113
Christian suburbia, 16, 20, 27, 29, 33, 71, 75, 121–22, 127, 129–30
Church and State, 3–4, 16–17, 45, 58, 65, 67, 69, 73–75, 92–93, 118–19
Church of Christ, 80
Church on the Move, 19
Coalition on Revival, 49, 55–60
Congregationalism, 75
Congregationalists, 6

Index

Conservative Christianity, ix–xi, 1–2, 14–15, 27, 32, 47, 51–53, 55, 64, 66, 75–76, 81, 119, 131; and education, 47, 72–74, 88–96, 97, 106; and the family, 58, 60–62, 73–74, 81–88; and sexuality, 63, 73–74, 82, 102–7; and work, 34–39

Conservative church, xi, 4–5, 11, 16, 25, 27, 37–38, 41, 48, 50–52, 64, 71, 73–74, 82, 84, 89, 91, 94–95, 98–99, 102, 104–7, 113–14, 117, 119, 121–23, 125, 129

Conservative judges, 53, 110

Contemporary Christian music, 32–34

Coral Ridge Presbyterian Church, 25, 71, 109

Coser, Lewis, x

Creationism, 95, 101, 113

Disciples of Christ, 80

Dominionist/Dominionism, 50, 52, 55, 67, 71, 78–79, 81, 132

Episcopal(ians), 3–4, 75, 113

Establishment clause, 67, 92

Evangelical(s), ix, 15, 53, 64, 99, 105, 109, 121, 126, 130–31

Evolution, 24, 48, 73, 94–96, 124, 128

Falwell, Jerry, 52, 76, 126–27

Family Research Council, 49, 89, 100, 102, 110, 112, 114, 123

Fornication, 103–4

Free exercise clause, 67, 92

Free will, 77–79, 119

Fundamentalism, 2, 8, 114

Gay marriage/same-sex marriage, 15, 46, 48, 63, 72–73, 104, 118, 125, 127–28

God-filled life, 21, 23–25

Godly life, 26

God's will, 22–23

Haggard, Ted, 60, 127

Homosexuality, 24, 26, 39, 84, 103, 105, 120, 127–28

Intelligent design, 15, 53, 74, 95–96, 101, 113, 118, 126

Jefferson, Thomas, 59, 66, 120, 130

Justice Sunday, 110–12, 114, 122–23

Lakewood Ministries, 23–24

Land, Richard, 6, 48

Luther, Martin, 9, 12, 33

Lutherans, 80, 113, 131

McGuire, Meredith, 14, 41

Megachurch(es), 13, 15, 23–24, 29, 45, 79, 109, 117, 130

Methodism, 12, 79

Methodists, 79–80

Middle-class religion, ix, 45, 52, 71, 75, 79–81, 103, 106–7, 113–14, 118–19, 122

Modernity, x, 1–2, 5, 15–17, 19, 21–25, 27, 32, 34, 41–42, 79, 97, 107, 117–18, 124–25, 129

Moral Majority, 52

National Association of Evangelicals, 49, 60–64, 127

National Religious Broadcasters Association, 99–102, 117

Niebuhr, Richard, 12, 79–80

Osteen, Joel, 23–24

Peace of Westphalia, 65–66, 68, 131

Pornography, 84, 88, 98, 103, 105–7

Presbyterian, 15, 108, 124

Religious marginality, ix, 5, 7–14, 20–27, 30, 32, 37, 41, 43, 45, 50–53, 59, 73, 77–80, 82, 94–95, 98–99, 102, 107, 111, 115, 118, 130

Religious particularism, 100

Religious wars, 9, 66, 68, 132

Republicans/Republican Party, 6, 47–48, 50, 52–54, 100, 117, 123–24, 126

Robertson, Pat, 24, 50, 127

Salvation, 13–14, 77–79, 109

Salvation history, 13–14

Schiavo, Terry, 47, 53, 110, 112, 114
School prayer, 24, 39, 71, 92–94, 100
Sectarian faith/practices/worldview, 2–3, 10, 46, 64, 66–67, 71, 74, 91–93, 96, 109, 113, 119, 121, 132
Southern Baptists, 6, 48, 50, 114
Southern Baptist Convention, 6, 48, 50, 121

Ten Commandments, 37, 46, 77, 101, 109, 125
Troeltsch, Ernst, 12

Virginia Act, 66–67, 120

Weber, Max, x, 12, 78, 81, 86
Wolfe, Alan, 53, 129
Working-class Christianity, 12, 52, 77–78, 80, 109, 118–19

About the Author

H. B. CAVALCANTI is Professor of Sociology and Anthropology at James Madison University. He has published many book chapters and articles in publications such as *Journal for the Scientific Study of Religion*, *Sociology of Religion*, *Journal of Church and State*, and others.